# RAISING THE
# WORST DOG EVER:
# A SURVIVAL GUIDE

# RAISING THE WORST DOG EVER: A SURVIVAL GUIDE

Tales of The Wylie One of Highbridge

&

Instructions on How to Live with

Your New Puppy

## Dale M. Ward

DDTA PUBLISHING

Published by DDTA Publishing
PO Box 67
South Mills, NC 27976
Place of Publication: South Mills, NC, USA

Library of Congress Control Number: 2019909909

Ward, Dale M.
Raising the Worst Dog Ever: A Survival Guide / by Dale M. Ward, MA.
Includes bibliographical references.
ISBN-13: 978-1-7331350-0-9
Ebook ISBN: 978-1-7331350-1-6

Printed and bound in the United States of America
First Published 2019, Second Edition 2021

# WHAT PEOPLE ARE SAYING...

## Dog Writers Association of America Maxwell Award
### Winner in the Category of Human/Animal Bond

"*Raising the Worst Dog Ever: A Survival Guide* is an honest and wonderfully entertaining look at the complex relationship between a woman and her dog. Readers will not only gain a better understanding of their own dogs by reading this book, they will empathize with all the challenges as well as appreciate the pure joys of sharing their lives with these incredible animals."

—**Victoria Stilwell** | dog trainer and behavior expert

"I am a veterinarian and work with people who have gotten new puppies every day. There are lots of great books out there but this is one of my new favorites! Perfect for all puppy owners with great stories and amazing step by step training details to help along the way!"

—**Amy Learn** | VMD Chief of Clinical Behavioral Medicine

"For years I have been looking for the perfect Puppy Guide to recommend to my clients, and at last I have found it! The heartfelt, easy to read stories, along with the practical dog training instructions make this book truly exceptional."

—**Abigail Witthauer** | CBCC-KA, CPDT-KA, VSPDT, Owner/Director of Training at Roverchase Service Dogs

"As a veterinarian who sees only behavior cases, I hear a lot of people tell me that they have the "Worst Dog" — but in their hearts they know they also have the BEST dog. This is the perfect book for finding that place where the science of helping our dogs learn to survive in this complicated world collides with the heart and soul and true meaning of sharing our lives with dogs. Dale Ward writes from her heart, while giving high-quality effective training advice. I highly recommend this book for anyone who loves dogs and anyone who works with dogs."

—**Lynn Honeckman** | DVM Veterinary Behavior Solutions, Orlando FL

"As a dog photographer who has had to help numerous rescues, animal shelters, and individuals rehome dogs with serious behavior issues that started because puppies were not sufficiently trained in the beginning, I sincerely wish this was required reading for every new puppy owner. So many sad cases could have been prevented with proper training in the beginning, and this book is a fun & entertaining way to learn about proper puppy training. This book is not your usual dry How to Raise a Puppy manual. Instead it is interspersed with personal heartwarming and hilarious tales about raising the worst dog ever. Everyone — from puppy newbies to experienced dog owners — can learn something from it."

—**Hannah Stonehouse Hudson** | public speaker, writer, old dog lover, Principal at HSH Communications.

"Dale Ward has written a beautiful and inspiring story of Wylie the dog, showing us her relationship to Wylie — facing their imperfections with grace and candor, and showing us the way forward when we face our own. Their relationship was well lived and well told. By integrating their personal narrative with insights about training, Dale teaches us much more than we realize! It's not a simple how-to, though there's plenty of that, it's a story that will stick with you long after you turn the final page. I feel like I know them both, and they are with me as I live with my own dogs."

—**Lynne Tirrell, PhD**

"My name is Tim and I am mentioned quite a lot in this book! Full disclosure, I am the writer's husband and lived through most of the experiences that Dale talks about in this book. Having said that, Dale would not share any of the details of her book with me as she was writing it and I did not get to read it until it was 99% complete! When she did finally let me read the book, I laughed, I cried, and I have no doubt that others will experience a similar range of emotions. Also, this book is arranged in a rather unique format that presents a great story that any dog lover will enjoy, but it also provides a wealth of training information, in separate sections, that can be referred to time and time again. Definitely deserves 5 stars!"

—Timothy J. Ward | husband and dog lover

This book is dedicated to the memory of Wylie.

She lives forever in my heart.

Now, may a little piece of her also live forever in yours.

# AUTHOR'S NOTE

This book is different from other books. No, I don't just mean that the story is unique, although it is. This book combines a memoir of sorts with a dog training manual. Each chapter begins with a piece of the story of Dale and her dog, the Wylie One of Highbridge. Immediately following are one or more sections on puppy training that directly relate to the story preceding it and the problems — and lessons learned — therein. The next chapter continues the story, followed by additional relevant training topics. If you want to read the story straight through, go for it! Just skip the training at the end of each chapter. Conversely, you may use this book strictly as a manual, navigating as needed through the training sections. Or, of course, you can read the whole thing straight through. This book will serve you well in any of these three ways.

# CONTENTS

# CHAPTER ONE

# The Beginning:
# And Then There Was Dog

She was the best of dogs, she was the worst of dogs, it was the age of good intent, it was the age of blunder, it was the epoch of hope, it was the epoch of sorrow, it was the season of unconditional love, it was the season of frustration, it was the spring of birth, it was the winter of dejection. We had everything to conquer, we had nothing to lose. She was wise, she was silly, she was devoted, she loved all humans, she was my light, she pushed away my despair.

People ask me all the time, "Which dog is the worst dog you have ever trained?" That is such an easy question for me to answer: my sweet dog, Wylie! She was the hardest, toughest, most difficult dog I have ever trained, and she was the BEST worst dog ever.

She was born a poor little dog, in a little log cabin, in the middle of a big, cold winter, way back in the big, cold woods of northern Wisconsin. Well, okay, that's not totally accurate. She was indeed born one of eight puppies in the midst of the freezing winter of February 2004, and the location of her birth was an extremely secluded cabin in the woods. However, the "little log cabin" was in fact a massive luxury log home, nestled in the woods by a fast-flowing river. And the puppies! They were all so adorable, so wriggly, so small, so soft, and so beautifully black.

Flash back two years. I had moved from a big urban city bustling with over a million people where I worked in corporate consulting to one of the most secluded, rural parts of northern Wisconsin. I had taken a giant leap of faith when I got married in June 2002. I left everything behind to follow my husband and my dreams of a new life. I had no job, no friends, and no idea what I was going to do with the rest of my life. As it turned out, my whole world would be turned upside down by one very special dog.

My first months in the northwoods were busy enough. Trying to establish a new home, scoping out the nearby towns, and getting the lay of the land consumed most of my time. You may be surprised to know that we lived in our garage for the first six or so months. It was a bit more than a regular garage though. It was a large pole building that Tim had MacGyvered, creating our first home out of one end of the cavernous structure. By the time I moved in, Tim had insulated it, added a wood stove for heat, and built a makeshift bathroom. We had no running water, a composting toilet, and a workbench that served as a kitchen. Our bed was at one end, and the other end was filled with everything he owned. At least we had electricity, but there was no television. We had to get our water from artesian wells, filling 55 gallon drums and hauling them home, even in the dead of winter. That water was the best I've ever tasted — cold, crisp, and clear. I affectionately called our place the Batcave because we could literally pull our cars right into our house. It was a primitive existence. We began the work of building a real house in earnest, as living in a Batcave soon loses its luster.

I was excited by the prospect of a new life and what it had to offer. What did people do in a place like this? I thought there would be all kinds of rural activity — you know, things rural people did. I must admit, there wasn't much of anything around. We lived in a place called Highbridge, population 525. The center of town consisted of a tiny post office and an old one-room schoolhouse that was used for voting at election time. Otherwise, there was nothing, just a few houses scattered around a bunch of fields, red dirt, and trees. Lots of trees.

I thought that since I wasn't working anymore, I would have tons of time on my hands to do whatever I wanted. It sounded like a dream come true. My problem was trying to figure out exactly what that was. I had a few ideas. I was a runner. I was knowledgeable in the field of physical fitness but had no formal qualifications. I decided to pursue that avenue, and so I signed up for an exam preparation course to become a Certified Personal Trainer at the nearby technical college, only a 2-hour drive away. See? Everything was so far away. It was a big effort to do anything in my new surroundings because of the distance and isolation. I would make the trip from Highbridge to Duluth, Minnesota, every Wednesday afternoon for my evening class and drive home, arriving late, around eleven o'clock. It was fun to be back in school again, and I looked upon it as an adventure.

Well, I finished the class, took the exam, and I passed! I was one of three in that class of twenty people who made it. I was now an accredited American Council on Exercise (ACE) Certified Personal Trainer. I somehow managed to get myself into the business section of the local newspaper. It was a half-page spread on my new business and me: The Ward Fitness Institute. Go big or go home, I thought. Soon, I was receiving calls from people who wanted my help. I had clients! Maybe this could work! There was a gym in the next town, about a thirty-minute drive away. I created programs for my clients and helped them workout and reach their fitness goals. It was fun at first, but I admit, I wasn't very busy. As you can imagine, in a very rural, depressed area, not many people had the money to hire a personal trainer. The per capita income in Highbridge was under $20,000 at the time. There wasn't much money being spent on luxury items, that's for sure. My career as a personal trainer was quickly fizzling out.

I tried writing a cooking column for a little newspaper called *The Northwoods Woman*. That lasted for a few months, but then the paper went under. I applied for a job as a 911 dispatcher. I thought I would be a shoo-in given my university education combined with my background working with law enforcement in my former city life. I got called to go in and take the test. It was pretty easy, and I thought I sailed right through it. When I didn't hear anything by the end of the week, I called them to find out the results. Nope. The job went to some guy who knew a guy who knew another guy. I was getting frustrated and increasingly disheartened. I had nothing to do. I was lonely, and I was bored.

Well, at least I had my running. It literally saved my sanity more than once before. I usually ran three or four times a week, about five miles each time. I'd leave from our house in the morning after the sun was up, all by myself, and run down the gravel road. It's a pretty remote area — beautiful, but quite wild. The dirt in this part of Wisconsin is clay the color of a rusty red wagon. When it was dry, it was dusty. When it rained, it was muddy. I rarely encountered a car or another person. It was desolate! I naively thought that running in the country would be so much fun and actually be safer than the running I had been doing in the city. I was never afraid to run in my urban environment. In the city, I typically ran early, before work. I would get up at 5 am and was out running by 5:30. It was dark but, there were streetlights everywhere and even at that early hour, there were cars on the streets belonging to people going to and coming from work, starting or ending their day. Sometimes, I saw a few prostitutes on the street corners along my route. I guess I became a regular early morning fixture because they would wave at me and yell a few simple words of encouragement: "You go girl!" I always waved back with a big smile. Running in the city was always interesting, but, in my mind, never scary. Besides, I rationalized that all the bad people would be out at night, not at 5:30 in the morning. At that time, they would all be crashed somewhere, sleeping off whatever they were into the night before. I usually felt pretty darned safe.

Running in the backwoods of small town Wisconsin was a whole different story. First, no more early morning or late evening runs. I could absolutely not run in the dark, even with a headlamp. If you have never been in the *real* wilderness, you can't imagine how dark it can get. On nights when there was no moon, it was black as pitch. It was so dark that I couldn't see my hand if I stuck it right in front of my face. I certainly couldn't see my feet! It freaked me out. The road was riddled with potholes, and, if you were not careful, you could easily land in one. There was no way to see the edge of the road in the dark, and the ditches were steep and deep. There were ravines for goodness sake! I definitely didn't want to fall into one of those. No one would ever find me!

I was also not prepared for the animals. In a grand sense, it sounds really romantic to be "one with nature," but let me tell you right now, it's not fun when you encounter a skunk, badger, porcupine, coyote, bear, or whatever else is out there, and you *will* encounter them. Sometimes, you just hear them in the woods near the road. You could be running along, minding your own business, and then CRASH, *crash, crash*. Some big animal gets startled and smashes its way through the brush, hopefully not crossing your path. Your heart races, and you can't breathe from the fear. You can't run because your legs go weak. It's really bad.

The other thing about living in the woods way up north is the profusion of bugs. Oh my Dog! All summer long! At dusk, the mosquitos were so thick you could hear the incessant humming of their tiny little wings through the screen doors. There would be hundreds of them, maybe thousands, just waiting for a chance to target you for a tasty meal. There was no way to go outside in the evening without being totally covered up, including wearing a mosquito net over your head. I never went for a run in the evening. Ever. Too many mosquitoes. Then there were the flies. Oh, so many kinds of flies! Did you know that there are over thirty species of blood-feeding deer flies and horse flies found in Wisconsin? Thirty. They hang around from May through September, basically until the first freeze kills them off. Do you realize that those big, biting horse flies and those insidious, blood-sucking deer flies are attracted to motion as well as carbon dioxide? So, what happens when you're running? You are moving *and* emitting lots and lots of $CO_2$. I was like a fly magnet out there. I always wore a hat and brought a towel with me for protection. I was swatting and weaving and smacking, but they always outfoxed me, and I'd be bitten on the neck or arm or leg anyway. For me, each bite swelled up like a golf ball. I'm allergic to a lot of stuff — fly bites included, apparently. It made me feel miserable.

And then there were the more familiar dangers. Loose dogs were a frequent occurrence, and most were definitely not friendly. At least wild animals will run *away* from you if they can. They don't want an encounter with a human. The dogs, on the other hand, seemed to relish it. There was this one dog that lived on the corner, about a mile from home. He was big, black and tan, with a little white patch on his chest. He had a really thick coat and the fur stood on end all the way down his back. He was some kind of shepherd mix, maybe German shepherd and Rottweiler. This dog was almost always outside. The owner's house was set far back from the road, and I would steel my nerve as I approached that corner, rounding it and emerging from the cover of the trees. I would try to sneak-run by it, which never worked. When that damned dog saw me, he would bolt straight for me, barking and snarling, running at lightning speed. He'd tear across the field, jump over the big ditch, and race up to me on the road. I put on my biggest, meanest bluster: "Stop! Go home! *Go!* Get outta here, you big brute!" I tried to keep running, but I dared not turn my back on him. So, I kind of ran sideways down the road, as he continued to bark at me, and I continued to yell at him. I hated that jerk of a dog. The worst of it was that in about a mile, I had to turn around and come back, with him lying in wait, ready to terrorize me yet again.

One day, after a particularly terrifying morning encounter, I decided to drive to his house and introduce myself to him and his owner. *Enough is enough! I am done with this dog!* I thought to myself. As I drove down the two muddy ruts that made up the driveway, my car was greeted in the same aggressive way: *bark, bark, bark, snarl.* I honked my horn and waited for the owner to come out, as his dog just stood there and barked at me. The thought crossed my mind that no one knew I was going there and that I could easily disappear, and no one would ever know what happened to me. *Shake it off. That's just silly*, I thought. When the man finally came out of his house, he yelled at his dog. The dog stopped barking. He came over, and I talked to him through my partially open car window, ready to slam it in reverse to make a quick getaway. I explained my situation. I didn't tell him that I thought his dog was rotten though. I tried to be sweet and nice. The guy seemed sympathetic and assured me that his dog would never hurt anyone; he was all bark and no bite. Yeah, right. The dog had wandered off as we were talking, so he called him over. I can't remember his name, but it was something like Hunter or Remington or Gunner or Tank or some other big, scary dog name. The Tank stood in front of my vehicle and slowly wagged his tail. He never took his eyes off me. I gathered up my courage, got out of the car, and let him come over and sniff me. He wagged some more. I scratched his neck. He seemed to like it. There we were, my nemesis and me, building a little relationship! I relaxed a bit. Tank was okay, and I was okay. I left thinking that maybe the next time I ran by their property, things would be better. I figured that I could just call his name, and he would recognize me. We were buddies.

Ha! That worked as well as you would expect. In other words, it didn't. As soon as that dog saw me running down the road, he came charging at me with the same intensity as before. "Hi Tank! It's me! We met just the other day! Good boy, good boy!" Nothing. Tank just kept coming. He stopped short, and I thought I saw a slight glimmer of recognition, but I still didn't trust him. He scared the living daylights out of me and made my runs a stressful kind of hell. I think he liked scaring me. I could see it in his beady little eyes.

So, to summarize, I had to contend with the wild animals, the bugs, and the loose dogs, but that wasn't all. I hadn't even considered the human obstacles yet! One lovely day, I was running with Tim. We never talked much when we ran, and I was deep in my head, thinking whatever thoughts runners think, when suddenly, there was a deafening *CRACK*.

"Jesus Christ!" I screamed. I swear that I jumped two feet in the air. I almost fell to the ground. "What the @#$% was that?"

Some idiot had shot a gun right beside me! It was fall, and that means hunting season in northern Wisconsin. He was wearing brownish clothes, camouflage, so I didn't see him at first. I guess he was hunting or practicing or something. He was standing about ten feet away from me, right at the edge of the woods. I know he saw us, but he fired his gun anyway. Idiot. I was so mad! Tim just kept running, like it was nothing.

"Come on. Let's go. You're fine", Tim said.

Um, no, I was not fine! Tim hates confrontation, so he was happy to just ignore it. Besides, he'd been living in the northwoods for over two decades. He was used to it. I just couldn't make my legs move forward. I doubled over and started crying uncontrollably. I was shaking. It all came to a head: the wild animals, the bugs, the dogs, the guns, and on top of all that, the loneliness. I just couldn't do it anymore. I had a bit of a meltdown, right there in the middle of the road. I think Tim was finally starting to understand that I was not doing well, that I needed something to help me cope. I had no idea what I was going to do.

One day, I was sitting at home — alone again — and I got the bright idea to get a dog. After all, I had lots of time on my hands. I could train it! I grew up with dogs! Tim's experience with dogs was much different than mine. He had only ever had outdoor dogs when he was growing up. He believed that dogs did not belong in the house. That made no sense to me. If the dog had to live outside, then why bother having a dog at all? I wanted a companion, a friend, to live inside the house, not some random dog that lived tied up outside. So, we agreed to disagree (me rather grudgingly) and *not* get a dog. If the dog had to live outside, I didn't want one. I guess I could have gone and bought one myself and just brought it home, but I knew I needed Tim's buy-in. I didn't want to raise a puppy by myself, and if he was going to participate, I somehow had to get him to opt in.

I used to wonder why I would get so emotional over dog tales. I'd read a book about a dog — and cry — watch a movie that had dogs in it — and cry — hear a dog story — and cry. I never got teary over stories of people or even other animals. Only dogs. Even today, when I see a dog working in harmony with her handler, especially when I can see the close relationship they have, the communication between the two of them, the respect and love they have for each other, it literally brings me to tears. It touches something deep down inside of me that I can't really explain.

I believe that this next part of my story explains why I connect so deeply with dogs, why I feel like my relationships with dogs go far beyond almost all human relationships I have ever had. I believe there is a deep, profound link between the dog-human bond and trauma. Whatever that trauma might be, whether it is childhood abuse, bullying, PTSD, or something else — anything else — the presence of a dog in your life can make all the difference in the world. We each carry our pain with us, whatever that pain is. No one's pain is any less worthy than another's. No matter what color or flavor your pain is, dogs can "see" it. They get it. Dogs offer acceptance. Dogs provide a non-judgmental ear. Dogs deliver unconditional love.

I hope this gives you some insight as to why I put so much heart and soul into the dog-human relationship, why I need dogs in a way that maybe someone without my history might not understand, and why I need them much more than they need me. Dogs help to heal a huge, gaping wound in my life that started at a very early age, and continues through to the present. These early experiences set me up for a life of struggle that led to a final diagnosis of major depressive disorder that I live with every day. There, I'm out of the *Mental Health Stigma* closet. It's scary to be out here, but it feels good too.

My family always had dogs when I was growing up. There seemed to be a steady stream of them drifting through my childhood. There were probably more, but the ones I remember are Skipper, the spaniel mix; Chum, the black Labrador retriever; Duke, the German shepherd; Chico, the Chihuahua; Sandy, the little mystery breed; and Roxy, the lab/border collie mix. They all lived indoors with us. There was never any question about it. Back then, most yards weren't fenced, including ours. When we let the dogs out, they were either tied out, or they were let out to run loose. We also didn't neuter our dogs back then, as it just wasn't a thing to be done. So many of our dogs just ran away, following their free-roaming instincts. Despite all of this, the dogs always lived in the house with us. They slept with me, they played with me, they kept me company, they loved me. I could always count on them.

As a child, I lived in a chaotic, unpredictable, turbulent world. I had two parents and an older brother. My mom stayed at home and took care of us, and my father drove a city bus for a living. He wore a uniform that made him look like a police officer and all the neighborhood kids were a bit frightened around him when he wore it. He was an old man, fifty-two when I was born. We were his second family, but that was a big secret I didn't find out about until I was a teenager, and even then, it was a taboo subject. My mother only ever mentioned the name of his other son in the heat of an argument. I never met him. My brother and I were to keep quiet and not tell any of the family secrets to anyone, and so I remained completely silent about our home life.

My father drank. He was an alcoholic and violent when drunk. I lived in a shroud of secrecy and a state of constant fear. My father went out alone at night and came back late. Fights often ensued. I would be in my room, sleeping, awakened by the crunch of gravel under the wheels of my father's car. I could hear it clearly from my bedroom window. That sound brought a lump of apprehension to the back of my throat every time and is still a vivid memory fifty years later. I would wonder, *Is this going to be a quiet night or a fight night?*

On bad nights, my mother's voice heightened to a fever pitch as soon as he entered the house. He would speak in slurred, muffled tones, and then, right before all hell broke loose, he became silent, trying to control his temper, like he was holding his breath. It was like the calm before the storm. Then, all of a sudden, the rage burst open like a hornets' nest. Objects were thrown, fists landed on flesh, bodies crumbled to the floor. Not my body. I rarely got hit. These were not my fights. Instead, I just had to avoid, listen and watch. Powerless.

I watched as my mother screamed and yelled at him, calling him names, accusing him of infidelity, throwing her full mug of hot tea at his head. He ducked, and the mug missed its target, splashing its contents down the wall and leaving a small ellipse of a dent as evidence to be seen the next day. He retaliated with clenched fists. I heard the sound of his closed hand connecting with flesh and bone, a dull thud.

Once, I remember my mother pushed him down the basement stairs and slammed the door. We heard him stumble and thump down the six stairs to the landing. Yay! My mother was my hero for a brief moment. But then, I knew there was no lock on the door to the basement and he was going to be coming back up any second like a raging bull. So, I ran over, dropped to the floor, braced my back against the door and pushed against the wall across from me with my legs as hard as I could to keep him from coming back up.

He pushed on the door, yelling, "Open this goddamned door!" My mom ran over and helped me hold the door shut, putting her full weight against it. He swore, "You bitch, let me in!" and he pushed again, but my little legs held. He yelled and pushed some more. The door would open an inch with each shove and slam shut, back into place. I held fast, shaking in fear. It was probably only a few minutes before he gave up and went out the back door, got into the car, and drove off, but those minutes felt like an eternity to me.

My mother always had a lot of bruises: black eyes, finger impressions on her arms, defensive wounds. I saw her cover them with makeup and long-sleeved blouses. I look back now, and I know that my mother did the best she could, but she was not available to me emotionally, so I was always lonely and afraid. She could barely cope herself. When I was about eight years old, she had a nervous breakdown. I remember her in hysterics, crying, screaming, totally out of control. An ambulance came and took her away. I cried and cried, hanging on to her hand as they wheeled her out of the house on a gurney. I didn't see her for two weeks, as, I was told, children were not allowed to visit in the hospital. A really old aunt on my father's side named Zelda, whom I had never met or even heard of before, moved in to take care of us. She smelled funny. I didn't like her, and I didn't want to be near her. I didn't understand what had happened to my mother, and I was confused and scared. After two long weeks, my mother came home, and Zelda disappeared, never to be seen or heard from again, like a figment of my imagination. For a short while, things were quiet in our house. We all walked on pins and needles, sensing the fragility of my mother's mental state. Soon though — too soon — the fighting resumed.

Each fight brought new, unique peculiarities. A full case of beer, twenty-four stubby bottles of Labatt 50 ale heaved forcefully out the kitchen window and onto the cement sidewalk below, smashing into a million shards of brown glass with silver and green labels holding some of the pieces together, skidding onto the lawn, leaving frothy foam bubbling up from the grass in its wake. A potted palm thrown carelessly out the front door and into the snowbank, landing roots first, looking oddly like some discarded tropical Christmas tree leaning heavily to the left. A stray lampshade lying on the living room floor, useless without its missing base, and bent almost in half, crushed by purposeful, angry feet stomping it to its hopeless demise. Destruction. I was never sure what I would find.

As I got a little older, I could escape the house more, maybe go across the street to a friend's house, to experience what a normal family was like. It was a reprieve, but I knew I had to eventually go home. On *those* nights, I could hear the noise even before I walked up our long driveway. Sometimes, I would just stay outside, sitting on the front porch for what seemed like hours on end, not wanting to go in. Sitting there, I could reach a state of serenity after a while, listening to my mother's dampened, shrill voice in the night. I could float away in my mind. One really cold night, I wondered if I should just stay outside, lie down in the snow, and go to sleep. It was such a peaceful idea. I would never have to wake up. While I sat on the steps, I would listen to them argue, yell, scream, slam doors, and I'd laugh to myself about keeping the secret. I'm sure all of the neighbors could hear what went on in our house. No one ever mentioned it though, and as a child, the burden of secrecy was very real and very isolating, and along with it came shame.

I had no one to turn to, no one to comfort me, no one to confide in. Wait! Yes, I did! I had the dog! Each nightmarish fight was made more bearable in its aftermath because I had a dog. I would sit on my bed in my darkened room when the fighting had ceased, and I would hug my dog. I could feel my hot tears stream down my cheeks and onto her furry coat, soaking up all my pain and misery. My dog, who loved me unconditionally, who listened to me, who was always happy to be with me. My dog, who never judged me, never hit me, never screamed at me, never made me feel less than worthy. My dog. Oh, how I loved my dog.

One afternoon, when I was fifteen, I was hanging out with my friend at her house across the street. We were doing what we usually did, blowing smoke from illicit cigarettes out her bedroom window, listening to our coveted LPs: The Rolling Stones, or Elton John, or Chicago, and complaining about our lack of freedom. Suddenly, there was a sharp knock on her bedroom door. We flicked our lit cigarettes out the window. Her father came into the room. His face was ashen and serious. We thought we had been caught sneaking smokes. He stood there, looking down at me. He choked out a few words in his gruff German accent: "Your father. He is no more."

I stared at him for a long minute. It was sinking in. My father was dead. My first reaction was joy. A smile briefly slid across my face. Was he really dead? Is that what he meant to say? I felt a huge relief. No more fighting! I could see the confusion in his eyes, so I wiped that smile off my face fast and adopted a more suitable, shocked expression. After all, you weren't supposed to smile when your father died.

He said, "You'd better go home right now."

I took off up the stairs, out the front door and ran across the street, jumped the ditch, and dashed across the lawn. I swung open the front door and burst into the living room, thinking I would find my mother in a state somewhat like mine: happy and relieved. After all, she was free. Free from the threat of physical harm, free from fear and worry, free from the tension, free from a life of dread. What I found instead was my mother sitting in the big living room chair and a neighbor lady sitting on the edge of it with her arm around my mother's shoulders. My mother had her head in her hands and was rocking back and forth, sobbing, choking on her own snot-laced words.

"What am I going to do now? What am I going to do? Oh God, what am I going to do?" I stopped dead in my tracks. My smiling face froze in place as they both looked up at me. My mother's eyes were red and watery, swollen with tears.

I stupidly asked, "What's wrong? Aren't you glad?" She froze and glared up at me. My joy changed to fear and confusion. I had made a huge miscalculation. My mother was not happy. She was filled with horror for the future.

I found out later that my father had died in a car accident on the highway near our house. The inquest showed that he had been drinking and that no one in either vehicle was wearing a seatbelt. He had drifted off the road, hit the shoulder and overcorrected, heading straight into an oncoming car. The driver of that car died of a heart attack several days later, and his family sued ours. My mother was at a breaking point. We had no money. There was no insurance money.

She was only a part-time store clerk and had a very small income. We owned our house, and it was paid for, but she feared we would lose it in the lawsuit. I hadn't thought of any of that stuff. My reaction was solely based on the respite his absence was going to bring. Deep down, I still felt relieved, but I knew it was taboo to express it. I had to pretend I was sad. I could do that. But I never cried. I just couldn't fake the crying. To this day, I've not shed a single tear over him, and I never will. I felt guilty and confused about my reaction to his death for a long time, thinking I should feel sad, but by the time I was in my thirties, I had reconciled my feelings.

Out of all the dogs, I was closest to Roxy, probably because I was a young teen when we got her, and she made sure I made it through a turbulent adolescence. Depression had already set in and she provided a nonjudgmental ear and so much comfort and security that I credit her with getting me through that stormy teenage era. She kept me present because she gave me purpose. I had to get up every morning, let her out, feed her, walk her, take care of her. I took her to training classes, I practiced with her, I taught her tricks. I did everything with her. Teenage me was trying to cope with the pains of living, and she was simply enjoying being with me, her person. I told that dog everything! I knew then what a dog could do for a human. Her death at age seven from immune-mediated hemolytic anemia sent me reeling for a long time. She died unexpectedly and quite suddenly. I missed Roxy with an intensity I had never experienced before, but which I was to experience again in the future.

When I moved out of the house as a young adult, I was too busy, too independent, and my life was too restrictive for the company of dogs. I was attending university and working full-time. I travelled a lot, I worked a lot, and I lived in apartments. I was also fearful of the pain of losing another dog. And so began the gap. No dogs for twenty years.

Flash back to Wisconsin, 2004. Did I mention I was really lonely in my new life? Tim went to work every day, and I stayed home in the house, in the middle of nowhere, without any friends, all by myself. There were no smart phones then, and we barely had an internet connection. Our computer was so slow that we had to install updates overnight, and sometimes, they would still be installing when we got up in the morning. I felt isolated and cut off from civilization. I was ready for a dog.

One day, seemingly out of the blue, Tim said, "I think you should get a dog."

I was shocked and eyed him suspiciously. "You mean an indoor dog?"

"Yes, an indoor dog."

He obviously recognized my loneliness and hoped that getting a puppy would help. Yippee! I had converted him! His change of heart was born of concern and pity, but I didn't care. I still won!

The search for a puppy was on! Based on my past experience, I knew I wanted a Labrador retriever, and I wanted a black one. I thought a black lab would remind me of my sweet Roxy, and, more practically, the dog hair would be more manageable and match my pants!

I am not sure how I found the breeder, but pretty soon the "Lab Man" was on my radar. This guy didn't live too far from us, and he had been breeding Labrador retrievers for many years. When I called him, he told me that three of his dogs had just had puppies. I made an appointment to go visit right away. I had done my puppy homework; I knew I had to meet both parents on site to make sure that they were nice, friendly dogs. I also had to be sure that the puppies were being properly handled and had lots of human contact and that they were clean and warm, well fed and safe. That was the extent of my puppy knowledge at the time.

That weekend, Tim and I drove down to meet them. The Lab Man was a builder of custom log homes, and he lived with his family in the home he was constructing until its completion. We pulled up to this huge riverside house, obviously in the latter stages of being built. The Lab Man himself met us and invited us in to meet the dogs. Each mama dog had her own room, and ours was adjacent to their son's bedroom. The boy was about twelve years old and had grown up raising dogs. These puppies happened to be the first litter that he was responsible for. He would feed them in the morning, and after school, he played with them, cuddled them and loved them. Of course, he had his parents as backup. When I saw this arrangement, I knew we were in the right place to select a puppy. We visited three more times before we made our final selection, and ultimately, we chose a litter of all black puppies. The mom was a chocolate lab, and the father was a yellow lab — you've just got to love genetics.

The last time we visited, the dogs had been moved to their outdoor kennels. I was immediately concerned. It was late March, but there was still a lot of snow on the ground and it seemed too cold for puppies to be living outdoors. My concerns were laid to rest when I saw the setup. Each of the three litters and their mamas had their own large fenced pen. The floor was raised concrete that was hosed down several times a day and kept very clean. In each pen, there was a roomy doghouse with a door that had a flap to keep out the cold. The whole roof was hinged so that it could be opened completely to allow easy access to the puppies. There was a thick layer of bedding on the floor and there were heat lamps inside that kept the dogs toasty warm at night. All of the puppies in each of the three pens were romping around being totally adorable.

I had my eye on the littlest pup in our chosen litter, a sweet, shy, calm ball of fur. Tim, on the other hand, liked what he called "the feisty one." We took both puppies and put them on a blanket in the back of my Toyota 4Runner to watch them interact with their surroundings. The little one was quiet and explored in a tentative manner, sniffing her way around the truck. The feisty one proceeded to prance around and jump into my shoes, pulling at the laces and dragging them around the blanket. She was obviously a very confident puppy.

"Let's get that one," Tim said, "She's got personality."

"Okay," I said, "She's the one!"

The Lab Man painted the tips of her ears pink so that they could tell her apart from her sisters in the litter, and she was ours. Little Miss Pink. We had to wait another week before we could bring her home. By then, she would be eight weeks old.

IT'S TRAINING TIME...

# Equipment and Supplies

 *Just a quick note, I use the terms "he" and "she" throughout the training portions of this book when talking about dogs. I use them interchangeably and by no means do I intend to infer a bias or preference for either gender.*

I made many mistakes when I first got Wylie. I am going to try to provide you with some solid advice to help you navigate the world of puppies and dogs. I want you to be proactive and prepared, not reactive and unprepared. Don't go shopping wearing puppy-scented, rose-colored glasses! This information should help you purchase wisely and avoid buying things you don't need.

Before you bring your puppy home, you should be thinking about advanced preparation. Being on top of things *before* you bring your new puppy home will go a long way towards helping you and your puppy adjust and settle in smoothly, with fewer bumps along the way. This is my list of equipment and supplies that I recommend to new puppy owners. It is by no means exhaustive and focuses on what I think will help you the most.

# XPENS

An Xpen is also sometimes referred to by its full name, an exercise pen. It is a multi-sided (usually eight panels), foldable, portable structure that you can use to confine your puppy. An Xpen is like a big crate but without a floor or roof (usually). They come in different materials; the most common is wire, just like many crates. The plastic ones are lighter but a little bulkier, so if you plan on traveling with it, this is a consideration. An Xpen gives your puppy much more room than a crate, but it still keeps them safe when you can't watch them or you just need a break. You can even use one as a makeshift gate (see below). I encourage everyone to use an Xpen for their puppies. They can be real sanity savers when dealing with a young dog.

# GATES AND DOORS

Limiting access to areas of your house is essential to puppy training, whether it's closing all the bedroom and bathroom doors or installing gates. If you are in a busy household, especially with children, the likelihood of someone leaving doors open is very high. Sometimes, it's just easier to put up a gate or two. Know that in most cases, gates are temporary, and that your dog will earn access to the rest of your house gradually and in a controlled and supervised manner. How long will this take? As with most things in dog training, it depends on you and it depends on the dog. Keep this in mind when selecting your gate. You may have to live with it for several months or even years.

Remember, that puppy is going to grow fast! Make sure your gate is high enough to prevent your adult-sized dog from jumping over it. Don't waste money on a short gate only to have to buy a taller one in a few months when your large breed puppy gets, well, large. There are gates for pretty much every situation, no matter the configuration of your house.

There are three types of gates: freestanding, pressure-mounted, and fixed gates. Fixed gates are the most secure since they mount directly into the frame of the door or the wall. Pressure-mounted gates are fairly secure but will fall through if leaned against or pushed hard enough. Freestanding gates are somewhat secure, but the ends are not attached to a surface, so clever dogs can move them out of the way and simply walk around them.

You should also consider what the gate is made of. Some gates are very beautiful and decorative but are made of wood. Many dogs love to chew on wood, so this material would likely not be a good choice for a dog that chews. Keep in mind that all puppies chew to some degree. Some are avid chewers and would not do well with wooden gates at all. If you want to be sure, select a metal gate to begin with. Then, if your dog doesn't chew, or when your puppy grows up, you can replace your metal gates with more decorative, wooden ones.

Many homes today are open-concept, and people are sometimes stumped as to how to gate off a portion for their puppy. There are freestanding, long barriers available to handle this type of home. You can even use an exercise pen as a makeshift gate, stretched out and secured at both ends, to cover really wide openings.

I don't recommend any type of gate without a door. Some baby gates are made without a door, and you have to step over them to get through. These types of gates are too short for all but the smallest of dogs anyway, and I know of many incidents where people have been injured trying to step over these kinds of gates. Get a gate with a walk-through door for safety reasons.

If you want a longer term, aesthetically pleasing solution, get creative! I have had many clients who decided to close off certain rooms to their dogs for various reasons. You can install French doors, put up a lovely iron garden gate, put in a half door, or one of a whole host of other ideas. You are limited only by your imagination. Remember, restricting your dog's access doesn't mean your decor has to be ruined.

## CRATES

Crates deserve their own section. See section entitled Crate Training 101 which follows.

## TOYS

There are so many choices when it comes to selecting toys for your new puppy, and it can be overwhelming. Toys are basically divided into three categories: toys for play, chew toys, and interactive toys. I include squeaky toys, balls, tossing toys, and plush toys in the play toy category. These toys are fun for your dog either to use with you or to play on their own. Chew toys are a very important part of puppyhood since young dogs go through a teething period and need to chew. Some dogs retain this need throughout their lives while others lose interest in chewing as they age, but most dogs like to chew at least some of the time. It is a natural, normal dog behavior. Choosing the right chew toys for your puppy will depend very much on the size of your dog. If your dog is going to be large, then selecting durable chew toys is a must. Kong® Company makes a variety of great chew toys. I also really like Puppy Teething Keys by Nylabone™.

Interactive toys include things like food puzzle toys (I really like the toys by Nina Ottoson®), and food stuffing toys (like the Classic Kong® by Kong Company, Tux® by West Paw™,

Busy Buddy® Squirrel Dude™ by PetSafe, and so many more!). These toys allow your dog to use their noses — and brains! — to obtain food. Using interactive toys is a wonderful way to keep dogs entertained when you aren't able to interact with them.

A few cautions:

- **Don't buy cheap toys from unknown companies.** They may contain toxic material; be of inferior quality, which could pose choking hazards; and/or may not last very long.

- **Take your dog's size into account.** Don't buy small toys for a big puppy. It could be dangerous due to ingestion potential.

- **Read third party, unbiased reviews by professionals.** A good source of information on toys (and many other dog related topics) is the Whole Dog Journal™. There you will find articles and reviews by some of the best dog trainers and veterinarians in the business.

## COLLARS

There are many types of collars out there, and I believe that your dog's collar should be primarily used for identification purposes. Even if they've been microchipped, your dog should, at minimum, wear an identification tag sporting at least a phone number. I choose to have my dog wear her rabies tag, her microchip tag, and her ID tag. That way, if my dog is lost, all her information is readily available. If your dog has allergies or other health concerns, consider adding a line to their identification tag that says, *Allergic to X* or *Medical Needs: Please*

*Call Immediately.* The more information your dog's finder has, the better it will be for your dog.

Some collars are to be avoided at all cost. They include any collar that is designed to inflict pain or cause suffering to the dog.

## Avoid

> Training (choke) collars
>
> Slip (choke) collars
>
> Choke chains
>
> Prong collars
>
> Pinch collars
>
> Electric/Electronic collars (shock collars)
>
> Remote training collars (shock collars)
>
> Underground fence collars (shock collars)
>
> Bark collars (shock collars)
>
> Citronella collars
>
> Ultrasonic collars

## Maybe

> Head halters
>
>> In very specific circumstances, head halters (sometimes called head collars) may be useful, such as when the dog and handler are roughly the same size. For example, a 100-pound person may have difficulty handling a 100-pound, reactive dog. Normally, we use a head halter in conjunction with a harness with a leash

attached to each. The first line of defense is always the harness; the head halter is the backup. Eventually, when the dog is less reactive and has learned to walk nicely on a leash, the head halter can be retired. I prefer the Halti® and the Top Paw® HOLT Walking Dog Collar if you need one.

## Yes, Use One of These

### Flat buckle collar (quick-release type buckle)

These collars are best because they are easy to remove in the event of an emergency. I don't recommend the old-fashioned buckle collars (called a Tang or Pin buckle). These buckles are like a belt buckle, with a "pin" that fits into holes to adjust the length of the collar. These collars can be more difficult to release if caught and pulled tight on an object. A quick release buckle minimizes your fumbling to free your dog when faced with a life or death situation.

### Flat buckle martingale collar (with quick release type buckle), caveats listed below.

The addition of a buckle on a martingale collar allows for quick release in case of emergency. The quick release buckle is a relatively new addition to the traditional martingale collars. Martingales were invented for dogs whose heads are smaller than their necks, like greyhounds, so that the collar would not accidentally slip over their heads. CAVEAT: Martingale collars are also known as "limited choke collars". If fitted tightly, these collars can and will cause distress. If you are going to use one of these collars on your dog, I recommend that the collar be fitted loosely, so that when it is tightened to the greatest degree possible, it still is not tight enough to cause any discomfort.

When this type of collar is tightened completely, it should feel the same as a regular flat buckle collar.

I use these buckle martingale collars on my dog because I don't want her collar to be tight. My dog has lots of loose skin and thick fur, and a regular flat buckle collar, properly fitted, would be uncomfortable for her. She wears the buckle martingale collar only to hold her tags. I do not attach a leash to the collar. When we go out, we use a harness.

## HARNESSES

Today, there are lots of harnesses on the market, so the choice can be overwhelming. I am going to discuss the general harnesses most of you will use to walk your dogs. I am not addressing specialty harnesses like sled dog harnesses, skijoring harnesses, search and rescue harnesses, etc. I am talking about your regular, everyday harness. First, ask yourself, "Does my dog pull on the leash, or does he walk nicely at my side?" This will steer you in the right direction when selecting a harness for your dog.

If your dog doesn't pull on leash, you can use any harness really, but a harness where the leash attaches on the top/back is preferable. You do not need a front attach harness if your dog doesn't pull. Look for good quality with comfort in mind. Make sure the straps don't chafe, especially between the upper arm and the chest (what we incorrectly refer to as the armpits).

If your dog is still learning to walk nicely on leash, I recommend a front attach harness. These harnesses usually have two points of attachment: one on the back and one at the front of the chest. By attaching the leash to the front of a pulling dog's chest, physics is on your side! When your dog is walking ahead of you and he decides to pull, the harness and leash will steer him around towards you since you are then walking behind him. Note that these harnesses are simply a piece of equipment, and your dog must still be *taught* to walk nicely on leash. This is not a skill that dogs have naturally. It should be taught using positive methods and it will take practice and patience on your part.

New harnesses seem to come on the market every day, but you are looking for something sturdy, comfortable, and easy to put on. Again, make sure that none of the straps chafe your dog. It will be extremely uncomfortable for your dog if skin is rubbed raw. I don't recommend any harness that requires you to pick up your dog's paws to put their legs through openings, unless it is a very small dog. Choose a harness that has clips that allow you to put the harness on without touching your dog's legs and feet.

## Harnesses I Like

Balance Harness® by Blue-9

Freedom No Pull harness

PerfectFit harness

RuffWear Front Range® harness

Both the PerfectFit and Freedom harnesses are customizable so that you can really get a good fit for your dog. With the PerfectFit, you select the size of each of the three pieces that make up the harness. If your dog's body size and shape doesn't fit standard sizes offered with the Freedom harness, simply contact the manufacturer (2 Hounds Design), and they will guide you through ordering a custom harness made just for your dog. For example, my dog Rhubarb wears a hybrid: a size medium Freedom harness with a size large girth strap. The RuffWear and Balance harnesses are not customizable, but all straps are adjustable, and the padding on the Ruffwear harness is a really nice feature

Do your homework. Read reviews from reputable sources. New harnesses come on the market all the time, so choose wisely.

## LEASHES

First, let me just say, in general, NO RETRACTABLE LEASHES. Okay, now that that's off my chest, let's talk about leashes. The purpose of a leash is to attach you to your dog. It is not meant to yank on, to steer, to stop, to control, or to correct your dog. Think of a leash as a security measure, a "just in case" mechanism to ensure that your dog doesn't somehow get away from you. A regular, four or six-foot nylon leash is all you need. You can buy one for under ten dollars. If you want to get fancy, you can buy a leather leash, a waterproof leash, a reflective leash, a waist leash, and more. Take your activities into consideration and choose one that's right for you. Just make sure it has a handle, is either 4 or 6 feet long, has a secure clip on the end, and is appropriately sized for your dog.

Why no retractable leashes? I believe they can be dangerous. Dogs can be too far away from their owners (some retractable leashes are 26 feet long!), and it is very hard to handle a dog that is so far away if an altercation were to occur. A loose or aggressive dog may be just beyond the next corner, and your dog will be way ahead of you before you can even see what's happening. These leashes can jam, making it impossible to retract the line. They can get tangled and cause serious burns, rashes, cuts, or worse. A person can easily drop the handle. The plastic can become slippery if it gets wet, and those handles are fairly big and heavy, especially on the larger ones. This makes them hard to manage. People think that they will be able to apply the brake with the little button on the handle before their dog takes off after a squirrel or a cat or whatever. I am here to tell you that you will *never* be faster than your dog. And what will happen if your dog is walking ahead of you and you drop the handle while the line is extended? That big chunk of plastic will race towards your dog, clanking and smashing against the pavement, scaring your dog, causing him to run away as the Evil Handle Monster follows him. It sounds funny, but it's not. It can be terrifying to your dog! So, as you can see, I am *not* a fan of retractable leashes.

## LONG LINES

Sometimes called a tracking line, this piece of equipment allows your dog to have some freedom while still being tethered to you. You can go on a wilderness walk and let out the line as your dog explores, coiling it as you close the distance between you. Note that I did not say urban walk. Long lines have no place in walking a dog on busy streets or sidewalks. You can use your long line as part of recall training (teaching your dog to come when called) to ensure that your dog is safe while you practice.

You can also us a long line as a drag line. If your dog has progressed in recall training to the point that you want to move to a more challenging environment, you can have your dog attached to a long line but let it drag behind the dog. Just make sure that if you do this, the line is attached to the back of a harness (not a collar) for safety reasons and that there are no obstacles in the environment that the line can get tangled in. An open, fenced field or an empty stretch of beach is ideal for this type of training. The drag line allows you to get close to your dog in case recall fails. You can pick up the line from a distance, so it allows you to increase the likelihood that you will be able to get your dog back.

These long lines come in a variety of lengths, anywhere from ten to fifty feet. For walking my dog on trails or beaches,

I prefer fifteen- or twenty-foot lengths. I find that anything longer gets too unwieldy for me to handle. Long lines are available in nylon, leather, cotton, and my new favorite, a synthetic leather alternative. The synthetic material comes in bright colors, floats, and doesn't absorb dirt or moisture in its inevitable dragging across the dirt, sand, and mud. Check out Brahma Leads™ from Bold Lead Designs® here: https://boldleaddesigns.com/shop/brahma-leads-training-and-tracking-leash-in-soft-grip-leather-alternative/ (link verified on 10/13/2021)

## TREAT POUCHES

You will definitely need a treat pouch. If there is more than one adult in the home, each person should probably have their own treat pouch to wear while training and interacting with the puppy. Isn't that overkill, you ask? Nope. Get one treat pouch for each adult (or older child) in the house. If you only have one treat pouch, someone else will have it when you want or need it!

There are four types of treat pouches, and each has a different closing mechanism: drawstring, magnet, spring hinge, and slit closure.

The drawstring pouches are my least favorite because they are difficult to open and close, and you must leave the pouch open if you are using it during training. This leaves a gaping opening for your treats to fall out if you bend over or if your dog happens to jump or paw at it. However, if you just need a second treat pouch to keep by the back door to take outside to reward your dog, a drawstring pouch is fine.

The second type of pouch has a magnet closure at the top of the pouch. The idea behind this is great, but in my experience, the magnet is sometimes not strong enough to keep the treat pouch closed. If you bend over, the treats may spill out.

The third type of pouch uses a spring hinge closure. It pops open and stays open until you tap it shut. It's easy to use and can easily be shut to prevent spillage. This is my favorite type of treat pouch. I can recommend the PetSafe® Treat Pouch Sport model. It's nothing fancy, but it does the job well.

The fourth type of pouch is fairly new on the market, and it's made of silicone. There is a slit opening in the top which allows you to slide your hand inside to retrieve the treats. This type of pouch has received mixed reviews thus far. It is definitely easy to keep clean, but people also have found that treats spill out when they bend over. When it comes right down to it, it's a matter of personal preference.

## FOOD

Food is such an enormous and often controversial topic. I can only hope to touch on some basics and provide you with further references. You will no doubt find that you are given a lot of advice about dog food. It seems that everyone, including veterinarians, trainers, groomers, dog walkers, and your long-lost cousin, swear by their favorite brands. Studies are continuously being conducted on the health benefits/drawbacks of certain ingredients, vitamins, minerals and other additives. It is a difficult road to navigate on your own.

I rely heavily on the annual dog food review carried out by *The Whole Dog Journal*™. The staff do the research and provide a list of their top food picks every year. I check yearly to make sure that the foods I am feeding my own dog are on that list. You never know if one food gets dropped or another added. It's good to keep up on dog food ratings at least annually.

Here are some things to watch for:

- Beware of unidentified protein sources (the label will list *meat*, or *poultry* instead of naming the actual animal, like *lamb*, or *chicken*). You want to see the actual name of the animal.

- Be aware of ingredient splitting. We know that ingredients are listed in descending order. You might see an ingredient listed two or three times with slightly different names (corn meal, corn gluten meal, whole grain corn, etc.) If added together, the three similar ingredients would be way further up on the ingredient list. So instead of a food containing mostly a protein source, in actuality, it contains mostly an inexpensive carbohydrate source, in this case, in the form of cheap corn. Tricky.

- Be aware of the addition of potatoes and pulses (peas, lentils, etc.) in grain-free foods. If you see potatoes in the top four ingredients, find another food. Grains have been removed from these foods and have been replaced by potatoes and pulses. There is little information on the health effects of these ingredients on dogs. There are very few studies on how dogs metabolize these new additions to the dog food pipeline. More research is needed.

- If you are interested in learning more about dog food and the dog food industry, I highly recommend the book *Dog Food Logic* by Linda P. Case and her online course offerings at *The Science Dog*.

## TREATS

Everything about dog food also applies to dog treats. I like to use your dog's regular food for everyday training purposes but sometimes something special is useful. Selecting treats for your dog can be a daunting experience. There are *so* many varieties! I look for wholesome ingredients, with no dyes or artificial preservatives.

Soft or crunchy? I prefer small, soft treats to use in training sessions. These treats are often called *training treats* and come in a wide variety of brands and flavors. Each small treat can be further broken into tinier morsels, either with your fingers or you can cut them up with a knife in advance. When I use treats that are soft and already considered small by the average person, I still break them into smaller pieces, even for large dogs! I will break one small training treat into three or four pieces.

On the other hand, I like to use crunchy treats if I am stuffing them into a food dispensing toy. The hard, crunchy treats fall out of toys better and faster than the soft ones, which can get stuck.

## BELLS

If you decide to use bells as a way for your dog to communicate that he needs to go outside to eliminate, you should consider their composition. Many bells found in craft stores can contain lead. Lead is toxic. Your dog will be ringing the bells with his little nose several times a day for ten to fifteen years. That's a lot of potential exposure! I highly recommend using lead-free bells.

For hanging bells, I recommend a company called Poochie Bells®. Their bells are made in the USA and are all lead-free.

For fixed bells, I recommend the *Mighty Paw All Metal Tinkle Bell* or the *Mighty Paw Smart Bell*. The *All Metal Tinkle Bell* is on an iron support arm that acts like a spring when hit and rings the brass bell. The *Smart Bell* consists of a wireless transmitter and receiver and works like a doorbell. It is wall mounted and has a large round surface, easy for your dog's paw or nose to push. There is no fabric used on either of these bell systems, so dogs that tend to chew may do better with one of these bells.

## JOURNAL

The journal you choose for tracking your puppy's habits doesn't have to be anything special. It can just be a spiral bound notebook or a pad of lined paper. Easy. Just make sure you keep it in a location that is close to the door, with a pen somehow attached. Don't trust yourself to fill it in later; it just won't happen. See Elimination Journal, Chapter 3.

IT'S TRAINING TIME...

# Puppy-Proofing Your Home

So you've got a new dog, now what? A very big piece of the dog training puzzle is *management*. Yes, management. You can't train everything at once and so you must accept the fact that you will have to manage your dog's environment for a good length of time. How long? It depends on the dog, and it depends on you. Some dogs are less inquisitive than others, but they can all get themselves into trouble given the right — or wrong — situation. Prevention of problem behaviors is a huge part of raising a dog. We often hear about "puppy-proofing" the house, but what does that mean?

## PICK YOUR BATTLES

It is unreasonable to think that your puppy will not get into things he should not be touching in your house and yard. It is also very frustrating for new owners to always be telling their puppies *no, ah ah, leave it, stop, off, don't touch that*. A dog is a very curious little being and will naturally be drawn to objects in your home that are not necessarily meant for his amusement. Trying to teach a puppy to not touch things is an exercise in frustration when a little prevention could mean turning that frustration into enjoyment and building a great relationship with your new dog! It is also impossible for you to foresee every single situation that could arise. Try your best to prevent, supervise, and adapt. Be flexible. The changes you make don't necessarily have to be permanent.

## TOO MUCH FREEDOM TOO FAST

The most common error new dog owners make is giving their puppy too much freedom too quickly. Giving a puppy access to all rooms in the house is a huge mistake. First, the dog is not house trained and will soil your floors and carpets if not properly supervised. A dog often eliminates in places that are less "lived in." Likely areas include, but are not limited to, the formal dining room or living room, a back bedroom or closet, bathrooms, spare bedrooms, etc. Dogs typically do not like to soil the area in which they live, so they quietly retreat to one of these lesser-used areas of the house to carry out their business. Instead of giving your puppy free rein of the whole house, close off an area like the kitchen with gates, or use an exercise pen to contain your puppy when you are not supervising him. Try to contain your dog in an uncarpeted area. That way, accidents are easier to clean up. Dogs will also chew items that you would perhaps not think to remove, like fringes on rugs. If you have area rugs in the puppy's designated space, consider rolling them up and storing them until your dog is housetrained. That way, your beautiful rugs will not become stained or chewed.

## CLEAR THE COUNTERS

If you have a large breed dog, you will definitely need to clear your counters, especially in the kitchen and dining areas of your home, or gate off those rooms. Remember the golden rule of behavior: all behaviors that are reinforced are more likely to be repeated. If your young dog jumps up on the counter and snags a tasty piece of food, that behavior is very likely to be repeated. That yummy food is *very* reinforcing to your dog. He loves that loaf of bread or piece of chicken and so will always go back looking for more. Also remember that your dog's nose is very powerful, and although you think those cookies you put in that sealed container are safe, your dog can still smell them. No measly plastic container is going to be enough to protect those cookies from a hungry dog! All food items should be stored in cupboards or in the refrigerator until your dog learns not to jump on counters and learns not to steal your food. Some dogs remain opportunists for their whole lives and will always be unable to resist temptation. Make life easier for both you and your dog. Clear your counters.

## PICK UP YOUR STUFF

One of the most common problems encountered in puppy-raising is that the dog chews an item that it was not supposed to touch. Not only is this dangerous for the dog, but it can be very expensive for the owners. Remember, dogs do not instinctively know what is acceptable to chew on and what is off limits. Their curious nature means that everything that is accessible is fair game!

Common items that dogs will chew include remote controls, eyeglasses, earbuds, cell phones, shoes, socks, and underwear. Why are these items sought out by your pooch? We don't know for certain, but my guess is because they smell like you! Remember, a dog's nose is incredibly powerful and so they can detect your scent on objects. Make a habit out of putting things in their place, up or away from your dog's inquisitive reach. One of the funniest cases I had involved a little one-year-old Yorkshire terrier. The dog had chewed up five pairs of fifty-dollar earbuds that belonged to the son, in succession. As soon as mom bought another pair, they were chomped on. Five pairs! To date, the replacement cost was over $250.00! The dog had pulled them out of an open backpack left at the front door or found them left on the sofa or on the floor — you get the idea. The remedy for this situation was so simple. *Pick up your stuff!* I also recommended that mom stop buying replacement earbuds for her son. Once her son knew that his current earbuds were going to be his last, he began ensuring they were out of the dog's reach!

Here are some useful tips to help you avoid problems:

- **Pick up all remotes as soon as you turn off the device.** Make a habit of placing them in a designated spot, on a mantle, in a box or closed basket, or on top of a cabinet.

- **Put a laundry hamper with a lid in every bedroom and main bathroom.** Make it easy for the humans to put their soiled clothing in its proper place.

- **Put a covered bin or basket by the front door for the humans to put their shoes in when they come in the house.**

- **Don't leave things on the floor.** If it's on the floor, it's fair game for the dog.

- **Close closet and cupboard doors.**

- **Put food items in high cupboards rather than in those at dog-nose level.** Dogs are clever, and many learn to open drawers and doors.

# THE OPEN-CONCEPT AND CHERISHED HOME

Many homes today have open-concept floor plans and are sometimes difficult to gate. Some of the openings that would need to be closed off for confinement, like the kitchen, can be ten or more feet wide. In those cases, check for free standing gates or play yards. Many of them span over one hundred inches. When searching the internet, include the terms "dog play yard" and "baby play yard" and the results should include options for blocking off large spans.

If you are averse to putting up gates that are not quite aesthetically pleasing, there are still ways to include barriers using perhaps more unconventional ways. Expand your mind and your imagination! Half doors called Dutch doors, garden gates, or wrought iron gates are all potential options. These are, by their nature, costlier and more permanent solutions, but they will afford you a whole host of options and ideas for keeping your beautiful home intact while adding to its aesthetic. I personally love the Dutch door idea. A Dutch door is a door that has been divided into two parts horizontally, allowing for one half to be shut and the other left open. If you are handy, you can even make one as a do-it-yourself project. There are detailed instructions available online for you to follow.

# ELECTRICAL CORDS

Electrical cords deserve special attention. One of the saddest cases I have ever encountered in my years as a dog trainer involved a beautiful, 6 month old golden retriever puppy. The owners had decided not to use a crate as part of management and training because the dog "didn't like it." They also had a lot of computer and stereo equipment that resulted in a myriad of wires and cords all over the floor. They were using plastic bins to try to keep the dog out of those areas. The puppy was big for his age, and whilst those bins may have worked for the first few weeks, the dog quickly learned to push them aside or jump over them. I warned them about the dangers of the puppy around the wires and cables. I told them over and over, in as many different ways as I could think of, that the dog was likely to chew on the cords. I pleaded with them to separate the dog in a more secure fashion. If they did not want to crate-train the puppy, they could use gates or tethers. Anything was preferable to their current situation. I only saw that dog once. I received a call from their veterinarian about a week later, letting me know that the puppy had been electrocuted and passed away while the owners were in the same room with him, working on their computers. I was so sad and so angry.

When I go into a house for a puppy consult, the first thing I do is take in the environment, scanning for potential dangers. I often point out a problem, only to have the person say, "Oh, my puppy never touches that," or, "My dog would never chew on that." My reply is always the same: "Not yet." Yes, they may never touch it, but in my experience, they eventually will. It is better to prevent a tragedy than to wait for one to happen. When it happens for the first time, it may be too late, just like in the case of that sweet golden retriever puppy. It only took one time; the first time.

There are many ways of hiding electrical cords. You can push a heavy piece of furniture in front of them, ensuring that your dog can't access the cords from the side or underneath. You can use tie wraps to bundle cords together and use duct tape to secure them to the floor or wall. You can get cable "tunnels" to securely hide cords and cables. The tunnels are cheap, easy to install, and look great. When you are installing these fixes, make sure the dog does not watch you do it. Dogs are curious, and if you draw attention to something, they will want to go check it out. So, craft your electrical cord fixes in secret.

## PLANTS

Many plants are toxic to dogs, including some indoor plants, some that can be found in your garden, and some found in the wild. Become familiar with what you have in your house and outdoor areas and check to see if any of them are toxic. Prevent accidental ingestion by supervising your dog or fencing off areas of concern. Place houseplants out of reach, whether they are toxic or not, to avoid having the puppy consume them or dig through the dirt, thereby making you an indoor garden that you really didn't want. The ASPCA maintains a list of the most common plants that are toxic to dogs here: https://www.aspca. org/pet-care/animal-poison-control/toxic-and-non-toxic-plants (link verified on 10/13/2021)

## DANGLING THINGS

Take a good look around your house as if you are seeing it for the first time. Pay attention to anything that hangs or dangles. We often overlook items like this simply because we are so used to seeing them. They just don't appear to be a potential dog toy to us. A good way to do this is to get down on the floor and crawl around, trying to look at things from your puppy's perspective. Puppies are immensely curious and are always looking for an engaging, fun activity. Pulling on things that dangle is a puppy favorite!

Some items that are of concern include:

- Tablecloth edges
- Electrical cords

- Blind cords

- Clothing hanging from chairs, wall hooks or a coat tree

- Kitchen towels hanging on the stove or cupboard door

- Chair pad or furniture slip cover ties

- Cushions with fringes

- Rugs or carpet with frayed edges or fringes

- Appliances like a hot iron, electric shaver, or curling iron

## GARBAGE

Dogs are opportunists. If food is present, they will likely try to eat it. If the food is in a garbage can, many dogs will raid it. Sometimes, I think dogs must be amazed at our generosity. "Wow! Look what my humans left for me! Leftover chicken bones and bacon grease! How thoughtful of them!" It is unreasonable to expect a young dog to not try to get into the smelly garbage when you are not looking. Remember, prevention is the key. When your dog finds delicious food in the garbage can, it is highly rewarding for your dog, and so he will continue to try to get to it. Leftover food is a powerful incentive for many dogs, so prevent it from happening in the first place, and your dog will learn not to try.

What can you do to prevent this from happening? First, get a garbage can with a lid. This may sound like common sense, but I know many people who expected their dog to leave their open, odiferous kitchen garbage can alone. They quickly found out that this was not going to happen. Try to get a garbage can with a lid that doesn't have a lip for the dog to flip open. Don't get a garbage can with a swinging lid. Your dog could still get into the garbage by sticking his head inside, and then he may get stuck. A dog with his head stuck in a garbage can lid may conjure up a funny picture in your mind, but the poor dog is likely to panic and may make a real mess of your whole house. I like the Simplehuman® semi-round garbage can. There are no corners on the front for your dog to grasp, it's smooth, and there is no lip to flip, but anything similar would work just fine. If your dog is big enough to knock the whole garbage can over onto its side and dump the contents, you can put some weight in the bottom of the can. A plate weight, like those used for weight lifting, works well. Simply put a 10-pound (or heavier, if necessary) plate in the bottom of the garbage can, between the bag and the hard, plastic liner. This will make the can heavy on the bottom and very difficult for your dog to knock over.

If all else fails, deny your dog access to the garbage can completely by putting the garbage can behind a closed door. Some people use their pantry or a broom closet to accomplish this. Alternatively, you can gate your kitchen off so that your dog does not have access to the room containing the garbage can at all! It's your choice. There are many solutions to this very common problem. Pick one and go with it.

You can do the same for bathroom and bedroom garbage cans. Dogs seem to have a penchant for soiled tissues and other bathroom trash. It's more than a bit disgusting from a human perspective, but most dogs do like bathroom garbage. How can you handle this unappetizing and potentially embarrassing problem? Either restrict access so that the dog cannot reach the garbage by gating or closing bathroom doors, put garbage cans inside cupboards, or change out your garbage cans for ones with lids. In my experience, the option of just keeping doors closed is not always successful because of human failure. We forget to close the doors! It is best to replace your open garbage cans with ones with lids or put the garbage in the cupboard under the sink. Simplehuman also makes mini versions of their trashcans that are great for bathrooms and bedrooms.

## THE GARDEN

Why does my dog dig up my garden? This is a very common and frustrating complaint. We spend so much time planting and tending our gardens, and in one fell swoop, the dog destroys our work. Most dogs like to dig in the dirt. Gardens are especially appealing because the soil is usually looser than the surrounding area, and so it is easier to dig there. Gardens are also very tempting because the soil has been amended with compost or other organic matter, and so it is full of pungent scents. Lastly, our dogs watch us dig in our gardens and just follow our lead! We dig and bury stuff there, so they do too!

In addition to the annoyance of dogs digging up our gardens, there is the risk of our dogs ingesting something toxic. You may want to look at changing your gardening and lawn practices to better suit keeping your dog healthy. Putting chemicals in and on the lawn and garden that are toxic is not a good idea. Remember, your dog is much closer to the ground than you are, and they walk barefoot in, roll in, sniff, and eat the grass and plants, so, unlike us, they are exposed to the lawn chemicals to a much greater degree.

## LIGHT AT THE END OF THE TUNNEL

In my experience, if you can prevent your puppy from getting into things or having access to potential trouble areas, the adult dog they become will not see those things as toys or entertainment. If your dog never has access to shoes to chew as a puppy, he won't chew shoes when he is an adult. If your puppy never gets food off the counter, he will stop jumping on counters as an adult. This strategy is not always one hundred percent foolproof, but it has been my experience that it goes a long way to raising a dog that is easy to manage and a joy to live with.

# CHAPTER TWO

# Wylie Comes Home

I had been searching for information on puppy raising for many months before getting my puppy and stumbled around from site to site, book to book. I didn't really know what I was looking for except that I wanted to find something with kind methods. It seems odd now, but there wasn't that much information on modern, science-based dog training available at the time. Dog training has come so far in the last two decades! My last exposure to dog training had been over twenty-five years prior, when I took my sweet Roxy to obedience class. I was taught "old school" methods back then, using a choke collar and a ton of "corrections" to get my dog to "behave." This was all that was available to me at the time. It was the only way I knew to train dogs, and so I did it. It was emotionally and physically draining every single week, and the practicing in between was almost as bad. I will say now, out loud, to my sweet Roxy, wherever you are, "I am very, very sorry that I hurt you while trying to train you. I didn't know any better at the time. I am sorry. I am amazed that you loved me anyway. Thank you, sweet Roxy".

Back to my new dog. We named her way before we got her. Whenever Tim and I were driving in the car during those weeks before we picked her up, we would play the Name That Dog game, running name after name past each other to see if one would stick.

I would start. "How about Gracie?"

"No way!" Tim would answer. "Not a people name!"

"Okay then, how about Midnight, or Magpie, or Magnolia? Those aren't people names."

"I don't like any of those." Tim would answer.

"Okay, you pick one!" I would challenge.

"Maybe Bella, or Daisy?" Tim tentatively suggested.

"Everybody names their dog Bella or Daisy. Those are too common."

And so, it would continue. Indigo, Licorice, Paisley, Poppy, Sugar, and on and on. Nothing seemed right. If I liked a name, Tim didn't. If Tim liked a name, I didn't.

Then, out of the blue, Tim said, "How about Wylie? As in Wyle E. Coyote from the Bugs Bunny cartoons?" Yes! Ding, ding, ding! It just resonated. That was the right name. We both loved it. Her full registered American Kennel Club® name eventually became Wylie One of Highbridge, because that is where we lived, in Highbridge, Wisconsin, and she certainly turned out to be a wily one!

As I hadn't trained a dog for so many years, I didn't know where to start. I found a book called *The Art of Raising a Puppy* by the Monks of New Skete*, and it became my handbook for all things puppy. The book (and the Monks) have since fallen out of favor in the positive, force-free training community for their punitive and aversive training methods, but they were spot on with their puppy development information and for making me try to see things from the dog's perspective. Much of the old school information that the

Monks prescribe just didn't sit well with me. I just did not want to inflict pain on my dog in the name of training. Those techniques didn't work for me when I trained Roxy, and they weren't going to work when I tried to train Wylie. I guess I wasn't "hard" enough, and more importantly, I didn't want to be!

I prepared for Wylie's homecoming: Little pink plastic crate — check. Three-foot tall baby gate for the stairs — check. Dog bed, chew toys, squeaky toys, plushy toys, rawhides, dry dog food, dog cookies, leash, collar — check. Yes, I had everything, and I was ready. I could hardly contain my excitement. We picked her up on a cold April day in 2004 when she was eight weeks old. Wow, she was so stinking cute, a little black bundle of licks, wags, and wiggles, and oh, that sweet puppy breath! It was enough to melt your heart. I was instantly in love with my dog.

The car ride home went smoothly. It was a two-hour, uneventful drive with Wylie either snuggled in my arms or on the floor of the truck, napping. When we finally got home, I brought her inside and let her explore. We had just finished building our house, and so our floors where brand new, shiny maple hardwood. Wylie navigated them confidently. She sniffed every nook and cranny and showed absolutely no fear when encountering new objects, surfaces, or scents. She was my brave little puppy.

Within ten minutes, she had peed on her fluffy new dog bed. That was my first mistake, the first of many, many mistakes. I made a mental note: buy a washable dog bed with a removable cover.

It became very clear to me that we needed to establish a solid routine for Wylie so that we would know when she needed to go out, when and how much to feed her, when she should nap, when we would play. We were just beginning potty training, and if I'm honest, I was a little lost on that topic.

We limited access to certain rooms, shutting all of the doors to rooms in the back of the house, the bedrooms and the two bathrooms. If Wylie was allowed back there, I wouldn't be able to keep my eyes on her and I correctly predicted that she would get up to no good. Eyes on the dog! Those back rooms were carpeted, and I knew that Wylie would no doubt have accidents. I didn't want her peeing on our new wall-to-wall carpet. It would be much easier to clean up her messes on hardwood or tile.

Dogs are opportunists and will chew on and play with just about anything that's available, and Wylie was no exception. As a matter of fact, she went to the head of the class in that department! It quickly became apparent that Wylie was a puppy who needed to have something in her mouth at all times. If there was nothing appropriate for her to chew, she would find something. We always kept a few toys handy, stashed all over the house, ready to put into her mouth if she decided she was ready to chew on something.

We were very diligent in watching her; we had to be if we valued our stuff. There were eyes on her at all times, and if we couldn't watch her, she was in her crate. This was for her safety, so that she would not have the opportunity to ingest something that could hurt her, and it was for our sanity, so that we could protect our belongings from the little jaws of certain destruction.

We had taken great care to puppy proof the main living areas and the kitchen, ensuring that everything was picked up off the floor or put away behind closed doors. We were lucky to have an entry that was closed off by a door so that all of our shoes and boots were not accessible to our alligator puppy. Even so, Wylie quickly and efficiently showed us where we fell short.

We found out that there were those white papery tags hanging down on the bottom of our living room club chairs. We snipped them off. There were tags on a lot of other things I hadn't noticed or paid attention to before too: sofa cushions, blankets, towels, clothing, dog toys. So many things! Wylie found them all. She loved to chew on them, shred them, and would swallow them if we didn't stop her. This was my first inkling into Wylie's lifelong desire to consume inappropriate things. Lots of dogs destroy things. That's a common puppy/dog thing to do. However, not that many ingest the items afterward. I found out that this is a common trait of the Labrador retriever. Lucky me. Tim and I went around the house looking for all the tags we could find and cut them all off. Done.

What else was our little angel puppy going to show us? She showed us that puppies had particular uses for common household items. Tablecloths were for yanking, rugs were for chomping, wood was for chewing, dog beds were for unstuffing, towels were for dragging, carpet was for unraveling, paper (any paper: toilet paper, tissues, paper towels, newspaper, magazines, books, printer paper) was for snacking. Luckily, we were quick learners and so we were able to keep damage to a minimum. I learned then that it was way easier to put things away rather than try to stop Wylie from getting them. Yelling *NO* at her a million times a day was just exhausting and frustrating and fruitless. In the end, it was so much easier to remove access to the sought-after items or remove the items altogether. We just put them away. Then we could enjoy our puppy.

 *\*DISCLAIMER: For the record, I do not recommend, condone, or use the training methods in the book entitled* The Art of Raising a Puppy *by the Monks of New Skete. That book was all I had at the time, and I did not know any better. We live, we learn and when we know better, we do better. This is one of the reasons I am writing this book, so that I can share my mistakes and point you in the right direction with your dog.*

# Puppy Preparation and the First Days At Home

No matter how much you prepare, no matter how much you read, no matter how much you think you are ready, things just won't go according to plan. Be ready to adjust your expectations and be flexible. If there is one thing your puppy is going to teach you in the next months and years, it's Patience with a capital P. Here are some tips, tricks and techniques to make your transition to puppy owner easier.

## YOUR FIRST NIGHT TOGETHER

Puppy's first night with you is often a very difficult one. Having a new puppy means you are going to lose some sleep. There is *no* way around this. It's part of being a new puppy owner, plain and simple. However, you can try to put everything in your and puppy's favor!

# WHERE SHOULD YOUR PUPPY SLEEP?

There are many different opinions out there as to where your puppy should sleep. I have strong feelings on this subject. Here are my thoughts and recommendations.

## First, let's look at where your puppy *should not* sleep:

- **Isolated in another room**. I do *not* think it is a good idea to put the puppy in another room, outside of your bedroom, especially one that is located far away from the humans, with the door closed. Many people choose this option so that they don't have to hear the puppy whining, barking, and crying. When a puppy is whining and carrying on like that, she is trying to tell you something! "I'm lonely!" "I need to go outside to potty!" "I'm scared!" Being left alone makes this worse. If you want a close relationship with your dog, now is the time you should be bonding with your puppy. You can't do this from another room. Dogs are social animals. We bred them to be social with humans, so they should be with us.

- **In bed with a child**. I do *not* recommend that a puppy be allowed to sleep in bed with a child. This is a safety hazard for both puppy and child. Here are a few hazards for you to consider. It will be very difficult to house train your dog if the puppy is in a child's room. Children sleep deeply and will not hear a puppy whining in the middle of the night. You also risk the puppy urinating or defecating on the bed. There is the danger of the child rolling over on the puppy and suffocating her, or the puppy could fall or jump off the bed, risking injury. If the puppy is bigger, she can wake in the middle of the night, jump off the bed, and get into trouble. Young puppies and dogs tend to chew on anything and everything, and a child's room is full of temptations. A child cannot be made responsible for supervising a dog overnight. So, it's just not a good idea.

- **In the garage**. Do I really have to explain this one? Do *not* isolate your puppy.

## Where your puppy *should* sleep:

The best place for puppy is in the adult's room, beside the bed. A crate can be placed in most bedrooms, at the head of the bed, next to the adult who is going to be responsible for taking puppy out to potty in the middle of the night. Yes, the puppy will have to go outside in the middle of the night. It is a rarity that your young puppy will be able to sleep right through until morning. Count yourself extremely lucky if that happens! So, be ready to deal with the sleep interruptions.

Plan ahead! If you are living alone, it's all on you. However, if there are two adults sleeping in the bedroom, you can split up responsibilities. Do this in advance so that each of you knows what the other is supposed to be doing. Assign a person to be responsible for:

- the last potty trip before bed (the night owl)

- the middle of the night potty trip
  (whoever sleeps closest to the crate)

- the first thing in the morning potty trip
  (the early riser)

If everyone knows and agrees to their role, things will go much more smoothly. No fighting, please!

Your puppy may already come to you from the breeder or shelter with some crate experience. Some breeders will start this process for you. If you adopted from a shelter or rescue, your puppy may be familiar with a crate but may not have ever been alone in one. She may have only slept with her littermates present. If your puppy is comfortable in her crate, then you can put her in it the very first night she is home. However, if she is not familiar with a crate, she will likely whine and cry. You won't do your puppy any favors by shoving her in the crate and letting her *cry it out*. This will only stress the puppy, and it will ensure that you don't sleep at all.

So, if your puppy is not familiar with the crate and is not comfortable in one, for the first night (and a few more after that), I recommend that you put your puppy's crate bed (not the crate, the bedding you put inside the crate) on your bed so your puppy can sleep with you but on her bedding. Having the puppy sleep on her own bedding, in your bed, will familiarize her with it so when you transfer her bedding to the crate, she will already know that it's her bed. You will eventually transition the puppy, after a few days, into her crate beside your bed, having spent some time crate-training her during the day (see section entitled Crate Training 101 which follows).

If your puppy is having difficulty making the transition from in your bed to in her crate on the floor, try elevating her crate to the same level as your bed. Put the crate on a large box or bedside table (make sure it's secure), at the head of the bed, for a few nights. Once she is comfortable there, you can transition her crate to the floor. This method will minimize the number of sleepless nights you are going to have and will reduce the puppy's anxiety, and with the puppy sleeping beside you, you will be able to feel or hear when she wakes needing to go outside to potty.

# SUBSTITUTE LITTERMATES

Your puppy is going to be really lonely — and chilly — for a little while. After all, she has just left her littermates behind. She is used to sleeping with warm bodies around her and the sound of multiple heartbeats. There are a couple of ideas you can try to recreate this environment for your puppy.

## Hot Water Bottle and a Clock that Ticks

Fill a hot water bottle with *warm* water (not hot). Put a cozy cover over it. Many hot water bottles now come with covers included. If you are purchasing a cover, look for one without any drawstrings, tassels, or pompoms on it. These will only be intriguing and potentially hazardous playthings for your puppy. Then, look for an old-fashioned clock, one that makes a ticking sound. You might have an old wind up one lying around somewhere. Wind up your clock and put it inside the hot water bottle cover. Put the hot-water-bottle-clock combo on puppy's bed for her to snuggle up to.

## Heartbeat Pillow or Snuggle Puppy

These toys are specifically designed for puppies. Both mimic a heartbeat and provide a heat source for puppy. Puppies will curl up with these toys and be more comfortable when sleeping alone. Both basically function the same way. Your dog won't care which one you get for her. The SmartPetLove Snuggle Puppy Behavioral Aid Toy and the PetZu Mother's Comfort Heartbeat Pet Pillow are available from multiple online sources.

By employing these strategies, your puppy will adjust to sleeping soundly in her crate. The transition won't be perfect, but it will be pretty darned close.

IT'S TRAINING TIME...

# Crate Training 101

I am a big believer in crate training. In my opinion, you are doing a disservice to your dog if you do not crate-train him. After all, there *will* be times when your dog must be in a crate. No, you say? Well, what about when he goes to the groomer, or must stay at the vet if he is sick, or if he needs to be boarded in the future? All these situations will require your dog to be crated.

Having worked in a veterinary setting, I have witnessed firsthand what can happen to a dog that is not crate-trained. The complete panic that can occur when they are put into a crate or dog run is heartbreaking. Some dogs refuse to eat. Others are so stressed that they vomit or have bouts of diarrhea. Some bark incessantly. This can be averted, or at least minimized, if you take the time to crate-train your puppy. Crate training will help him be more comfortable and less anxious in these settings.

We already talked about your first night home with your puppy (see previous section on Puppy Preparation and the First Days at Home). The question remains: how do you train your puppy to love his crate *during the day?*

# SELECT A CRATE AND BEDDING

First, choose what kind of crate you want: wire crate (most popular), plastic airline-style crate, or soft-sided crate. Wire crates are convenient since they collapse for ease of storage and travel. They can be heavy to move though, especially if you have to get a large one. They also let your puppy have a great view of what's going on in his environment.

If you think your dog will ever have to travel by plane in cargo, an airline crate might be a good choice. This type of crate is made of heavy plastic and is more enclosed, so your puppy will have to get used to this darker environment. It's better to start now rather than wait until your dog is an adult to introduce this type of confinement.

The soft-sided crates are a really nice option for dogs who will not chew or scratch. This may be an option for your dog as an adult, but it is rarely a good one for puppies. Puppies are naturally curious and will chew on anything they can find. They may be able to chew a hole through the fabric or find a small seam or tab that sticks out to chew on. Therefore, I don't generally recommend a soft-sided crate for a puppy or any dog that tries to get out of their crate. A determined dog can destroy a soft-sided crate.

You could easily use both a wire crate and an airline crate together. I would recommend the airline crate for the bedroom and the wire crate for the family room. That way, your dog becomes familiar with both types.

Regarding bedding, most puppies will chew or destroy dog beds. To puppies, beds are mostly just big, fluffy stuffed toys. I know many, many owners that, once their dog destroys one bed, simply buy another one to replace it, and guess what? The dog destroys that second bed too, and on and on. I recommend trying a crate pad instead of a fluffy bed. A pad provides a nice surface for puppy. I would also suggest that you look for a crate pad that is waterproof or has an optional waterproof liner. Remember, your puppy will not be house-trained for several months, so accidents are bound to happen. Be proactive, buy a waterproof liner! If you think your puppy will be cold, you can also use a towel as a blanket. They are cheap and easy to wash. Make sure you remove all tags and loose threads from the towels though. Puppies tend to find these little items and chew on them.

## Select the Crate Size

Now, select an appropriately sized crate. It should be big enough for your dog to sit, stand, and turn around comfortably. Your dog's head should not touch the roof of the crate. You can buy an adult-sized crate if the crate comes with a divider to adjust the space available to your puppy instead of needing to purchase a new, larger crate as your puppy grows.

## Find the Best Location

Start by placing his crate in a location where the family spends leisure time together. This is most often in the kitchen or family room area. When you are selecting a spot for the crate, look for a place where the dog will be able to see what is going on in the household, will not be isolated, but will be out of the way of heavy traffic. Make sure that the crate will not be in direct sunlight and will not be too close to heating and cooling vents, or in the path of heavy drafts. Once you have selected your location, put the crate in place with the crate door open. Make sure the door does not accidentally close; use a zip tie, bungee cord or some other kind of fastener if you must. Okay, now you are ready to begin crate-training your puppy.

## Puppy Crating Times

In general, during daytime hours, puppies can hold their urine for one hour for every month old they are, give or take an hour. Little ones, like Yorkies, can hold for less time. How long can you leave your puppy in his crate? Use these guidelines.

- 8 to 10 weeks → 30 to 60 minutes

- 11 to 14 weeks → 1 to 3 hours

- 15 to 16 weeks → 3 to 4 hours

- 17+ weeks → 4 to 5 hours

*But I have to go to work,* you say! See section on housetraining for how to handle this situation.

## Stop! Don't Do This Stuff!

- Never force your puppy into his crate. You will only scare him and make him fearful of you *and* the crate. That's a double *no-no.*

- Never use the crate as a punishment. You want the crate to be a happy place where your puppy can relax. Punishing a dog by forcing him into his crate will backfire on you.

- Don't try to hurry. Train at your puppy's pace. You cannot rush this process. If you do, you will create fear and anxiety around the crate. This is *not* what you want to do.

- Don't overcrowd the crate with a thick, fluffy bed. Your puppy may get too hot and have nowhere to cool off.

- Don't expect your puppy not to pee just because he is in his crate. A puppy can only hold his urine for so long. If you leave your puppy in his crate longer than he is physically able to hold it, he will pee. This will likely prolong and complicate the housetraining process.

## Yes, Do This Stuff!

- Make the crate a comfy place. Use a semi-flat crate pad, one that is not going to envelop your puppy and make him overheat. You can add a towel or two inside the crate for your puppy to snuggle up in if he chooses. Some examples of good choices for beds include:

  - Kong® Durable Crate Mat

  - P.L.A.Y.® Pet Lifestyle And You Chill Pad and waterproof Outdoor Chill Pad

  - K&H™ Pet Products Self-Warming Crate Pad is a nice choice for young puppies

  - K9 Ballistic Tough Crate Pad™ has an option of a warm side (velvet-like) and a cool side (ripstop nylon) side, making it ideal for winter/summer use

  - Vetbed® by Petlife has the advantage of having drainage properties, good heat retention (important for a young puppy), and it is machine washable

- Make sure you take your puppy outside to eliminate before putting him in his crate.

- Feed your puppy in his crate. Your puppy will make a good association between food and his crate.

- Give your puppy a long-lasting food treat in his crate while you sit beside him and watch television or read a book. Tip: get a short length of rope and tie a knot on one end. Get an empty Classic Kong®. Feed the other end of the rope through the large hole in the Kong, then through the small hole. The knot will act as a stopper so that the rope doesn't come out. Stuff the Kong. Now use the long end of the rope to tie the Kong in the back of puppy's crate. This will keep the Kong inside the crate, keeping him inside, voluntarily, with the crate door open. He will be free to leave but won't want to. Make sure to call him out just as he finishes eating. Don't let him wander out on his own if you can help it.

- Once your puppy is staying in the crate for longer periods of time, make sure you take him out to eliminate as soon as you take him out of his crate.

## Seed the Enchanted Crate

Secure the crate door open. You want to prevent the door from accidentally closing or bumping into your puppy. When your puppy isn't looking, plant some treats in and around the crate. Don't make it too hard for him by hiding them or putting them way at the back of the crate. Just drop them around the outside and just inside the crate door. Make sure you are using something your puppy loves to eat. Let him discover the treats all by himself. Repeat this a few times. Make sure he doesn't see you put the food inside. You want it to seem like the crate is sprouting delicious treats. The crate will seem magical to him!

## Entice Puppy Into the Crate

Next, sprinkle some food in the crate and sit on the floor next to it with your puppy. When he puts his head or paws inside the crate, drop a few more treats in from the top of the crate. Praise him. *Good boy!* When he finishes eating and investigating, call him out of the crate with a release word. I suggest using *Okay*, but you can choose another word if you like. *Out, Release, All Done*, whatever you prefer, but be consistent. Once you pick a word or phrase that will mean "you can come out of your crate now," stick with it.

Once your puppy is comfortable going in and out of the crate on his own, you are ready for the next step. Choose your cue phrase. It can be something like *In your crate*, or *Kennel up*, or *Go to bed*, whatever you like, but you must be consistent with whatever you choose. Sit beside the crate. Call your dog over to you and toss a treat inside the crate as you say your cue. When your dog goes inside, praise him and give him another treat while he is still inside. Then, call him out with your release word/phrase. Don't give him a treat when he comes out. We want him to think that the good stuff happens *inside* the crate, not outside of it. Repeat ten times or so. Take a short break to play with your dog. Then, repeat another ten times. You're done for now. *Good job!*

## Cue Your Puppy

Later in the day, you'll be ready for another session. Get your treats and go sit by the crate with your dog. Do a bit of a warmup by repeating what you did in the previous step. Say your cue, toss the treat in, call your dog out. Repeat a couple of times. Now, instead of dropping the treat in first, say your cue and point to the inside of the crate. It helps if you use a similar hand motion to point as the one you just used to toss the treat inside. Wait. Give your dog a few seconds to puzzle this out. You may need to cue this again, but don't rush. Your dog needs time to think! When your puppy goes in, heap on some praise and a few treats, then call him out. Repeat ten times. If your puppy doesn't go in, go back to the previous step and practice a little more. Remember, your dog sets the pace, not you! Take a break and do another ten repetitions. *This is going really well!*

## Close the Door

Warm up with a few repetitions of the previous step. Now, when your puppy goes inside, close the door and feed a few treats through the top or back of the crate. Immediately open the door and call your puppy out. Repeat ten times. If puppy seems scared or anxious with the door completely closed, make it easier by only closing it halfway for a few repetitions, then three quarters of the way, then close it completely. Again, your dog sets the pace. Take a little break. In your next set of repetitions, gradually lengthen the time you keep the door closed. When I say gradually, I mean *really* gradually! Everything moves slowly in the dog world. Start with one second, then two, then five. Count in your head. If at any time your puppy seems scared, it means you're going too fast. You may need ten repetitions with the door closed for just one second. There's no rush. *You're both doing great!*

## Stand Up and Move

Warm up with the previous step. Next, with the door still closed, stand up and pop a treat in the crate, take a few steps back, and then return and treat again. Open the door and release your puppy. Repeat ten times, each time backing away in a different direction, adding steps, turning your back. Take a break and repeat, this time lengthening the time your puppy is in the crate. Keep it short. Five seconds. Make it variable. Five seconds, then eight, then ten, then back to five, then fifteen, back to ten seconds. You get the idea. Open the door and cue your dog to come out. Repeat ten times. *You are both amazing!*

## Reduce the Treats

Keep it up with short little sessions like this but reduce how often you give a treat. Take a few steps left, then a few more to the right, wait ten seconds, then treat. The more comfortable your dog gets, the fewer treats you will need to give.

## Leave the Room

You are making it more and more difficult, so watch your dog for any sign of discomfort. If all is well, start leaving the room, but only for a second. Pop out and right back in. Go back to the crate, treat, and release your puppy. Your job then becomes to leave for longer durations, gradually stretching the time out, almost imperceptibly, so that your puppy barely notices. If puppy cries or barks, you are moving too fast. Return to an easier step. Then, you're done! *Wow, that went really well!*

## Add Time

Over the next few days, use a long-lasting food toy in the crate to increase the amount of time your puppy spends in the crate when you are home. Cue your dog to go in and give her the food toy. Close the door. Sit down and relax. Read a book. Fold the laundry. Surf the net. Whatever. Every once in a while, calmly praise your puppy. *Good boy, Levi.* Levi will likely ignore you, but that's okay; he heard you. When your puppy finishes, he will likely look at you or stand up, expecting to be let out. Wait a few minutes. Stretch it out. You can ask your puppy for a sit or a down if you've trained that skill. Wait. Your goal is thirty minutes. Yes, that's a long time. *I know you can do it!*

## Leave the House

This is it. The Big Show. You are going to cue your puppy inside the crate, give him a stuffed Kong, close the door, leave the room, leave the house. Go sit in the car for ten minutes. Return as if nothing happened. Gradually extend the time you leave your puppy alone over the next several days. Remember to follow the guidelines based on your puppy's age. You're done. *Congratulations! Good job!*

IT'S TRAINING TIME...

# Socialization Dos and Don'ts

I'm sure you've heard people say that it's really important to "socialize" your puppy. Everyone seems to have an opinion on this socialization thing. Some people think that an adult dog who is fearful just needs to be "socialized." Others think that you should not begin to socialize a puppy until they are fully vaccinated, usually after sixteen weeks of age. Yet others believe that the best way to socialize their puppy is to just bring them everywhere, whether or not the puppy is scared. Who to believe? As you can see, this process of "socialization" is fraught with pitfalls into which well-meaning puppy owners can stumble!

The American Veterinary Society of Animal Behavior (AVSAB) recommends that puppies begin socialization outings as soon as a week after they are given their first set of vaccinations and first deworming. The trick is to balance the risk of illness and the risk of developing behavior problems due to a lack of proper socialization. "Behavioral issues, not infectious diseases, are the number one cause of death for dogs under three years of age,"[1] and that includes puppies.

My goal in this section is to give you sound resources you

[1] *AVSAB Position Statement on Puppy Socialization:* https://avsab.org/resources/position-statements/ *(link verified on 10/13/2021)*

can trust and to fill out the edges, so to speak, by providing some tips and pointers based on my years of puppy experience. By no means is this chapter meant to be a complete guide to socialization. For detailed information on puppy socialization, I urge you to check out *Puppy Culture*. You can find information on this great program at www.puppyculture.com.

First, let's look at the dictionary definition. According to Merriam-Webster, socialization is defined as follows.

https://www.merriam-webster.com/dictionary/socialization:

> *The process beginning during childhood by which individuals acquire the values, habits, and attitudes of a society.*

But there is another definition! I could hardly believe that it was included, but here it is:

> *Exposure of a young domestic animal (such as a kitten or puppy) to a variety of people, animals, and situations to minimize fear and aggression and promote friendliness.*

And this example is included:

> *Some adult dogs, because of a lack of socialization combined with genetic tendencies, can never transfer certain individuals from the "unfamiliar" to the "familiar" category.*
> *— Dog Watch*

In terms of your puppy, there is no more important aspect to raising a well-adjusted dog than a solid socialization process.

There is general agreement that the prime period of socialization is between two and sixteen weeks of age. Yes, you read that right, *two weeks*. That's why you hear dog professionals harp on the importance of finding a good breeder. Puppies should be with their mother and littermates until they are at least eight weeks old, so socialization from two to eight weeks rests solely with the breeder. It's totally out of your hands! If your puppy comes from a puppy mill or a backyard breeder, she will have had little to no opportunity for socialization. These puppies are behind the curve right from the start. At a time when their little brains are so receptive to new experiences, they receive few to none.

Socialization begins with the breeder and continues when you bring your puppy home. Your puppy is learning from you every moment that you are together. As soon as you get your puppy, she will be exposed to your home, yard, car, family members, perhaps another dog or cat. That's already a lot to take in! Your first concern with your puppy should be to focus on building a relationship based on trust, patience, love, and understanding. The easiest way to do this is through gentle play and hand feeding. After you have spent a few days getting to know one another, you can start to venture out.

Why is this socialization thing so important? Well, dogs don't understand the world the way we do. We understand concepts. If I say the word *shoe* to you, you can immediately conceptualize shoes. Maybe it's the ones you're wearing at the moment, your favorite ones, your running shoes, dress shoes, red shoes, black shoes, leather shoes, boots, moccasins, work boots, etc. And if you happen to see a stray shoe in the middle of the road (Who the heck loses one shoe while driving down the road? What's up with that?), you are able to recognize it as a shoe. It fits into the shoe category, even though it is totally out of context in the middle of the highway. It doesn't scare you. You know what it is because you have the concept of shoes in your head.

Dogs don't understand the world that way. I believe dogs understand the world in pictures.[2] When you are socializing your puppy, I like to think it's your job to create a catalogue of positive experiences (pictures) for them. Everything your puppy sees, smells, tastes, feels, and does, goes into that catalogue, one page at a time. Your job is to create as big a catalogue as possible, so that in the future, your dog will be able to better cope with novel experiences. Having that big catalogue will allow your adult dog to have a vast frame of reference, and they will be able to call upon their previous experiences to accept the new situation and pull it into the world of the familiar.

Now, socialization doesn't only mean *exposure* to the world. It means exposure in a *controlled and thoughtful manner*. Many people miss this point and over-expose their puppy to too many situations too quickly. Puppy becomes overwhelmed and fearful and can't cope with the overload of information. This creates negative catalogue pictures. We want the catalogue entries to be positive and happy or at least neutral. If your puppy does encounter something that scares him (see section on body language), it's your job to help him through it. How? With tasty food, of course!

There is a well-known saying in dog training circles: food overcomes fear. Whether a dog will eat a tasty morsel or not has long been used as a means of determining if a dog is in a fearful state. Dogs suffering extreme fear won't eat. If you are out with your puppy and you come across something that puppy is scared of, move her *away* from the scary thing to help her cope. Then try feeding a piece of yummy food. If your puppy eats it, you can start moving forward from that point. If she doesn't, you need to move further away. Let her look at the scary thing, then feed, look, feed. Repeat. If she relaxes (and she should), then move

[2] *See the work of Dr Temple Grandin. Her books, "Thinking in Pictures" and "Animals in Translation" provide amazing insight into how dogs may perceive the world.*

a step closer and feed again. Once puppy is relaxed around the scary thing, you can move on. Don't ignore your puppy when she's scared. She is telling you she needs your help! If you leave these situations unattended, your puppy may very well retain that fear into adulthood. That fear can also bleed into other circumstances. It's best to address these situations as they arise.

There are good socialization checklists to help you track your progress. Two of them are available here: https://www.petprofessionalguild.com/PuppyTrainingResources https://drsophiayin.com/app/uploads/2015/12/Socialization_ Checklist.pdf (links verified on 10/13/2021)

Sometimes, the auditory aspect of socialization can be difficult to accomplish. How does one expose puppy to sirens, for example? Wait outside the fire station until an emergency call comes in? It's just not practical. For these hard to find sounds, there is an app for your phone called *Sound Proof Puppy Training* that is available through Google Play and the Apple App Store. At the time of writing, it cost $3.99. You will need to use an external speaker to obtain more realistic sounds (phone speakers just don't create convincing sound). Instructions for training with the app are included.

In all cases, do *not* overwhelm your puppy!

## FIND A WELL-RUN PUPPY CLASS OR STRUCTURED PUPPY PLAYGROUP

If you can, take your puppy to school — puppy school, that is! A well-run class or playgroup should focus on developing the bond between you and your puppy. There should be some controlled and well supervised off-leash play, interaction with other people, and some environmental exploration, but this should be interspersed with teaching some basic skills such as sit and a hand target, and the opportunity for frequent check-ins with the owners. This will help build your bond and teach your puppy to focus on you.

Stay away from classes that use outdated equipment like training collars (also known as chokers), use compulsion to teach (for example, pushing down on the puppy's rear end while pulling up on the leash to make the puppy sit), or use barbaric techniques (like spraying bitter apple in the puppy's mouth to punish biting). Remember, you are your puppy's advocate. There is no place for using aversive techniques like this in a puppy class (or any class)! If something doesn't feel right, leave. Do not risk harming your puppy.

## WHAT TO BRING

Get some kind of bag that will be your *Dog Gear Bag*. It can be a special one designed just for dogs (like the Ruffwear Haul Bag™) or a baby diaper bag, or any other bag that will hold your puppy's stuff. What stuff? This stuff! You should bring your gear bag with you on all puppy outings.

- Poop bags (lots of them)
- Wet baby wipes (for you and puppy)
- Paper towels
- Hand towel
- Treats
- Single meal (in case you get delayed)
- Water bowl and bottle of water
- Clean towel (to put under puppy to reduce environmental exposure)

- Chew toy(s)

- Large plastic bag (to hold soiled items)

## PLACES TO GO

When you take your puppy out, there is no requirement for puppy to actually interact with people or other animals. You can go to a farm and just watch the horses, cows, and chickens. You can go to a pond and watch the ducks. You can go to a playground and watch the kids from the comfort of your vehicle. You get the idea. Focus on exposure rather than firsthand experience. With people, it's a bit different. You want your puppy to love people, but not necessarily learn to go say hello to everyone they meet. There is no doubt that your puppy needs to see a lot of different looking people. You can have some of them come over and toss your puppy a treat. Others, you can ask if they would like to pet if your puppy volunteers, meaning your puppy initiates the interaction. Never push a puppy towards someone or something. Most people need *never* interact with your puppy. Puppy can just watch them come and go. Your puppy should learn to focus on *you,* not on other people. Here are some ideas.

- Car rides anywhere

- Restaurant with outdoor patio

- Outdoor cafés

- Drive-throughs (bank, fast food, etc.)

- Big box hardware stores

- Kids playing at a playground

- Outdoor baseball or soccer game

- Parking lots

- Motorcycle dealership

- Farm

- Forest

- Fire Station

- Friends' home with no dogs

- Friends' home with a dog-savvy cat

- Barking adult dogs behind a fence

## WHAT TO AVOID

I suggest avoiding the following places until your puppy is fully vaccinated and has developed a good immune system.

- Pet stores

- Stores that allow dogs inside

- Dog parks*

- Doggie Day Care

- Streets frequented by lots of dogs

- Dirty floors or other soiled surfaces

- Dog shelters

- Dog events where other dogs will be present

 *I avoid dog parks completely, forever, unless they're deserted. Too many people bring their untrained dogs to dog parks and fights often break out. Dog parks are fraught with danger from disease and other dogs. A puppy should never be taken to a dog park.*

## BE READY FOR THE UNEXPECTED

You just never know what's going to happen! You will see the environment in a whole new light, from your dog's perspective! Here are some examples of weirdness in the human world that we take completely for granted and hardly even notice.

- Some mannequins have no heads and are frightening versions of human beings.

- You will be shocked at how much gum is squished on pavement and under tables and chairs.

- Goose poop is tasty!

- Fire hydrants are scary, and then scary again when they're painted a different color.

- Burning food in the kitchen makes the house smoky, thus terrifying the dog.

- The smoke detector!

## KEEP IT UP

Socialization doesn't stop at sixteen weeks. The prime window may have passed, but your socialization must continue at least until your dog reaches social maturity at eighteen to twenty-four months. Training and socialization should both continue for the life of your dog. Remember, skills that are not regularly practiced will fade away.

# CHAPTER THREE

# Wylie Pees-A-Lot

Those first weeks and months with baby Wylie flew by in a blur of joy, exasperation, love, and doubt. It was a real eye-opener for me. I had no idea of the time and energy that went into taking care of a puppy. It was 24/7! The last time I lived with a puppy, I was a child myself, and so I guess puppy-raising fell into my parents' domain. I don't remember anything about it except cleaning up a lot of soiled newspapers that had been placed by the door. Otherwise, I was oblivious. I just enjoyed having a dog without any of the responsibility.

Wylie was a handful right from the start. She was almost six months old before she could even sleep through the night without having to be taken out to pee, usually somewhere between two and three in the morning. Tim and I split the late night/early morning potty training responsibility; I got up in the middle of the night and he took the early morning shift. Tim had to get up early for work anyway, so he took Wylie out then. To many people, this may not sound like a big deal. So what? Please, let me clarify this for you.

# Dale M. Ward

We lived on forty-seven acres in the northwoods, adjacent to the Chequamegon National Forest, way up in the top left corner of Wisconsin. One of the things about living in a secluded, wild place is, well, that it is secluded and wild. We had no fenced yard and we were totally surrounded by forest. There were a multitude of wild animals living all around us that could easily harm a defenseless puppy: badgers, coyotes, wolves, bears, cougars, deer, porcupines, skunks, and more. We saw footprints and other evidence of their existence quite regularly, and we often spotted deer and black bears foraging in our woods.

So, the idea of letting Wylie go outside unsupervised was just out of the question in my mind, even on a tie out. Unless we wanted to risk her being attacked, mauled, skunked, or injured, one of us had to go with her. I know other people did it, just opened the door and let their dogs out, and I also know that other people's dogs were gravely injured or died as a result. Not my dog!

We wanted to teach Wylie to urinate and defecate in a particular area, so as to keep the poop bombs in one place. Wylie's elimination area (we called it the Poop Zone) was about a hundred feet from the house, right beside our big pole building, where it was somewhat sheltered from the winter weather. We had to keep that area clear of snow, so we plowed and shoveled it. It was often cold when we took her out. I mean really, really cold, windy, or snowing, or all three. Putting on boots, coat, hat, scarf, mittens and going outside with your puppy into minus thirty-five degree cold, sometimes with a wind chill factor that made it feel much colder, at three in the morning is not fun. Not one little bit!

To successfully housetrain a dog, you must know if your dog has actually peed or pooped and reward that activity on the spot, not after you and your dog come back into the house. If you wait until you're back in the house to give your dog a treat, all your dog learns is that he goes out, he comes back in and he eats food. What do you think is going to happen next? You can so easily end up with a dog that asks to go outside, stands on the porch, scratches to come back in, goes right over to the cupboard where his treats are kept, and sits there looking at you, waiting for you to give him his reward for *walking outside and coming back in*! Trust me, you do not want this to happen. There is nothing more annoying than a dog who has learned to do this. What makes it worse is that *you* taught him to do it! Remember to give your dog his treat *outside*, right after he has done his business.

So that means going out with your dog on a leash and rewarding with a small food treat. Every. Single. Time. If you just open the door and let your dog out by herself, you will never know if she really eliminated or if she just went out to play or sniff. She then may come back in to get her treat and promptly pee on the carpet. This would be the human's mistake, not the dog's.

Housetraining is really pretty simple, but it is not so easy to execute. As humans, we mostly want to take the easy way out, but that results in less successful housetraining and an unreliable dog. I stuck with it. I am tenacious by nature and I don't give up easily. I think it was because it was so cold and miserable those first few months that I came up with the idea of the Elimination Journal. I didn't want to be out there with my puppy when I didn't have to be. I wanted efficiency. I wanted data! Also, there were two of us that were responsible for taking her out at different times during the day. How was I supposed to know if Wylie peed or not when she went out with Tim? Impossible. I know it sounds kind of crazy, but I kept track of every pee and poop that came out of my dog. I knew the times she was likely to go and the times she likely just wanted to go outside to play.

Gathering that data over several weeks allowed me to know when I needed to take Wylie out and when she was just trying to get me to take her outside to play. In the latter cases, I could distract her with a toy or a game inside instead. It made housetraining so simple, so reliable, so bomb-proof. The number of accidents Wylie had in the house was minimal. She never pooped inside the house, not even once. She did come really close one time though.

I had just taken Wylie to the vet for her second set of shots and deworming. The vet had warned me that I might see some worms in her poop over the next few days. "So, watch for them. They'll mostly all be dead so don't worry. They look like spaghetti." "Oh, okay. How lovely," I thought to myself. I had never seen roundworms before and had no idea what to expect. I kind of forgot about it until the next afternoon. Wylie was on the living room floor, just walking around looking for trouble, when I saw her start to circle, a sure sign that a poop is imminent. Looking to interrupt and keep her stellar record intact, I jumped up off the couch and made one beeline for her, scooping her up in my arms turning to run outside. I heard Tim behind me exclaim "Oh my god, what the hell is that? Be careful, she's pooping right now!" I held her out, away from my body, only to see what a huge infestation of roundworms actually looks like. I thought the vet meant that I would see one or two short whitish strands but no, I saw a whole bowl of pasta, and it was ready to explode out of a puppy bum at any moment. We just made it out to Wylie's poop spot when I put her down on the ground and she squatted to expel one of the vilest things I have ever seen. I was truly shocked. That stuff came out of my little, tiny, sweet puppy? Wow. And that's all I'm going to say about that! If your vet warns you about worms, listen. Having a puppy isn't always pretty.

When Wylie did pee in the house, it was my fault for not paying enough attention. I missed her signals or got busy and forgot a time when I should have known that she had to go out. Gathering the data in her Elimination Journal helped me predict when Wylie had to go, and I could help ensure she was successful. Setting your dog up for success is so important. That way, the opportunity to make a mistake is minimized, and Wylie learned quickly from her successes instead.

## Wylie Pees-A-Lot

Once Wylie was reliably peeing and pooping outside, I needed a means for her to let me know when she had to go out. I didn't want her to bark. Barking can be so annoying, and we hadn't heard even a little *Woof* out of her so far. I apparently had a silent dog. I didn't want her to scratch at the door. I wanted to keep my new home intact and scratch-free. I decided to try hanging a bell on the doorknob for Wylie to ring as a means for her to communicate her need to go outside to pee. I had purchased a couple of bear bells because of the danger posed by startling a bear when out on a walk. These are bells that dogs wear on their collars to warn bears of their approach, to hopefully avoid any surprise encounters. I took one of those bells, tied it on a ribbon and hung it from the doorknob. Poochie Bells®, which I love, had not yet been invented, but I must have read somewhere that training a dog to ring a bell was possible. I don't think I thought of this amazing technique by myself, but I don't know whom to credit for it. In a very short time, Wylie was ringing that bell reliably. Whenever she needed to go out, she nosed the bell. *Ding-a-ling-a-ling!* What a smart dog I had! *Good girl, Wylie!*

Because of the cold weather in the spring, winter, and fall, and because of the mosquitos and biting flies in the summer, I wanted to be able to take Wylie out quickly and efficiently. I did not want to be out there in those unpleasant conditions if I didn't have to be, so adding a verbal cue — ours was a cheerful "hurry up" — allowed us to train her to eliminate when we asked. This made it so easy to manage her when we were visiting or traveling or when the weather was bad. It takes approximately one hundred-ish repetitions for a dog to learn this, and those one hundred repetitions went pretty quickly. Within a month, Wylie knew what *hurry up* meant.

For the rest of her life, all I had to say was *hurry up!* a few times and she would squat and go. It made traveling easy, visiting easy, gathering a sample for her veterinarian so easy. Put simply, it was pee and poop perfection. She was the best dog I have ever met in the housetraining department. Mission accomplished.

There is one more chapter in Wylie's elimination history and it has to do with her spay. When she was six months old, at the recommendation of her vet, I booked an appointment to have Wylie spayed. Of course, I was nervous when I brought her in that morning. She was totally unaware of what was going to happen as she bounced into the waiting room. We checked in and sat down. Wylie was so happy to be there. She loved everyone. I was feeling conflicted. Should I be doing this? She was so young. I pushed my doubts to the back of my mind and stayed positive and happy for Wylie's sake. Soon, the vet and a tech came out to get my dog. The vet was wearing a white lab coat. She greeted me and Wylie as she took the leash from my hand. At that moment, a flood of memories came rushing back.

Twenty-five years ago, when Roxy got sick with immune-mediated hemolytic anemia, the last time I saw her was when I brought her to the vet and handed over her leash to a man in a white coat. I didn't think anything was seriously wrong with her at the time. I had noticed some small spots on her belly, like tiny round bruises. I found a drop of blood on the floor. When I checked Roxy's face, I saw a drop of blood coming out of her nose. That was enough to scare me and take her in to be examined. The vet said they wanted to keep her overnight and run some tests. I gave away the leash and watched them take my dog *to the back*.

Roxy went without a fuss, as usual, but before she went through the door, she stopped, turned her head and looked at me with her deep brown eyes. That image is burned into my mind. Her tail was still. I said to her, "What's wrong? It's okay, you're going to be fine. I'll be back tomorrow. Go on, go!" Her eyes were trying to tell me something. I couldn't read them. I had never seen that look before. "Go, you silly girl. It's okay!" I tried to smile. She stared at me for a few moments more, then she slowly turned and walked away, out of my sight. I never saw her again.

# Wylie Pees-A-Lot

When I handed over Wylie's leash that day, all those memories came flooding back and I started crying. The vet was surprised and told me Wylie would be fine. I explained why this was difficult and told her about Roxy. I felt like an idiot. The vet was lovely and told me I could wait in the waiting room or go grab a coffee and call back in a few hours. I chose the latter, thinking time would go by more quickly. I went to the Black Cat for a coffee and waited. And waited. It seemed like an eternity but by eleven o'clock, I couldn't wait any longer. I called the vet. Wylie was out of surgery and recovering well. Everything went fine, and I picked a groggy Wylie up that evening.

As Wylie recovered, I started noticing that she was leaking urine. I took her out to pee frequently but that had no effect on the leaking. I made an appointment and took her back in right away. The vet examined her and told me that sometimes a leaking problem occurs after the spay but usually resolves in a few weeks or months. Well, it did not resolve for Wylie. What I did not know, nor was I told by my vet, is that between five and twenty percent of spayed female dogs can develop urinary incontinence as a result of the spay procedure. It is caused by the procedure itself and the absence of a hormone called estradiol in the body. Dogs that are spayed under the age of six months are more susceptible. Wylie could no longer control her uterine sphincter muscles. Spay incontinence develops right after the spay or within a few months of the surgery.[3]

When the vet told me that Wylie would be leaking urine, possibly for the rest of her life, I was really angry. Why wasn't I told about this possibility? What was I supposed to do now, let her walk around dribbling pee all over the place? I was frightened. How could a dog live like that? Diapers forever? It freaked me out. The vet told me that the leaking might stop on its own, but that for now, we could put her on a drug called Proin® to see if it would help. It did! Proin

[3] https://www.vetinfo.com/symptoms-of-spay-incontinence-in-dogs.html *(link verified on 10/13/2021)*

is phenylpropanolamine hydrochloride, whatever that is, and it helps tighten the muscles in the bladder[4]. Wylie took it for a few months without any noticeable side effects. Then I tried to wean her off the medication. Nope. The dribbling immediately returned so I put her back on the drug. I tried to stop, on and off, a few more times, but it never worked. Wylie was on Proin for her entire life. There was nothing else I could do about it. I often wonder if knowing about this possibility would have made a difference in my decision to spay my dog. I don't know. Maybe. I probably would have waited until she was a little older, at least.

---

[4] https://prnpharmacal.com/product/proin/ *(link verified on 10/13/2021)*

IT'S TRAINING TIME...

# Housetraining Tips & Troubleshooting

House soiling is one of the main reasons that dogs are relinquished to shelters by well-meaning owners. People are often at a loss as to how to train their puppy to eliminate outdoors, not in the house. The puppy grows into adulthood and is still peeing and pooping inside. It becomes intolerable. Here are some practical tips and troubleshooting advice that will help you navigate this stage of puppyhood as seamlessly as possible.

1. If your puppy is urinating frequently, squatting multiple times to empty her bladder, or straining to urinate, she may have a urinary tract infection (UTI). Take your puppy to see your veterinarian right away. There is no point trying to housetrain a puppy who is ill and physically can't hold her urine. UTIs are more common in female puppies than males because bacteria can more easily enter their urinary tracts through their much shorter and wider urethras.[5]

[5] http://www.pethealthnetwork.com/dog-health/dog-diseases-conditions-a-z/urinary-tract-infections-dogs *(link verified on 10/13/2021)*

2. Times provided in the elimination schedules that follow are approximate and should be adjusted to your own lifestyle. Create your own schedule based on these examples.

3. Be consistent. Supervise. If you can't supervise, confine. Confinement includes using a crate or Xpen, or tethering to your waist using a leash so puppy is not out of your sight.

4. Feed and water on a schedule. What goes in on time comes out on time. Always offer water when you feed, three times a day. Always offer water after vigorous play and after a walk. Offer last water three hours before bed unless it is hot outside and your puppy has been outside playing. Always offer cool water in the heat. Remember, you are **not** restricting the amount of water your puppy drinks, you are scheduling when puppy drinks it.

5. Post your elimination schedule somewhere prominent, like on the fridge or on the door you use to take your puppy out, so that everyone in the household is aware of the times that your puppy needs to be taken out to eliminate. Set alarms on your phone if you need to.

6. Hang a leash and a full treat pouch right by the door that you use to take puppy out. That way, you are not hunting around for your leash and treats when puppy has asked to go out. If you are running around trying to find your stuff, your puppy may eliminate by the door while waiting for you to get ready.

7. Put your shoes on outside so your puppy doesn't pee inside while waiting for you to get your shoes on! Get yourself some Crocs™. Easy on, easy off.

8. Keep your Elimination Journal close to the door with a pen attached so that whoever takes the puppy out can easily record what occurred.

9. When you take your puppy out, especially first thing in the morning or in the middle of the night, pick your puppy up and carry her to her potty spot so that she doesn't have a chance to make a mistake and eliminate while walking to the door.

10. When you take your puppy out in the middle of the night, do not interact with her. Do not talk to, pet, treat, or cuddle her. Simply take her out to her spot while leashed, repeat your verbal cue, and reward with verbal praise (no treat!). Then, bring her directly back inside and put her back in her crate. You do not want to give the puppy the idea that there is an opportunity for food or fun interaction with you in the middle of the night. Be boring. No fun should happen on this middle-of-the-night trip outside.

11. Female puppies usually empty their bladders all in one go. Male puppies rarely empty their bladders all in one go and may urinate two or three times before they are empty. Be patient with your male puppy and give him enough time to finish.

12. Make sure you reward with a treat as soon as your dog has eliminated. Do not wait until you go back inside to reward your dog in case your dog thinks the reward

is the result of going back in the house. In order to make an appropriate association between eliminating outside and the treat being given, the treat must be delivered within about a second or two of her finishing. She will never associate a treat given in the house with eliminating outside.

13. If you find that your dog has made a mistake and eliminated indoors, simply clean it up with a good, odor-eliminating, enzymatic cleaner. Do not scold your dog. Count it as your mistake since you missed the opportunity to take your puppy out when you should have.

14. If you catch your puppy in the act of eliminating indoors, simply interrupt the mistake by picking your puppy up and taking her directly outside to her potty spot to finish. Reward on the spot when she is finished. Clean up as described above.

15. During the day, puppies can typically hold their urine one hour for every month old they are, plus or minus one. So, a two-month-old puppy can only hold their urine for two or three hours, *maximum*. During the night, when they are sleeping, they can usually go a little longer but often must be taken out in the middle of the night. Puppies typically defecate three times a day, usually after eating. Don't expect more than what your dog can physically do.

16. Watch for the following opportunities to take your puppy out. Dogs typically have to eliminate upon waking up in the morning, after longer naps during the day, after vigorous play sessions, after vigorous chew

sessions, after eating, before bed, and in the middle of the night. Puppies typically have to defecate five to fifteen minutes after they eat and after a vigorous chewing session. In addition to these key times, young puppies should be taken out every hour or so, to be given the chance to empty their bladder.

17. Small breeds have small bladders and often take longer to housetrain. They simply cannot hold their urine for very long. Be patient, especially with the little ones.

## YOUR ELIMINATION JOURNAL

Whenever I go see a client with a new puppy, or one that has an older puppy who is having trouble with housetraining, I bring a notebook for them to use as their Elimination Journal. When I tell them that I want them to write down the time of every pee and poop for two whole weeks, they sometimes think I'm crazy. I'm not crazy; I'm gathering data, and you can, too!

When you put your puppy on a feeding and watering schedule (see preceding section on Housetraining Tips & Troubleshooting), what goes in on time comes out on time. By gathering data for at least two weeks (sometimes you need more information to identify a pattern so keep your journal longer), you will discover your dog's pattern of elimination. Once you have that information, you can be proactive and take your puppy out just before those times and ensure that no accidents happen in the house.

This is an example of what an Elimination Journal looks like:

| Monday 11/19 | |
| --- | --- |
| 6:45 am | Out — 1 Pee 1 Poop |
| 7:30 | Feed and Water |
| 8:10 | Out — 1 Pee |
| 9:30 | Out — Nothing — Offer Water |
| 10:50 | Out — 1 Pee |
| 12:45 pm | Feed and Water |
| 1:30 | Out — 1 Pee — Kitchen Floor! Oops |
| 1:35 | Out — 1 Pee finished outside |
| 3:00 | Out — 2 Pees, 1 Poop — Offer Water |
| 4:35 | Out — Nothing |
| 4:55 | Out — 1 Pee — Offer Water |
| 6:00 | Out — 1 Pee |
| 6:10 | Feed and Water |
| 6:30 | Out — 1 Poop |
| 8:30 | Out — 1 Pee, 1 Poop — Last Water Offer |
| 10:30 | Out — 1 Pee |
| 11:10 | Bedtime — Crate |
| 4:25 am | Out — 1 Pee |

Also include any notes on your puppy's health or behavior that could be related to their elimination. For example, note soft stool, if puppy ate something inappropriate like some dandelion heads, etc. Notes like this will help you determine whether your puppy's pattern has been affected by a one-time occurrence and therefore can be ignored when trying to find a regular pattern.

So, if you look at the journal and find that your puppy almost always poops three times a day, at times that are very similar, you know that when you take puppy out around that time, you should wait outside until she poops. If you take your puppy out at around 9:30 am every morning and she never pees or poops, you can skip that time. You get the idea. This will help you ensure that your puppy's accidents are kept to a minimum. Strive for perfection, but know that even if you are diligent, your puppy is bound to have a few accidents in the house. That's okay. It's all part of the learning process.

This is an example of a page from my dog's Elimination Journal:

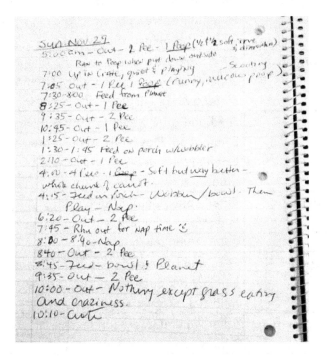

# SAMPLE PUPPY SCHEDULE (HOME ALL DAY)

| Time | Activity |
| --- | --- |
| Early Morning | Wake up. Go out (on leash). Elimination. Free period in bathroom with you, supervised. |
| Morning 7am | Feed and offer water. Go out (on leash). Elimination. Free period in kitchen while you eat breakfast, supervised. |
| Midmorning 10am | Offer water. Go out (on leash). Elimination. Supervised play and learning. Confine to crate/Xpen in kitchen/living area. |
| Noon | Feed and offer water. Go out (on leash). Elimination. Play/Walk. Offer water. Confine to crate/Xpen in kitchen/living area. |
| Midafternoon 3pm | Offer water. Go out (on leash). Elimination. Supervised play and learning, followed by quiet crate time. |
| Dinner 6pm | Feed and offer water. Go out (on leash). Elimination. Supervised play and learning, followed by quiet crate time. |
| Evening 8pm | Offer water. Go out (on leash). Elimination. Supervised play and learning. |
| Bedtime | Go out (on leash). Elimination. Confine to crate, overnight, in bedroom. |
| Middle of Night | Go out (on leash). Elimination. Confine to crate, in bedroom, for rest of the night. |

# SAMPLES PUPPY SCHEDULE
# (AWAY ALL DAY)

| Time | Activity |
|---|---|
| Early Morning | Wake up. Go out (on leash). Elimination. Free period in the bathroom with you while getting ready for work, supervised. |
| Morning 7 am | Feed and offer water. Go out (on leash). Elimination. Free period in the kitchen while you eat breakfast, supervised. |
| 8am | Go out (on leash). Last elimination opportunity. Fill water bowl. Confine to Xpen in kitchen/living area with potty pads. Leave for work |
| Noon to 1 pm | Dog Walker arrives (or you do). Go out (on leash). Elimination. Feed and offer water. Go out (on leash). Elimination. Play/Walk. Change potty pads. Confine to Xpen in kitchen/living area. |
| 5pm | Arrive home from work. Go out (on leash). Elimination. Change potty pads. |
| Dinner 6 pm | Feed and offer water. Go out (on leash). Elimination. Supervised play and learning, followed by quiet crate time. |
| Evening 8 pm | Offer water. Go out (on leash). Elimination. Supervised play and learning. |
| Bedtime | Go out (on leash). Elimination. Confine to crate, overnight, in bedroom. |
| Middle of Night | Go out (on leash). Elimination. Confine to crate, in bedroom, for rest of the night. |

# CHAPTER FOUR

# Wylie Hates Cars

That initial car trip when we brought Wylie home from the breeder went very smoothly with no problems at all. Subsequent car rides did not go quite as well. I knew that it was a good idea to get a puppy used to riding in the car. Dogs don't naturally or instinctively love car riding. If you don't start early and make it fun, the dog will likely develop some car riding issues. So, like a good puppy owner, I bundled Wylie up into her little pink plastic carrier crate and put her in the back seat of the 4Runner with the intention of going to get the mail at the post office just a few miles away. *That will be a good first trip*, I thought to myself. *Nice and short and not too stressful. She'll like it. It will be our first adventure together. It will be fun.*

As soon as I started the engine and put the truck into gear, the screaming started. When I say screaming, I mean real, full-blown, high-pitched shrieking. I tried to soothe her with my voice. "It's okay, it's okay," I cooed out loud, but clearly, it was not. We drove to the end of our 700-foot driveway, but the screaming and her obvious distress were just too much. I had to turn around and go back to the house as the screeching continued. I remember saying out loud,

# Wylie Hates Cars

"Oh great, now what?" My poor little puppy was having a total panic attack. I thought this was odd since just a few days before, we drove for two hours when we brought her home from the breeder without so much as a peep from her. I parked the car, turned off the engine, and her screaming instantly stopped. I started the car again and rolled forward, and the screeching began anew. It was definitely the motion of the vehicle that was causing this reaction. I brought Wylie inside, totally perplexed as to what to do next. The thought crossed my mind that I would never be able to take my dog anywhere. This was obviously not an option! She would, at a minimum, have to go to the veterinarian now and again! I certainly did not want to torture my innocent little puppy, but somehow, I had to get her to feel comfortable and secure while riding in the car.

This was the first of many times I felt a whole host of emotions surrounding my dog's behavior: frustration, sadness, disappointment, anxiety, stress, and confusion, all mixed together. What do I do now?

Determined not to give up, I tried again the next day. This time, I put the crate in the front passenger seat, right beside me, thinking that maybe if she could see me, she would feel better. I set a goal of only going around our driveway circle. My plan was to keep it short. Hahaha, go ahead and have a good laugh. My idea of "short" was very different from Wylie's! This was my first lesson in how time and perception differ greatly between dogs and humans. You have probably figured out by now that I got the same screeching results. I had to break the experience of going on a car ride down into smaller pieces, ones that could be handled by Wylie with less distress.

And so began the two foot excursions. It went something like this:

> start the truck
>
> turn off the truck
>
> start the truck

drive two feet

stop, wait

drive three feet

stop, wait

drive six feet

stop, wait

scream, wait (mistake: too far too fast)

drive two feet

stop, wait

drive six feet

stop, wait

Well, you get the idea. I did that for several days until we could get all the way down the driveway. Once Wylie realized that nothing bad was going to happen, we were able to get to the post office. Success!

It took me about two weeks, working with her every day, to accomplish this seemingly simple task. Never underestimate the power of baby steps! It takes time and patience, but the payoff is big. Wylie became the best car rider ever. For the rest of her life, she was able to go on very long trips, days at a time, and ride happily, comfortably, and sleepily in her crate in the back seat. Nothing bothered her while she was in the car, even the odd time she rode loose in the back. She just curled up and slept. She would sit up, look around for a bit, then go back to what she was so good at doing, snoozing the ride away.

IT'S TRAINING TIME...

# Systematic Desensitization and Classical Counterconditioning: The Basics

What I was doing without knowing it when I set out to help Wylie get over her fear of riding in her crate in the truck was a combination of what is called *systematic desensitization*, with a bit of *habituation* thrown in for good measure.

> *"**Systematic desensitization** is a process in which a conditioned emotional response (CER) such as fear is extinguished by exposing the animal in a graduated manner to the fear-eliciting stimuli."*

(From the Encyclopedia of Animal Behavior, Vol.1, 2nd Edition, page 206 "Overview of Animal Training: A Welfare Perspective" by Melissa Bain)

*Habituation* is defined as

> *"the process of people or animals becoming used to something, so that they no longer find it unpleasant or think it is a threat".*

(From the Cambridge Dictionary) https://dictionary.cambridge.org/us/dictionary/english/habituation (link verified on 10/13/2021)

These two techniques sound very similar, but they differ in one very important way. In habituation, the animal simply gets used to something with repeated or continuous exposure. There is no graduated plan used to keep the animal calm and relaxed. There is a danger of causing real stress through over-exposure (this is called flooding). That would have been like me continuing to drive while Wylie screamed, until she stopped screaming and got used to driving in the truck. That would have been cruel. It can also backfire and make the animal even more fearful, actually *sensitizing* them to what was already a scary experience. We don't want to do that.

The key to successful *systematic desensitization* is gradual, increased intensity of the stress inducing stimuli. How gradual? That's not so easy to answer because it depends on so many factors including the human doing the training and the individual dog.

Wylie had had an adverse *conditioned emotional response* (CER) to the car. There is no way to know exactly what was going on in her little head, but she was likely scared to be alone in her crate when she could feel movement underneath her. Maybe her crate vibrated. Maybe she got sloshed around. Who knows? We can take an educated guess and say that her CER was fear based. That much I could tell. In the moment, Wylie was likely thinking something like, *Lalala, here I am, cozy in my crate.* Then bam, vehicle moves! *What the heck was that, get me out of here, I'm going to die!* The car was traumatizing her.

|              My Truck              | Wylie's Interpretation of |
|                                    |          My Truck         |

*(Mechanik/Shutterstock.com)*

My plan was to gradually expose Wylie to the movement of the vehicle (fear-eliciting stimulus) with the goal of making her enjoy car rides thereby extinguishing her fear. Simple. I also didn't know that I would likely have had more success if I had paired the systematic desensitization (most often referred to simply as desensitization — people drop the "systematic" for the sake of brevity) with another technique called *Classical Counterconditioning* (you will see this referred to simply as counterconditioning — most people drop the "classical" also for the sake of brevity but for our purposes they are the same thing). In dog training, these two techniques (desensitization and counter-conditioning) are usually paired together to help dogs overcome their fears.

*Classical conditioning* is defined as

> *"A learning process that occurs when two stimuli are repeatedly paired: a response which is at first elicited by the second stimulus is eventually elicited by the first stimulus alone."*

**Oxford Dictionary** https://www.lexico.com/definition/classical _conditioning **(link verified on 10/13/2021)**

Think Pavlov and his salivating dogs. When we add the word "counter" to classical conditioning, it implies that the first stimulus has already taken on negative meaning to the animal and must be *countered* with the second stimulus so that it produces a favorable emotional response and loses its negative connotations.

At its core, counterconditioning involves exposing the animal to the scary thing (at an intensity they can handle without losing their mind) and feeding them some delicious food. Expose/Feed. That's it. You present the scary thing (stimulus) and follow it up with some roast chicken. Easy. You don't ask for or expect any particular behavior from your dog, not a *sit*, or *look at me*, or anything. It doesn't matter what your dog is doing, they get the chicken anyway. In fact, if you ask your dog to perform a behavior (like sit or look, for example) and then feed the chicken, you're not doing classical counterconditioning. Getting the chicken would be contingent on the *sit* and that would be something else entirely (something called *operant conditioning*, but we don't need to talk about that right now).

If I had amended my desensitization routine with Wylie to include counter-conditioning with food, it would surely not have taken two full weeks to get her to be okay in the car. My guess is that I could have been finished in a few days, maybe less. The new plan would have looked like this:

start the truck, *feed*

turn off the truck

start the truck, *feed*

drive two feet

stop, *feed*

drive three feet

stop, *feed*

drive six feet

stop, *feed*

scream, wait (mistake: too far too fast)

drive two feet

stop, *feed*

drive six feet

stop, *feed*

The addition of the food would have made a huge difference in Wylie's response. She would have quickly made a positive association between the car movement and the chicken, and she would have begun to happily anticipate the vehicle movement because it predicted that chicken was coming.

Car Moves → Chicken → Nice Feelings

Once this positive association had been cemented into her little brain, it became...

Car Moves → Nice Feelings

No more chicken required. See? Simple.

I give another example with detailed instructions on desensitization and counterconditioning in Chapter 8 called *Wylie Tames the Lawnmower Monster*, so I won't repeat the step by step instructions here. However, I want you to know that you can apply this technique to *anything* your dog is afraid of or anxious about. You just have to manage the exposure, then think of how you can set up controlled exposure to the trigger (the thing your dog is uncomfortable/anxious/scared of), arm yourself with the tastiest food you can find, and go for it.

People are often at a loss as to how to change the steps in the example given above to fit their particular situation. They can't imagine how to set things up. Let's take a minute to dream up some more sample set-ups so that you can see how this idea morphs to accommodate your unique situation. We already discussed the car, and I will give you detailed instructions on the lawnmower. Here are a few more.

Your goal is to make the stimulus *small*, low in intensity. How do you do that?

- If it's an object like a fire hydrant or storm drain or a statue, move far away so that it looks *small*.

- If it's a person, make that person move far away, turn sideways, sit down, avert their gaze so that they look *small* and non-threatening.

- What if it's thunder? Record the sound, play it on a good speaker so that it sounds realistic, but at a very, very low volume, so that it sounds *small*.

- What if it's other dogs? Find a dog that's behind a fence (neighbor dog, dog park) and move far away from it so that the barking dog looks *small* and sounds *small*.

- If it's the person at the drive-through window, find a bank with multiple lanes, go when the bank is closed, drive right through without stopping, so that the process of going to the drive-through is made *small*.

- If it's people walking by your car, find a helper, go to a big parking lot and park at the back, have your helper park far away, walk past your car from a distance, making the person look *small*.

- There could be many parts you may need to work on individually for any given stimulus: the sight of it, what it feels like, how it moves, what it sounds like, and then you may need to work on them in combination.

Don't fret. Break it down. Let's take the example of a dog who is scared of motorcycles.

- Start with *static* first. Start with the motorcycle turned off, not moving, and from far away.

- Add *touch*. Work up to having your dog comfortable eating treats on the ground next to the motorcycle or even off the wheel rims.

- Add *movement*. Once your dog is okay with the static motorcycle and being close to it, walk your dog far away again and have a helper move the motorcycle back and forth, just a few feet at first.

- Add *sound*. Once your dog is okay with movement, move away again and have your helper turn the motorcycle on and off. Gradually increase the amount of time the motorcycle is running.

- Combine *movement and sound*. Move away again, and have your helper ride the motorcycle at a distance.

In each of these examples, you follow the same principles. Expose your dog to the scary stimulus, feed chicken (or whatever yumminess your dog prefers). When the dog appears to happily look at the stimulus and back at you for her chicken, gradually increase the intensity; move closer, have them move closer, add movement, raise the volume, etc.

Raise your criteria slowly. If you think you're going slow enough, *go slower*. Everything moves slowly in the dog world. Don't rush. Humans always want to go too far too fast. Let your dog tell you when she is ready to progress. Look for that happy change in her response; when she sees the previously scary thing, she stays relaxed and looks to you for her treat. This is called a *conditioned emotional response* (CER). Wait for that CER before you move on to a more difficult stage. If you go too fast, your dog will likely explode into a barking frenzy. You can't rush this process. You just can't.

## THE ABSOLUTE RULE OF COUNTERCONDITIONING

In the presence of two stimuli, the second one *always* affects the first.

What does this mean in reality?

This is important so pay attention. If you present the scary thing first followed by the food, then the scary thing starts to predict that delicious food is going to follow. The dog starts to like it when the scary thing appears because it means a piece of roast chicken is coming! The second stimulus affects how the dog feels about the first. The rule holds.

**CAUTION:** This is where it gets tricky. If you present the food first followed by the scary thing, the food will start to predict that the scary thing is about to appear. The food will start to take on negative connotations and will make the dog fearful even before the scary thing appears. The second stimulus affects the first. The rule holds, but with totally unintended consequences. The effect will be the opposite of what you want. Your dog will know that as soon as she sees the food, something bad is going to happen. She may stop eating the food and she may even try to run away as soon as she sees the food.

As you can clearly see, the ORDER in which you present the stimuli is VERY important. Don't make the mistake of presenting the food first.

There are other problems to consider in successfully using desensitization and counterconditioning to help your dog overcome her fears.

- Make sure the associations your dog is making are as clear as possible.

  - Bad thing appears > Food appears

  - Bad thing goes away > Food stops

  - Repeat

- Make sure there is a clear end and a clear beginning to each association. You don't want to confuse the dog as to what came first.

- Avoid rapid succession. It gets confusing. Don't do this:

  Bad thing > Chicken > Bad thing > Chicken > Bad thing > Chicken >Bad Thing

  Which came first, the chicken or the bad egg? If this string goes on long enough, it will be hard to tell. Then you enter into the danger zone described earlier; the dog may get mixed up and think that the food is predicting the bad thing. Uh oh. So, try not to repeat in rapid succession. Your set ups should allow for proper timing of the appearance and duration of the bad thing. Take breaks.

- Make sure it's the bad thing that predicts food and not some other unintended event in the environment. You may inadvertently add other predictors like your hand reaching for the food, or turning your head towards the bad thing, or tightening up on the leash every time the bad thing appears. Your dog could easily think that one of these stimuli is predicting the food, not the bad thing. Try to keep your actions constant and neutral.

- Your dog needs to experience the pairing of the two stimuli in many contexts. Change up other variables; time of day, leash/harness combination, your shoes, whether you are standing or sitting, etc. The only variables that must remain consistent are the two stimuli you are intentionally pairing. This will help your dog realize that all the other stuff in the environment doesn't have any impact on his association of the bad thing with the chicken.

Although this desensitization and counterconditioning sounds simple, as you can see, there are many pitfalls to avoid and trying to implement a plan on your own can be daunting. A couple of sessions with an experienced force-free dog trainer/ behavior consultant that is adept at behavior modification will set you up for success. It may be worth your while and save frustration for you and your dog.

# CHAPTER FIVE

# Wylie the Alligator Puppy

L abrador retrievers are bred to be mouthy. That's their job. They work with humans by retrieving items — usually birds or tennis balls — with that ever-present, handy tool, their mouth!

Contrary to popular belief, Labrador retrievers are not gentle dogs, nor do they come with a "soft mouth." They are large, unruly bruisers that require a lot of early, positive training. They grow quickly in the physical sense, but mentally, they remain puppies for a very long time.

My Wylie puppy was settling in nicely. We had the sleeping arrangements down: she was in her crate beside our bed. We had the housetraining solidly in progress. Wylie went out, on leash, many times a day and once in the middle of the night. Elimination was on cue after ringing the bell each time. It was not really that complicated. It was simple but just not that easy to execute. But I was managing. She was time consuming, bothersome, and sometimes just a plain pain in the rear end, but my love for her grew each and every day and made it all worthwhile.

# Dale M. Ward

One of the most annoying and painful behaviors began to appear almost from the day we brought her home: the dreaded puppy biting. Every time I went near my dog, her mouth was on me. Those little, needle-sharp teeth on my tender human flesh were so painful and they left bloody wounds on my hands and down my arms on a daily basis.

I tried giving her a toy, shoving rawhides into her mouth, the tennis ball, a stuffed animal, whatever I could find that I thought she might like, all to no avail. Apparently, nothing was as good as my hands and arms, except maybe my legs and feet. I tried the "yip like a puppy" method, but that seemed only to encourage her more. When she heard my voice screeching "OUCH!" she became even more excited and jumped on me, open-mouthed, with even more gusto. I pushed her away, trying to protect myself, and she came right back at me. It was all a game to her.

I became increasingly frustrated. It got to the point where I couldn't even pet my dog! Unless she was totally exhausted and half asleep, she would twist her head around, following my hand until she could latch onto it. I stopped trying to pet her when she was awake. I didn't know how to make her stop. I simply had no idea what to do and no one to ask.

# Wylie the Alligator Puppy

My hands and forearms were a total mess for months. On any given day, I sported several bandages covering fresh wounds, multiple gashes in various stages of healing, and an assortment of bruises. Some were scratches from her sharp nails, but most were made by her razor-sharp little teeth. I could hardly wait until those evil things fell out and were replaced by her adult teeth.

There were a few times during those first months when I thought I had come to my wits' end. Tim didn't understand what my problem was. It was just a puppy. What was so hard? He would leave and go to work every day and I would take care of Wylie all day long. I had no help. It was hard. I put up with the biting and scratching. I fed her, tried to train her, played ball with her, entertained her, and she appreciated exactly none of it! I'm not going to lie; there were at least two times that Tim came home after work and found Wylie in her crate and me curled up in a ball on the couch crying my eyes out.

"Take her away! Put her in a garbage bag and put her out with the trash," I said through crocodile tears.

Tim and I both started to laugh. I tried to explain how frustrating she was, but he didn't get it. He would let her out of her crate, and she would come bouncing out, all innocent and happy to see him. She was a little devil so much of the time when she was with me.

There was one occasion when Tim found out what a problem she could be. It was a weekend, so Tim was at home. We were eating lunch at the kitchen table. Wylie was under the table, trying to chew on her Nylabone™. It was one of the big, hard ones with a knot at each end. Little Wylie was having trouble holding onto her bone while she chewed it on the slippery hardwood floor. If she bit down on one end, it would skitter across the room in the opposite direction. Tim, being the kind person that he is, decided to hold Wylie's bone between his two feet so that she could get a better grip on it with her teeth.

I told Tim, "I don't think that's such a great idea."

"It's fine. Stop worrying."

"Okay!" I said. "But don't say I didn't warn you!"

Well, you can probably already predict what happened next. Wylie bit down hard, full force. Her teeth slid off the bone and landed on Tim's big toe. Chomp. Don't ever doubt that a young puppy can bite hard. Tim let out a blood curdling scream. "Jesus Christ!" he yelled as a startled and slightly frightened Wylie leapt up and ran into the kitchen. Tim stood up and started hopping around on one foot. I asked him if he was okay. "No! What do you think?"

It took everything in my power not to say, "I told you so." I suppressed a smirk.

Wylie certainly brought out the extremes of our emotions. I loved her so much, but she made me so mad! What a weird combination of feelings: love and hate sitting side by side in my heart.

IT'S TRAINING TIME...

# Puppy Biting Survival Strategies

If you have ever watched a bunch of young puppies playing, you would notice that they bite each other pretty much non-stop. It's how they play. When your puppy leaves the nest and comes home to you, you become the new puppy substitute. Your puppy's mother and littermates started to teach your puppy not to bite, and it becomes your job to finish that lesson. First, let's look at what you should *not* do.

## WHAT **NOT** TO DO TO STOP YOUR PUPPY FROM BITING YOU

*Never* hit your puppy. Do not pop them on the nose or tap them on the snout. Hitting a puppy is always inappropriate, but it can also do a lot of damage not only physically, but also psychologically. It can damage your relationship and teach your puppy not to trust you. It can make them fearful and hand-shy. It can also incite them to bite you harder.

*Never* hold your puppy's mouth closed. Again, this can make your puppy fearful and hand-shy, and it can also result in your puppy biting you harder as soon as you let go, which is not what you wanted at all!

*Never* stick your fingers down your puppy's throat or push your thumb down on his tongue. I know, this sounds so barbaric that surely it can't be possible that someone would do this. Believe it or not, this advice is still being given by "professionals" in some circles. This is so dangerous, and it could really hurt your puppy. This is abuse. Don't do it. Ever.

*Never* spray your puppy in the mouth with < insert awful thing here: water, bitter apple, vinegar, lemon juice, window cleaner >. No explanation required. Plain and simple, this is also abuse. Don't do it.

*Never* yell at your puppy or use noisemakers like an empty soda can that contains a few pennies. You may frighten your puppy, or, in some cases, you may excite your dog, and the biting may actually increase.

*Never* push your puppy away in an attempt to make them stop. Most puppies will just come back stronger, perceiving the push as an invitation to play and bite more. Pushing just doesn't work at all.

## WHAT TO DO INSTEAD

After all that, you are certainly wondering what to do instead! So many "don'ts"! The strategies to work on teaching your puppy not to bite are simple but not always easy to carry out. Dogs learn through repetition and consequences of their actions, and so doing these things only once will not teach your dog anything. You must repeat, try, and try again for your dog to finally start understanding what you want. Remember that it is not realistic to expect to completely eliminate this behavior until your puppy has grown and developed a little more (and lost their puppy teeth). Your goal is that by the time your puppy is around six months old, puppy biting will pretty well be over.

## Be Proactive

When you reach for your puppy, it's because you want to touch her, right? Your puppy wants to touch you too, but she doesn't have hands, so she uses the only thing she can: her mouth. You need to teach your puppy that approaching hands do not mean a chance to bite. Make sure to start this training when your puppy is not over-aroused or cranky-tired.

## Get Started

To begin, sit on the floor or in a chair with your puppy in front of you. Have about 20 small pieces of food in your hand. You can use your pup's regular food for this. Reach your empty hand forward toward your puppy's shoulder as if you are going to pet your dog. At the same time, reach toward your puppy's mouth with your other hand, holding a piece of food in your fingers. As you lay your hand on your pup's shoulder, feed her the piece of food with your other hand. Try to do this simultaneously. Hold your hand still while it's on your puppy. At this stage, you're not trying to actually pet your puppy. You are just letting your hand rest on her. Repeat several times. Move your hand to other parts of your dog's body (chest, leg, back, top of head) as you continue to feed simultaneously. When your dog is happily eating food from one hand while ignoring the hand that is touching her, you can move to the next stage, adding some actual petting.

This time repeat the same sequence, but add deliberate movement to the hand that is touching your puppy. Move your hand along puppy's fur — just once — as if you are petting her.

Give her the food simultaneously. Repeat until she is happily ignoring that single stroke of petting. Next, hold the food in one hand, and move the other hand to pet puppy *first*, not at the same time; stroke your puppy just once, and then follow with the piece of food. Stroke, then feed. Repeat several times. Move your hand to stroke other body parts, all while repeating the stroke-then-feed sequence. Do this in several short sessions daily. If your puppy is still biting your hand, you likely have progressed too quickly. Go back and work on just touching her as you feed her a piece of food at the same time. Change your location, body position, and time of day as your puppy becomes accustomed to petting without biting. Your puppy will soon learn that petting is not an invitation to bite your hands, but a simple pleasure exchanged between the two of you.

## Manage

What do you do in the meantime, while you are training puppy not to bite? When puppy starts to play bite on your hands, you can allow some soft mouthing. Be prepared with a plethora of toys. If puppy bites hard enough to hurt, redirect onto a toy. If puppy bites on the toy, praise her. If puppy bites your hand again, give her the toy one more time. Keep repeating this process until puppy remains focused on the toys instead of your hands. Remember to play with your puppy with her toys, not with your hands! This applies to everyone who interacts with the puppy. If your puppy is getting overly aroused and is biting too much, place her in her exercise pen or crate with something to do, like chewing on an appropriate toy or stuffed Kong for a little while.

## Stop Reinforcing the Behavior

If puppy bites you again, stand up and remove yourself from play. What does this look like? For some dogs, this means that you stop playing and become still. For others, it means you stand up. For yet others, it means standing up and turning your back. For the tenacious puppy, it means standing up, turning your back, and stepping behind a gate or door. In all cases, though, wait about ten seconds, and then resume calm play. If puppy bites hard again, repeat. Your puppy will learn that if she bites you too hard, she will lose you as a playmate. Remember, your puppy is learning through consequence and repetition. You will have to repeat this scenario every day, multiple times a day. It will not happen overnight.

## WHAT ABOUT MY KIDS?

Puppies and children may sound like a good combination, but left unchecked, things can quickly get out of hand. Children cannot be made responsible for a puppy. It is your responsibility as the adult to manage your dog and your kids so that a good relationship based on trust and respect is encouraged to develop. A child must be old enough to show competent basic dog-handling skills and understand dog body language so that they can recognize when their dog is uncomfortable to be trusted with the puppy. How old is old enough? It depends on the child. Babies, toddlers and young children should *never* be left unsupervised with a puppy or dog.

Kids are often the target for puppies to bite and chase. Kids tend to try to run away from a puppy who is trying to bite them, making the puppy want to chase them even more. When the puppy is small, kids will often run and jump on the couch to get away from the puppy, but the puppy will grow quickly and soon be able to jump up and follow, continuing to bite them.

Kids should be taught not to run in the house when the puppy is loose. If the puppy starts to chase, the child should be taught to stop and stand still so the puppy finds them boring, loses interest, and walks away. You can also make or purchase long braided fleece toys for your kids to drag behind them as they walk. The puppy will usually be distracted by the toy and leave their dangling arms and pant legs alone.

Young children do not understand or know how to control the pressure they put on a puppy when petting or playing. They do not know what will hurt a puppy and they will often treat the puppy like one of their stuffed animals, squeezing too hard, poking inappropriately, or lifting puppy up by a leg. They may put their faces too close, and the puppy may innocently lunge at them with a nip to the face. Puppies love to lunge at faces!

It is just not safe to leave a young child and a puppy alone together. In fact, active supervision must be in place. A responsible adult must be present to guide the child and watch the interaction up close. An adult watching television, on their phone, reading, just being in the same room as the child and puppy is not enough.

Supervise, supervise, supervise and teach, teach, teach.

If you can't supervise, separate. That's what exercise pens, crates and gates are for! Simple.

Puppy biting is a difficult phase to live through and can be really tough to handle. If you are having trouble, call in a professional force-free positive reinforcement trainer to help you. For excellent information on dogs and children, consult the Family Paws Parent Education website.

# THINGS TO REMEMBER

- Don't play rough games with your puppy like wrestling or rough-housing with your dog's head or mouth. Make sure no one who interacts with the puppy plays rough.

- Curbing puppy biting takes time. Be patient. Children don't learn overnight, and neither do dogs.

- Actively supervise your children when they are with the puppy.

- Teach young children not to follow or chase a puppy that has walked away from them. When a dog chooses to leave, let the dog leave.

- You do not have to spend all the time you are at home with your puppy loose in the house. Use gates, exercise pens and crates appropriately. We all need a break from puppy sometimes!

- Have a lot of toys on hand. Learn what kind of toys your puppy loves best and use those to distract your puppy from biting human skin.

- Remember that your puppy is teething and might enjoy something cold to chew on like a hollow rubber toy that has been stuffed with yummy food and frozen.

By employing these strategies, you and your puppy should come through the biting stage with flying colors!

CHAPTER SIX

# Wylie the Social Butterfly

By the time Wylie was four months old, she was a handful and a half. She had grown into a beautiful, sleek coated, young dog with a real zest for life. She went in for regular vet visits, as all puppies should, in a nearby town called Ashland. Wylie loved visiting with everyone. She didn't seem to care that the vet and technicians were poking her, prodding her, giving her vaccinations, taking her temperature, or looking in her ears. All she wanted to do was eat their hands and launch herself at their faces. They were all worthy targets for her sharp little teeth. At one appointment, the vet called her "a mouth on four feet." I will never forget that. Oh, wait, that wasn't a compliment. "She's the mouthiest puppy I've ever seen!" he said. I wasn't sure what to say. That was certainly not helpful.

Wylie wiggled and wagged and played, pooped and peed, ate and slept, oblivious to the chaos she caused around her. When she was awake, she always had something in her mouth. It was either a toy, a stick, or me. Tim and I had managed to teach her a few of the basics: sit, down, and fetch, but we were at a loss when it came to the biting, walking on a leash without pulling my arm off, jumping up on people, and generally crashing around in the world. She was a brute. So, as soon as Wylie was fully vaccinated, I decided to take her to doggie daycare. I needed some time away from her for my own sanity, and I also thought it would be good for her to play with other dogs in a controlled, monitored environment.

Since we lived in the middle of nowhere in northern Wisconsin, what was the likelihood that the little towns around us would have a doggie daycare facility at all? Whatever the odds, we beat them. The vet had recommended a place not far from his office. I really wanted her to go so that I could have some downtime, but then again, I didn't. I had no idea what to look for when trying to find a reputable, safe facility. I had to take a giant leap of faith and trust that they knew what they were doing. I thought I was being selfish, wanting to get rid of her for a few hours. I felt guilty, but I needed a break. I called and made an appointment to go visit.

I was so nervous taking Wylie there for the first time. I felt like a mom taking her only child to kindergarten for the first day of school. I was worried Wylie would get hurt by all the other dogs. I was worried she would miss me and cry. I was worried she would get sick. I was just worried. I pulled into the parking lot and sat there, debating. I could hear all the dogs barking. It was definitely loud and sounded so out of control! I started to second guess my decision. *Is this a good idea? Should I really be leaving my dog with these strangers?* I almost left several times, but I finally gathered up my courage — and my dog — and went inside. After all, I told myself I was just going to visit.

Wylie and I made our way across the parking lot and stumbled through the front door with Wylie in the lead, as usual. She was pulling so hard against her collar that she was making loud coughing and choking sounds. You would think that this would be uncomfortable enough for a dog to make them stop pulling. Nope. At least not for my Wylie! So, in we went, my little beast and me.

I opened the door and looked around the big room, Wylie four feet ahead of me. On the left, there was a reception counter. Straight ahead of me, there were two grooming tables, right there for everyone to see. There was a little schnauzer getting a haircut on one of the tables. I liked the transparency! No hiding behind closed doors. A very pretty young woman with long blond hair greeted me.

"Hi, I'm Natalie. How can I help you?"

I tried to hide my nervousness. I explained that I was interested in putting Wylie into doggie daycare and inquired about hours and pricing.

"Would you like to drop her off right now?" she asked.

"Now?" I said, incredulously.

"Sure, we could take her now."

*No way*, I thought to myself. "Um, no." I asked if she could give me a tour instead.

She introduced me to the owner, who stopped clipping the schnauzer for a moment to shake my hand. She smiled and welcomed me warmly. Next, Natalie took me into the back, where the boarding runs were. It was really, really clean and smelled nice and fresh, not something I thought would be possible in a kennel. Each roomy indoor kennel run had a Kuranda® bed in it so that the dogs could be off the cold concrete floor when they slept. That was nice. We walked around to the other side, to the doggie daycare area. There were sliding glass doors on the front and sides of two adjoining rooms, and more glass doors that led to a fenced outdoor area. Inside, there were approximately fifteen dogs milling about. Some were playing together, chasing each other around the room and then running outside, some were sitting up on one of those children's plastic play sets complete with slide, some were sleeping in corners, and others were just walking around. There was one staff member sitting off to the side, keeping an eye on things. When the dogs saw us at the window, they all came running over, obviously curious about the newcomers. Wylie seemed a bit scared and backed away. More doubt crept into my mind. We went back to the reception area.

Suddenly, I opened my mouth. "Okay, take her," came out. *Who said that?!* Was that me talking? Had I just entrusted my little, sweet, four-month-old puppy to these strangers? Why yes, apparently, I just had.

Natalie went behind the counter and checked Wylie's vet records and said that all was in order. The staff was wonderful, and they all fussed over Wylie, my cute, sweet, wiggly, black puppy. I glanced over at the two large sliding glass doors that faced the playroom. All the action was visible from the lobby and grooming area. I liked that. No secrets. I could see the dogs in the room, having a blast, running, jumping, playing.

I told Natalie how worried I was, and she tried to put me at ease. "Don't worry. We'll introduce her gradually," she said, "and we'll keep a close eye on her for you. We'll take good care of her."

I passed her the leash. I think I was sweating. I know my heart was beating a bit too fast. She led Wylie to the side door, took off her leash, scooped her up in her arms, and walked into the fray as I watched from the lobby.

As soon as they entered, they were rushed by all the other dogs who were intent on investigating the new arrival. She kept Wylie in her arms, only allowing the other dogs to get a quick sniff as she walked around the room. Wylie looked scared and clung to her shoulders. I was scared. The dogs in the room all looked happy to be there and seemed to be enjoying the whole experience. The staff assured me that the dogs were all very dog-friendly and welcomed new playmates. They said Wylie would be okay. They told me to leave. I didn't want to, but I did. I took a deep breath, swallowed hard, turned, and walked out. I sat in my car with the windows open, listening to the dogs in case I heard puppy screaming. All I heard was the same barking as when I arrived, so I left.

Like a worried mom, I drove around for a few hours. I went to the grocery store and wandered the aisles aimlessly. I went for coffee. I drove to the marina and paced the docks, thinking of my little Wylie. After three hours, I couldn't stand it anymore, so I went back to pick her up.

When I arrived, most of the dogs were gone, already picked up by their owners. I could see three or four dogs wandering around in the playroom. I didn't see Wylie. A surge of panic began to rise up in my throat. *Where was my dog? Did they give her away to the wrong owner?* I looked into the room through those glass doors and saw the woman in the chair. She saw me looking for Wylie. I mouthed "Where is Wylie?" through the glass, my eyes wide with worry. She smiled and pointed to the kiddie play structure with the green slide. There, underneath the slide, crashed out on the floor, was my sweet sleeping dog. I slid the door open a crack and called her name. Wylie opened her eyes and her tail started thumping against the concrete floor. She jumped up and ran over to me as I opened the door and bent down to greet her. She looked so happy to see me. She jumped up and licked my face then ran from person to person in the lobby, giving everyone kisses and full body wags. The staff reported that Wylie had had a blast and that she played and played with lots of dogs. A little pug named Deogie (that's the phonetic spelling of D-O-G, by the way) was by far her favorite. She romped around until she ran out of gas and then crawled under the slide and fell asleep. I was so happy and more than a little relieved! My dog was happy, too.

I continued to take Wylie to that doggie daycare at least twice a week for the next three years. I was there so often, I figured I might as well work there! They actually hired me, and I worked as their Kennel Manager until we moved away. Wylie absolutely loved it there. She enjoyed all the other dogs, and I believe this played a huge part in shaping Wylie into the social butterfly that she eventually became. Wylie made friends with every dog she met. She loved them all: big, small, furry, hairless, young, and old. Wylie learned to adjust her play style depending on who the other dog was. She was especially gentle with small dogs. They became her favorite playmates.

IT'S TRAINING TIME...

# Canine Body Language

There is a lot of great information available on canine body language, including some wonderful illustrations and excellent videos. I really don't want to reinvent the wheel here, so I encourage you to look up information produced by credible sources. *The Family Dog, Dog Sense*, and *Fear Free Happy Homes* all have excellent videos to help you learn what to look for to be able to identify fear, anxiety, and stress in your dog. When you are looking for information on any dog behavior, please make sure you look for current, force-free, science-based sources. That applies to all things dog!

What I want to do here is to summarize what you should be looking for in your dog's demeanor that will let you know that they are fearful, anxious, or stressed. Why is this important? Dogs, if pushed beyond what they can handle, may resort to biting to make the scary thing go away. You really want to avoid pushing your dog, or any dog for that matter, beyond what they can handle. You can think of this as going past the tipping point, or in dog training jargon, going over "threshold." Think of it as a glass of water. Each stressful event, no matter how small, adds water to the glass. Eventually, too many stressful events will make that glass overflow. So the tipping point is not some abstract point in time, it's the culmination of stress that finally makes your dog go over threshold.

The term "threshold," according to the Merriam-Webster dictionary, is defined as "the point at which a physiological or psychological effect begins to be produced." https://www.merriam-webster.com/dictionary/threshold

When your dog is anxious about a specific situation or the presence of a certain person, there is a point at which they may tip over into the fearful zone. They may go "over threshold." We always want to try to help our dogs cope before things go that far. If you know what to look for, you can mitigate the situation and help get your dog through it.

You may or may not see all of these signs in your dog. However, your dog will most likely show at least some of these signals if they are feeling anxious and uncomfortable. It is always important to take note of the context in which these behaviors occur. If your dog just wakes up from a nap and yawns, it is not likely due to stress. If your dog licks his nose right after eating peanut butter, it is not likely due to anxiety. You get my point. Context is important.

## SIGNS THAT YOUR DOG IS *NOT* HAVING A GOOD TIME

1. **Furrowed Brow**: Dogs will get a "worried look", just like people do, when they are feeling uncertain or scared. They will tense their brow (forehead), and small wrinkles will temporarily appear.

2. **Ears Flattened**: Dogs have a variety of ear shapes, from long and floppy to sharp and pointy. When dogs are scared or uncomfortable, their ears move down and back, regardless of shape. The floppy-eared dogs

will flatten their ears back and against their head. The pointy-eared dogs will move their ears backwards, and the tips might fold back, too.

3.  **Tail Carriage**: The tail talks! Tails tell us a lot about what a dog is feeling, so learning what they are communicating through their tails helps us better understand them. Some dogs have very short tails and are limited in what they can 'say' with them. Keep this in mind if you have a dog with a docked tail. You must read the other signs more closely to know how your dog is feeling in that moment. When a dog is happy and comfortable, their tail is carried in a neutral position (roughly parallel to the ground), and it wags from side to side. If they are really happy or excited, that wagging speeds up and can involve their whole body. Their tail may even start to whip around in a circle, what we call a "helicopter tail". They look loose and wiggly when they are happy. When a dog is uncomfortable or scared, the wagging slows down or stops, and their tail lowers and gets tucked between their back legs. When a dog gets really angry or on guard, that tail can change into one that is held high and stiff, like a flag, sometimes with the end wagging back and forth quite rapidly. That high, tense tail carriage is a sign of extreme tension and says, "Back off now!" A dog that is posturing like this is set to go on the offensive, so be very careful. Back away from the dog!

4.  **Hunched Posture**: Dogs that are uncertain, shy, or afraid will arch their backs, almost like a cat. This has

the effect of lowering their head closer to the ground. A tucked tail often accompanies this hunched posture.

5. **Lip Lick/Tongue Flick**: These terms are often used interchangeably. You will see uncomfortable dogs stick their tongues out, sometimes almost imperceptibly. These licks and flicks may be more pronounced and reach all the way up to their nose. With these types of stress licks, the tongue usually comes out of the front of their mouth, not the sides. These licks or flicks are also generally very fast.

6. **Repetitive Yawning**: When a dog yawns because they are tired or just woke up from a nap, their mouth opens wide, and the tongue usually comes all the way out and curls inward. When a dog stress yawns, the mouth opens wide, but the tongue usually stays inside the mouth, back and down against the floor of the mouth, or is only partially extended. A dog may repeat these stress yawns several times.

7. **Piloerection (sometimes called raised hackles or fur standing up on their back)**: Piloerection refers to the raised hairs on the dog's shoulders, and along the back and (sometimes) the tail. This is an involuntary reaction, sometimes referred to as bristling, and is similar to how we humans get goosebumps. It is usually a sign that the dog is excited or aroused in some way. It is not always, but may be, associated with anxiety and fear. Context is important here. This bristling can also happen during play when a dog becomes over-aroused.

8. **Adrenaline Shake Off**: This looks like a dog that is shaking off water, but they are not wet. It's a whole body shake off. You will often see this happen when two dogs meet, they sniff each other's rear ends, then part ways; a shake off will often follow. It's a stress reliever. We humans even have a saying that is similar. When we say, "shake it off," it means to get over it and move on. That's what your dog is trying to do!

9. **Pacing**: Dogs will pace back and forth or in circles when they are feeling anxious or stressed. This is sometimes accompanied by a tucked tail, excessive panting, and hypervigilance.

10. **Panting**: Dogs that are anxious will pant even though they are not hot or out of breath. When dogs pant to cool themselves, their tongue lolls outside the mouth, fully extended with a flat tip shaped like a spatula. If a dog is stress panting, the panting will be rapid, and the tongue will usually be kept inside the mouth or only partially extended. You will not see the *spatula tongue* in a stress pant.

11. **Hypervigilance**: The Merriam-Webster definition is: "the state of being highly or abnormally alert to potential danger or threat." https://www.merriam-webster.com/dictionary/hypervigilance (link verified on 10/13/2021) When a dog is hypervigilant, you will see them standing with their head held high, looking around from place to place, air scenting, nervous. They constantly look behind them, as if to ensure nothing

or no one sneaks up on them. They are hyperalert to any potential danger that may arise in their immediate environment.

12. **Shaking**: Some dogs will tremble. This is an involuntary reaction often seen in small dogs, but large dogs will also tremble in fear. Humans do it, too.

13. **Slow Motion Movement, Paw Lift**: Dogs will sometimes walk very slowly, almost as if they don't want you to notice that they are moving away. They may stop and lift a front paw and let it dangle in the air. I like to think they are saying, "Okay, I'll just move over this way for a second, okay? Nothing to look at here. Move along, please."

14. **Turning Head Away, Moving Away**: A dog that is uncomfortable with the situation will turn their head away from it. We often see this when people hug dogs. If the dog could, they would walk completely away in an attempt to remove themselves from the stressful situation. Leaving the stressful environment is a good strategy for a dog. They just move away from what is bothering them. It's simple and efficient! However, problems occur when the humans follow them and continue the unwanted interaction or when the dog is on a leash and can't move away.

15. **Refusing Food**: The majority of dogs will eat tasty morsels of food most of the time. Bits of chicken, liver, or steak are irresistible to most dogs. When dogs are too stressed, they won't eat. They simply can't. A dog's

"seek" pathway (their olfactory system — scenting, eating, sniffing) and their fear pathway in the brain are mutually exclusive. When one is turned on, the other is turned off. Like a switch. So, when a dog is fearful, they won't eat. As fear lessens, the dog will begin to take the food, sometimes more rapidly and roughly than usual. When fear subsides, the dog will eat normally[6]. This can be an extremely useful guidepost in determining your dog's stress level.

16. **Whale Eye and Dilated Pupils**: Stressed or fearful dogs will show the whites of their eyes, called the sclera. They will turn their head away but keep their eyes fixated on the threat, thus showing some of the sclera at the side of their eye. A 'whale eye' is often accompanied by a 'freeze'. Also, a frightened dog may have dilated pupils, an involuntary stress response that happens in humans, too.[7]

17. **Freeze**: The dog's body goes completely still, their jaw closes tightly, and they seem to hold their breath. The 'freeze' is a clear warning to stop what you are doing.

18. **Lip Lift, Baring Teeth**: Often accompanied by a growl, a dog will retract the corners of their mouth. The corners of a dog's mouth are called the commissures. The mouth will usually be open, and the commissures

---

[6] Animals Make Us Human *by Dr. Temple Grandin, Houghton-Mifflin Harcourt, New York, NY, 2009*

[7] *The Eyes Have It - What Can Be Seen in a Dog's Eyes by Karen London* https://www.dogbehaviorblog.com/2008/05/the-eyes-have-i.html *(link verified on 10/13/2021)*

become tightly stretched towards the back of the head when the dog is fearful. The commissures will be pushed forward if the dog is taking a confident, offensive posture. Either way, it's not good. Stop what you are doing and slowly back away from the dog. The commissures may also pucker, exposing the teeth.

19. **Growl**: This is a low, guttural vocalization that sounds like a rumble. Growling is a clear mode of communication that is telling you to stop immediately and assess the situation. Never punish a dog for growling. Doing so just silences the dog; it does not change how the dog is feeling. You want the dog to be able to communicate this level of stress so that you can avoid a possible bite situation. Note that many dogs *play growl*. When a dog is playing tug, many will growl. This is nothing to worry about when it is done in play and all other signs indicate that the dog is relaxed and happy.

20. **Air Snap**: The dog snaps its teeth close to the victim but makes no contact. Many people think that the dog actually tried to bite them but missed. If a dog wants to bite a person, they don't miss. Dogs are incredibly fast and accurate. An air snap is another warning to back off. If these final warnings are ignored, a bite will ensue if whatever is happening at that moment does not stop.

21. **Bite**: This level of stress is to be mitigated and avoided at all costs. When a dog has tried to communicate its discomfort and all signals have been ignored, they

may resort to biting. Bites are classified using a scale of severity from level 1 to 6 as developed by Dr. Ian Dunbar. It is important to note that all dog bites that fall into the first two levels and are not considered severe, must be addressed to prevent escalation. (see Bite Scale for further analysis and information). https://www.dogstardaily.com/training/bite-scale (link verified on 10/13/2021)

So much communication! We humans miss so many clues that our dogs give us to let us know that they are not feeling comfortable. Learn to watch your dog. Watch other dogs. Leave your dog at home and go to a dog park. Watch the body language to see how many signals you can identify. You will be surprised. And once you learn to see what dogs are telling us, you can't unsee it. You will see at least some of these signals anywhere there are dogs.

So, what should you do when you notice that your dog is not comfortable? Help them through it. You can give them some space by moving away from what is scaring them. Crouch or sit down with them, pet them, reassure them. No, you will NOT reinforce their fear. Fear is an emotion, not a behavior. If a child was afraid, we would certainly comfort them. A dog is no different in this respect. Once you have identified something that your dog needs help to cope with, use the principles of desensitization and counterconditioning discussed in Chapters 4 and 8.

# CHAPTER SEVEN

# Wylie Flunks Out

N ow that I had found an appropriate outlet for some of Wylie's boundless energy, I needed to focus on training. The only type of training I knew was based on classes that I attended with my dog Roxy almost twenty-five years earlier. I wasn't looking forward to that type of harsh training. It was hard on the dog and hard on me. When my vet suggested that I go to a *positive reinforcement* dog training class in Iron River, about a 45-minute drive away, I had no idea what he was talking about, but it sounded like a kinder, gentler training method to me. He said that the trainer was excellent and that I should try and get Wylie into her next class. I called right away to see if we could sign up. I was so frustrated with all the jumping, pulling and general craziness. I needed help. I spoke to the trainer on the phone, and she told me that dogs had to be at least six months old for basic obedience class and that she was sorry, but the class was full anyway. Wylie was a little over five months old. I explained my problems, and I basically begged her to let us attend. She finally gave in, no doubt recognizing the desperation in my voice. Yay, a ray of hope! Things were finally going my way.

The instructions for the first class were simple: no dogs, only owners. Phew, that was easy! It was an eight-week class held outdoors on Wednesday evenings for an hour throughout July and August. The class size was limited to eight dogs; the addition of Wylie made nine. I arrived a bit early, as usual, and was nervous to meet the instructor and other students. I was hoping that I would be in common company, all of us having out of control, young, large dogs that needed help.

Jennifer was great. My first impressions of her were that she was a kind, competent, and knowledgeable trainer. The other owners were friendly and nice. We talked about rules, expectations, and equipment. We talked about motivation. Jennifer demonstrated how to teach sit and sit/stay with a release word with her own amazing dog, and our homework for the week was to teach our dogs the sit/ stay command (we were still calling them *commands* back then, now we call them *cues*). We were all to bring our dogs the following week equipped with a properly fitted flat collar, a six foot leash, and kibble to use as treats. Okay, I could do this! After all, Wylie already knew how to sit! I was already way ahead.

I spent that whole week working on sit and sit/stay with Wylie, and she was awesome! I used my hand signal, said "sit," and she sat, so I gave her a piece of food. She had that skill nailed, perfect every single time. She was one smart dog.

Wylie had already mastered a semblance of "stay" from the time she was a very young puppy. She loved to eat so much that she would gobble her meal at breakneck speed. Then, she would gulp water and throw it all up. We quickly realized that we would have to slow this feeding process down for her since she seemed incapable of doing so herself. Tim and I came up with a solution. One of us sat on the floor with Wylie, asked her to sit, put a few pieces of food in her bowl, asked her to wait, and then released her with "Okay!" letting her go to her bowl. We repeated this until she had finished her entire meal.

We generally split up her meal into five or six portions. I didn't know it at the time, but this little ritual set her up for developing a really solid "stay." So, teaching sit/stay was easy. Wylie and I did really well on our Week One homework.

The next Wednesday afternoon, I loaded Wylie into the car and off we went to school, our very first formal training adventure together. I was excited to learn with Wylie yet apprehensive about Wylie's behavior. After all, there were going to be a bunch of other dogs that Wylie would no doubt want to play with and a bunch of new people that she would want to meet.

I got there early so I would be the first to arrive. As I walked up to the yard with Wylie by my side (sort of), I could see people walking around with their really well-behaved dogs. I was hoping that they belonged to another class, one that was obviously more advanced than my beginner class. I looked more closely and recognized a few people from my class in there. Apparently, other people were either eager to show off their amazing dogs or they were also nervous, so they got there early too. As I approached the fenced training area with my enthusiastic dog, I saw four or five dogs on leashes, calmly walking around sniffing the ground, being good dogs. There was no pulling, no barking, no lunging, nothing! As soon as Wylie spotted the people and dogs, she went ballistic, pulling like a freight train, gagging, and choking, and not caring one little bit. She seemed totally oblivious of me, her human annoyance, on the other end of the leash. She was so incredibly happy to be there and just couldn't wait to get inside the yard. With Wylie, everything was a wonderful new adventure! Everyone in the class stopped and just stared at us. I felt the blood rush to my face. I was mortified. Was I the only one with a dog like this? Wasn't this a *beginner* class? Why were all these dogs here if they were already so well behaved? This was ridiculous.

Jennifer saw me frozen outside the gate with my alligator puppy. I saw her smile. Wylie darted left, lunged to the right, spun in circles, jumped, and chomped at the leash. Let's face it: she partied. The only thing she didn't do was bark. I had yet to hear my dog bark at all. Jennifer motioned for me to come in. All the other owners and dogs scattered to give us some space. How nice of them and how humiliating for me!

Inside we went, my crazy dog and me. We all settled into our places in a big circle. There was a *six-foot rule* in class. That meant that no dog was to come within six feet of another dog. Everyone else's dog was sitting nicely beside their owner. Wylie was pulling, choking, and panting, trying to get to the other dogs. I was trying my best to control her enthusiasm. I tried to calm her, talk to her, pet her, keep her close to me. Nothing worked. I could feel everyone's eyes on me. I'm sure they were thinking that Wylie was some crazed, out of control maniac and that I was an idiot who didn't know what I was doing. That last part would have actually been pretty accurate.

So, we all started by practicing our sit/stay that we had learned in Week One. All the other dogs sat, and they all stayed. Guess what Wylie did? Well, let's put it this way, she did not sit, and she did not stay. What was a perfect, solid skill at home was totally unobtainable in this environment. I am pretty sure that Wylie did not even hear me ask her to sit. She was focused on everything but me. It was so incredibly frustrating. Wylie and I did not manage one single sit during that entire class. On top of that, Jennifer added a new skill we were supposed to learn, "Down." Since we couldn't even manage the sit command, I didn't even try that one! I watched how we were supposed to teach it, and I made a mental note to work doubly hard on it at home so we would be ready for the next class. Onward!

The next skill that we were going to start learning that evening was what the teacher called the "controlled walk." *Oh My Dog!* Fear shot through my whole being. I could actually hear my heart beating. A controlled walk? With my Tasmanian devil dog? What does that mean anyway? *No way is this going to be possible*, I thought, *but okay, we're here, and so we will try! Maybe some magic will happen.*

We were instructed to start walking in a big circle, and so off we all went. We were to keep up a brisk but leisurely pace and not crowd those in front of us. So, there we were, Wylie and I, walking in the ring of temptation. Everyone else was walking the circle with their dogs happily trotting beside them. Then there was Team Wylie. There I was, trying to walk with Wylie, but she was having none of this "controlled walk" business. Picture it: Wylie is darting left to the dogs across the circle, bolting forward to the dog ahead, dashing backward to the dog walking behind us. We were in a state of total chaos. The leash was getting tangled and we both stumbled over it. It got so bad that instead of continuing on the circle, I walked straight ahead and went to the far end of the yard, away from everyone else, just Wylie and me, all alone. I was hot. I was sweaty. I was frustrated. I was embarrassed and totally discouraged. How come everyone else could do this? What was wrong with me? Why couldn't I handle my dog?

Jennifer instructed the class to continue working as she made her way over to us. She told me not to worry, that Wylie was okay and that I was okay. This was "normal." She suggested that I might want to use a Gentle Leader® on my dog. She pulled a tangle of thin, pink nylon webbing out of her bag. I had no idea what it was, but she explained that it was a head halter, like a halter for a horse.

Wylie *was* kind of like a horse, but I said, "No way. I should be able to handle my own dog without that contraption!"

Jennifer was patient and kind and said, "Okay, no problem," and the three of us walked back to join the rest of the class together.

So many thoughts were running through my mind. I could see everyone else working just fine with their dogs on flat collars. Why would I need something "special" to help me? My own feelings of inadequacy surfaced. I was not used to such public failure. When I decided to tackle a project, I always found a way to succeed. Class finally ended, and we went home. I was hot, my clothes were damp from sweating so much, and I was totally frustrated. Wylie, on the other hand, was happily exhausted.

Wylie and I resumed our daily training sessions at home with renewed vigor. I was going to get this right if it killed me! We practiced several times a day, keeping sessions short and fun. I was nothing if not a good student. I did everything the trainer taught us to do and more. Wylie absolutely loved the training. When I asked for a behavior, she executed it flawlessly and got some yummy food as a reward. What could be better? Wylie was giving me hope that next week would be different. She was responding to the training incredibly well! *Good girl, Wylie!*

We worked on sit and down and stay. We worked on walking. Living in the middle of nowhere made it easier for Wylie to focus. There were no other people or dogs around. It was just Wylie and me and nature. We worked in the house first, then outside in the driveway, then down the long lane. I could ask Wylie for a sit/stay and walk twenty or thirty feet away from her. She wouldn't move. I'd walk back to her and she'd look at me with adoring eyes and a wagging tail. She'd stay put until I released her. Wylie was becoming really good at this stuff. I was so happy. I was ready for the next class. No one would be better than us. I just knew it! So, when the next Wednesday rolled around, we loaded up the 4Runner and went to class.

We arrived early (of course), got out of the car, and entered the training area. As soon as Wylie saw another person, it all fell to pieces. Gone was the focus, gone was her willingness to work for food, gone was her ability to sit or down or stay. Wylie was her "classroom" self again, all twists and lunges and craziness. It was like I wasn't even there except as an annoying fixture attached to her leash. Again, I sweated in the heat, trying everything to get her attention back to me. Nothing I did worked. Again, we fumbled on the controlled circle walk, all the other dogs happily strolling alongside their owners, while Wylie darted and lunged at them with her fun-loving puppy exuberance.

Again, I left the circle. I walked to the very back of the property and started to cry. I was so frustrated, angry, embarrassed, exasperated, and totally discouraged. Wylie was oblivious, and it made me feel even worse. *Oh no! Here comes Jennifer. Crap. I didn't think she'd come over again!* I dried my eyes as best I could and took a deep breath. Jennifer came walking over to us with that bright pink Gentle Leader® in her hand.

"I think you should try this." At this point, I would have tried just about anything. She slipped the head halter on my dog and the change was instantaneous. Wylie just stopped acting like an idiot. I walked her around, and she was calm. *What? How could this be?* We all walked back to join the class and merged into the walking circle. Just like that! I was in shock and disbelief. A little magic.

Wylie still had her moments in class though. One of the funniest was when Jennifer was explaining how you could use food to distract and manage your dog. She had a wooden spoon full of peanut butter in her hand. She asked for a volunteer.

"Oh, oh, please, pick me, pick me!" Wylie and I always volunteered for the demos, but Jennifer never picked us. This time, we were the only ones who offered.

Since no one else volunteered, Jennifer walked over to us, and I passed her Wylie's leash. As soon as she was within striking distance, Wylie started jumping up on her, reaching her paws up onto her chest, trying to lick her face. She tried to get Wylie to notice that she had a yummy peanut butter stick for her by waving it close to her face. Wylie did not care. She stole a quick lick and continued to jump. Wylie could totally ignore food if it meant she could have fun with a human. Wylie jumped, ignored the peanut butter, and jumped some more. Jennifer kept explaining how well this distraction with food worked as she walked my bouncing dog back to me and handed over the leash. Although I felt a bit bad for Jennifer because her demonstration had not gone as planned, I felt vindicated. *Thank goodness, it's not just me! She couldn't handle her either!* It was not just my inept handling that was the problem, it was Wylie herself, in all her unruly puppy glory!

As the weeks of class progressed, we learned more new skills. Wylie was learning how to control herself a little better, but I still had to use the head halter if we were going to be even remotely successful. I will say that I don't think Wylie liked wearing it. After all, it dialed down the fun for her. I also noticed that it pulled to one side as it often tightened around her snout. She did, however, stop pulling most of the time. I still felt badly for putting it on her, but I used it for her safety and my sanity.

In hindsight, I think the class was too much for Wylie at her age, but I just didn't know what else to do to work with her. I also think that all the rule-free time spent at doggie daycare contributed to Wylie's wild side. In any case, we were able to complete the remaining five classes.

When test day came, we had to perform all the skills we had learned. The hardest one for Wylie was the three-minute down/ stay. We managed to get to two minutes and forty-five seconds, and then Wylie stood up and started to walk towards me. I am sure she must have been wondering, *Why are we all just lying here? This must be a mistake. Silly human, I will get up and come to you.* We were allowed three attempts to get it right, but Team Wylie just couldn't do it. So, we didn't pass this Basic Obedience class. Team Wylie flunked out. We got a "Certificate of Attendance" instead. However, in my mind, we did way more than just pass that class. We triumphed! And although we didn't technically pass, we were voted "Most Improved Dog/Handler Team"! *Go, Team Wylie!* This was the first of Wylie's many awards to come. I was so very proud of my puppy. What a good dog she was! *Good girl Wylie!*

IT'S TRAINING TIME...

# Treat Magic!

You will no doubt encounter criticism for using food when working with your dog or puppy. Many people will tell you that you're just bribing your dog or that your dog won't listen if you don't have food with you or that your dog will get fat or that you need to dominate your dog instead of spoiling him and on and on and on.

Please ignore all of this advice. You can say something like, "Thank you so much for caring about me and my puppy, but I've got it covered." Be secure in knowing that science is on your side!

So, why is food so powerful, and why do we use it in positive reinforcement dog training and behavior modification? The answer may surprise you. We know for a fact that food has the power to actually change a dog's brain chemistry. Food boosts your puppy's ability to not only learn basic cues, but also to overcome stressful and fearful situations by increasing the release of dopamine — a neurotransmitter that elicits a positive emotional response — in the brain. This increase in dopamine stimulates your puppy's desire to sniff, hunt, and eat. As discussed in the previous chapter, two of the systems in a dog's brain are Seek and Fear. Sniffing/hunting/eating are part of the Seek system. These two systems are mutually exclusive. When one is turned on, the other is turned off. If you turn on

Seek, you turn off Fear. Using food turns on the Seek system and therefore has the power to turn off the Fear system. Simple.

If you give your puppy a piece of delicious food right before they become overly stressed, anxious, or fearful in a given situation, you turn on his Seek system, resulting in the production of dopamine, which in turn creates a positive emotional response, thereby mitigating the fear. It's a chain reaction.

Present food → *Mmm, yummy!* → Dopamine increases → *Ahhh, I feel good!* → Calm and happy

That's why we use food to help dogs overcome their fears. It really works! Food turns on a dog's thinking brain (using their noses) and deactivates their emotional brain. This enhances their ability to focus and learn. As you can imagine, this is incredibly valuable to you as the teacher! Who wouldn't want their dog to be calm, feel secure, be attentive to you, and learn new skills faster? No one that I know! So, use food to train.

## WHAT KIND OF TREATS SHOULD YOU USE?

It depends on your puppy. Some pups (Labrador retrievers come to mind) will find their regular kibble rewarding enough in situations with low distractions. Other dogs will require added incentive. I have heard many people say, "But my dog isn't food motivated!" Every dog eats! I believe you just have to do a little research into what your dog loves to eat. Tip: train your dog when he is hungry, not right after he has eaten an entire meal!

Keep in mind that the harder the task, the better the food reward should be. What I recommend you do is test out some foods on your dog. Rate them on a scale from 1, the lowest, to 10, the highest. I would put most dry dog kibble down as a 1. Watch your dog's reaction to each food item. Do they sniff it and slowly eat it? Or are they super excited for another bite? Does their body language say, "ho hum, fine" or "oh my goodness, that's yummy" or "give me another bite, please, please, please!" You decide.

So here are some ideas based on most dogs I know, rated from lowest to highest.

1. Regular dry kibble
2. Dry dog biscuits
3. Plain Cheerios™
4. Soft, meaty treats
5. Meat jerky (low salt/spice)
6. Dehydrated liver
7. Hot dogs
8. Cheese
9. Scrambled egg
10. Cooked chicken

Other popular food items include carrots, green beans, lean roast beef, water packed tuna, plain yogurt, canned pumpkin (not the pie filling), banana pieces, chopped apple, and canned dog food. All food treats should be small, even for large dogs. Pieces should be about the size of a pea or even smaller for the little pups. Although most soft treats already seem small, you can further break them up into three to five pieces. Remember, you'll be using a lot of them, so make them small. You don't want to cause any digestive upset by overfeeding.

Soft, runny or gooey snacks can be dispensed from a large syringe (without a needle, of course) or a Food Tube or Pouch[8], one little squirt at a time. If the soft food is too thick to squeeze out, dilute it with a little water, and process it in a blender. You are only limited by your imagination and your dog's tastes.

Remember to avoid all foods that are toxic to dogs. The list of foods that you should never feed your dog is available from ASPCA Animal Poison Control[9]. If you are not familiar with that list, go to the ASPCA website and review it.

[8] *Nature's Little Squeeze Double Zipper Reusable Food Pouch by WeeSprout is a great product that you can use again and again. Available on Amazon (verified on 10/13/2021).*

[9] **ASPCA Animal Poison Control Center Phone Number is (888) 426-4435.** *Post this number somewhere in your home in case of emergency. Their website is https://www.aspca.org/pet-care/animal-poison-control. (link verified on 10/13/2021)*

# CHAPTER EIGHT

# Wylie Tames the Lawnmower Monster

In her first few months of life, the only weather Wylie knew was COLD with lots of snow and ice. In those early days, I worked hard on socializing my dog. I tried to make sure that Wylie had been exposed to a wide variety of things and people, adding to her socialization repertoire. When it came to vehicles, Wylie had been exposed to a lot of different ones. We owned a huge, orange Kubota® tractor with a back blade for snowplowing and front loader for scooping and dumping the piles of snow around our property, and Wylie had watched Tim clear snow many times. There were our personal vehicles, a Chevy truck and a Toyota 4Runner. There were snowblowers and four-wheelers that belonged to neighbors. There were all the cars and trucks we saw when we went to town, the snowplows, the transport trucks on the highway, the bicycles people still rode in town in the snow. Wylie took everything in stride, showing mild curiosity for some or taking no notice of others. She showed neither fear nor a desire to chase. She mostly just ignored them.

# Dale M. Ward

By the time Wylie was four months old, spring had arrived in northern Wisconsin, melting the snow and creating a muddy mess. As the weather warmed, the flowers bloomed, trees leafed out, and the grass grew. Wylie was having a wonderful time discovering new sights, sounds, and smells. For Wylie, it was a little bit of heaven. By the time June rolled around, it was time to mow the lawn for the first time. (I know that those of you who live in the south are wondering about waiting until June to cut the grass, but up north, summer comes late.)

Wylie and I were outside in the driveway playing fetch when Tim went into the garage, about a hundred and fifty feet away from the house and wheeled out the lawnmower. Wylie noticed him from a distance but did not pay much attention, preferring to hang out with the tennis ball and me. Tim tinkered with the lawnmower, getting it ready for the summer's work, checking the oil, filling the gas tank, checking the sparkplug. Within half an hour, he was ready to start it. I did not pay any particular attention when I heard him start the mower. After all, I had heard lawn mowers my whole life. Wylie, on the other hand, had not.

As Wylie happily played with me, chasing her tennis ball, chomping on the grass, and sniffing all the great scents that only a dog can smell, a deafening, grinding noise exploded in the air. Wylie startled and bolted toward the house in sheer terror as fast as her little legs could carry her. She jumped and scratched at the front door, seeming to fear for her life, trying to get away from the noisy, relentless monstrosity of a lawnmower. She was literally screaming for dear life as she clawed at that door, trying to get inside. I ran over as quickly as I could, my heart pounding, and opened the door. Wylie bolted inside in what I can only describe as a state of pure terror. I ran outside and told Tim to turn off the mower. He did. I ran back inside to my frightened puppy. Wylie came to me looking for comfort and reassurance. I snuggled her quaking little body and stroked her fur. I held her close to me, repeating over and over again,

"It's okay Wylie, it's okay." She calmed down after a short while, relying on my reassurance to let her know that her world was not coming to an end. Tim came running in to see what had happened, thinking that Wylie had somehow been injured. He had no idea that it was the lawnmower that caused this extreme reaction. When I told him, he was as surprised as I was. After all, Wylie had been around so much machinery, and much of it was bigger and noisier than a little lawnmower! Wylie never balked at our big tractor, so why would a lawnmower elicit such a strong, fearful response? I was totally perplexed.

As it turns out, dogs, unlike people, do not generalize well. Just because Wylie had seen a variety of vehicles and machinery, she had not yet seen a lawnmower and, to her, it was a brand new monster. I knew I had to do something to help her overcome this fear. I just didn't know what that was. I was out of my depth. Again.

I know many of you have heard that you should not comfort a fearful dog because you will reinforce that fear. I am happy to report that this is another old, outdated idea that we now know to be false. No, you can't reinforce fear by comforting your dog! Not comforting a fearful dog would be akin to not comforting a small child who is afraid. It makes no sense and could definitely harm your relationship with your dog. If your dog is afraid, help her! Give her a safe place to retreat. In Wylie's case, I let her in the house, Tim shut off the lawnmower, and I held her close.

That said, don't overdo it. Your behavior can definitely influence your dog. Be calm, speak softly and slowly, and stroke your dog in a peaceful manner. Long, slow body strokes mimic a sense of tranquility. Talk softly. You do not want to add to your dog's anxiety by petting rapidly or speaking in a loud, excited manner. You want to instill a sense of calm to reduce the fear and anxiety your dog is feeling. Think of comforting a small child, then do that.

So, back to Wylie. What to do, what to do! I now had a dog that was terrified of a weekly activity that was going to take place all summer and fall, in perpetuity. I searched for a way to help her and was drawn back to our efforts with the car when she was a really small puppy. Could I use the same methods for the lawnmower? Yes! Through regular sessions, Tim and I managed to help Wylie overcome her fear so completely that she was able to romp and play while we cut the grass for the rest of her life. She even developed a new game all on her own. She would drop her tennis ball right in my grass-cutting path. She knew I would have to stop to pick it up and toss it out of the way. When I did, she chased and retrieved it only to drop it in front of me again. This is how Wylie taught me to play fetch while I mowed the lawn. *Smart puppy!*

No matter what your dog is afraid of, you can do it too! Whether it's the lawnmower, the vacuum cleaner, other dogs, or people, counterconditioning and desensitization techniques can be applied to help your dog cope in the scary human world. Check out the instruction guide that follows.

# How to Use Desensitization and Counterconditioning to Help Your Dog

Desensitization and counterconditioning are how I helped Wylie overcome her fear of the lawnmower (among other fears). As described in Chapter 4, you can apply these same principles and techniques to whatever your dog fears: the vacuum cleaner, plastic bags, fireworks, other dogs, whatever. It doesn't matter. The principles remain the same. You may have to get creative in how to make the feared object or sound small enough in intensity to allow your dog to be in a state of mind conducive to learning and not out of their mental safe zone. It is also very important that while you are trying to get your dog to overcome a fear, you must prevent exposure to that fear-inducing stimulus. It makes zero sense to try to get your dog to be okay around, for example, children playing if you allow children to overwhelm your dog between training sessions. This just won't work. You must manage and control the environment in between sessions.

Let's take a closer look.

**Counterconditioning:** *Counterconditioning involves the consistent and repeated pairing of a stimulus that evokes an unpleasant response (the lawnmower) with something that is emotionally positive (cooked chicken) until a positive association is made between the two. To achieve maximum success, counterconditioning should be performed in conjunction with desensitization.*

**Desensitization:** *The process by which the fear-invoking stimulus is minimized or reduced to a level that does not evoke the fear response (for example, by reducing volume, increasing distance, changing the environment, or modifying the stimulus to something less threatening). Once a positive association is made, rewards can be paired with stimuli of gradually increasing intensity.*

(Definitions from the Merck Veterinary Manual) https://www.merckvetmanual.com/behavior/behavioral-medicine-introduction/treatment-of-behavioral-problems **(link verified on 10/13/2021)**

|  |  |
|---|---|
| What I saw: simple grass-cutting machine | What Wylie saw: The Lawnmower Monster |

*(istock)*        *(istock)*

My job was to turn the lawnmower monster into the small, nonthreatening, grass-cutting machine that I took for a walk on the lawn every week.

# COUNTERCONDITIONING AND DESENSITIZATION STEP BY STEP INSTRUCTION GUIDE

1. **Establish the Threshold**

   The "threshold" is the level (distance/volume) at which the dog can be in the presence of the scary thing while being alert and aware of it, but not showing signs of extreme fear (cowering, running away, barking, or lunging). It may be different for each scenario, each dog, and each fear-inducing situation or sound. It may also change day to day depending on what the dog is feeling or experiencing at that specific time. The point is that the "threshold" is not static. Ideally, you always want to work just *under* this threshold. For Wylie, we were approximately one hundred feet from the non-running lawnmower for her to be aware of it but not too concerned about it. This is the distance at which we began the counterconditioning and desensitization process.

### 2.   Expose and Feed

Ensure that your dog is on a comfortable, well-fitting harness with a leash attached so that he is safe. If you have an assistant, have them bring the object, in this case, the lawnmower, into view. It helps a lot to have somewhere to "hide" the object between exposures. We used the garage as our screen. A parked car or separate room also work, depending on the situation. Alternatively, you can move your dog behind a barrier of some kind so that your dog can no longer see the scary object between exposures. This technique works well if you don't have an assistant. As soon as your dog sees the object, feed bites of chicken (or other high-value food that your dog *loves*), one bite after another, for five seconds (count to five in your head). Shorten the time to two seconds if your dog is having difficulty. Take your cues from your dog. If it is too difficult for him, increase the distance, lower the volume, or shorten the time.

### 3. Remove and Stop Feeding

After five seconds, have your helper remove the object, or you can remove the dog. Tim wheeled the lawnmower back into the garage, out of sight. I stopped feeding. The idea is that when the object appears, chicken appears, and the dog eats. When the object disappears, chicken disappears, and no food is given. If you are working at a great distance like we were, it helps to have walkie talkies, or you can use your phones to communicate with your helper. An alternative method of communication would be to establish some hand signals that indicate to your helper when to retreat and when to return. It is not a good idea to yell out instructions when your dog is already feeling uneasy. Yelling may increase your dog's stress level, something you want to avoid doing.

### 4. Repeat Steps 2 and 3

Repeat steps 2 and 3 until your dog is consistently looking at you in a relaxed, eager manner, looking for his chicken every time he sees the object (lawnmower) at this distance. When this happens, you have created what is called a Conditioned Emotional Response, also known as a CER. Your dog's emotions are changing from bad to good, from seeing the lawnmower at a distance of one hundred feet as scary to something that brings good things in the form of chicken. As the dog is being conditioned to associate the lawnmower with a high-value food item, the dog is beginning to look forward to seeing the lawnmower.

## 5. Increase Intensity

Now that your dog is comfortable at this intensity (how loud, how close, etc.), you slowly and gradually increase the intensity. You do this either by decreasing the distance or increasing the volume of the fear-inducing object or sound. For us, we began by allowing Wylie to move about five feet closer to the lawnmower and repeated steps 2 and 3. We continued until we achieved a CER from Wylie at each new distance. We gradually moved closer and closer until Wylie was happily eating pieces of chicken directly off the stationary, non-running lawnmower. We successfully closed the distance from one hundred feet to zero.

## 6. Add Sound

In the case of an item that also moves and makes noise, you must add these variants separately. Every time you add sound or movement, it is more difficult for the dog. A stationary, silent lawnmower is one thing, but a moving, roaring one is quite different. Return to your original distance before adding sound. At our original distance of one hundred feet, Tim started the lawnmower for just a split second, then I rapidly fed chicken to Wylie. Tim then turned the lawnmower off, and I instantaneously stopped feeding chicken. He started it again, and I fed; Tim shut it off, and I stopped. Initially, sound "on" intervals should be extremely short. Very gradually, we increased the time the lawnmower stayed on, each time looking for that CER from Wylie. Eventually, she was able to be comfortable with the motor continuously running from a distance of one hundred feet.

### 7. Add Movement

Once we had a good response to the sight and sound of the running lawnmower at one hundred feet, we added movement. Again, at our original distance of one hundred feet, Tim pushed the running lawnmower forward one foot. I fed Wylie. Tim moved it back one foot. I fed Wylie. We watched for the CERs and progressed at Wylie's speed, never pushing her beyond her comfort level, until Tim was able to push the lawnmower freely with only good reactions from Wylie. Wylie was now able to be in the presence of the moving, running lawnmower without showing any fearful response.

### 8. Combine the Variants

Now I combined sight, sound and movement while closing the one-hundred-foot gap. With the motor running and Tim pushing the lawnmower back and forth as if cutting the grass, I gradually allowed Wylie to close the gap. Wylie looked at the moving, running lawnmower and I fed her chicken. I was carefully looking for that CER each time before moving closer.

### 9. Maintenance

You must continue to expose your dog to the newly accepted, non-threatening stimulus from time to time while pairing it with something your dog loves. You can continue to pair it with food, but you can also use other things your dog enjoys like a game of fetch, a food puzzle toy, or whatever your dog loves. If your dog shows any fear, revisit the counterconditioning and desensitization process. The good news is that the process should be much faster and easier the second time since you have already created a good base. You should only have to remind your dog that the stimulus makes chicken happen! For us, Wylie was exposed to the lawnmower on a weekly basis for the rest of the season, and so it was easy to keep up that exposure. By the next summer, she was running and playing while we were cutting the grass, having completely overcome her fear of the lawnmower.

## Troubleshooting the Counterconditioning and Desensitization Process

a.  **How long is this going to take?**

The short answer is this: it depends. There are so many variables! How fearful is your dog? How easy is it to set up the training scenarios? How frequently can you work on this? Can you control exposure to the scary thing between training sessions so that the dog is not scared over and over in between training? All of these factors will affect your success. It took us approximately one month to work with Wylie on overcoming her fear of the lawnmower. We worked short sessions a few days during the week (five to ten minutes in the evening) and increased the number of sessions on the weekends. In the meantime, when we needed to mow the lawn, Wylie stayed in the house in her crate (her safe place) with a stuffed Kong® toy to keep her busy and music to drown out the sound and help keep her calm. Alternatively, I took her for a drive or out for a walk while Tim cut the grass. I managed to keep her away from the noise while we were training.

b. **My dog continues to bark and lunge before I even begin.**

You are likely starting when your dog is already *over* threshold. Either increase the distance, lower the volume, or find another way to lessen the intensity of the exposure. When a dog is over threshold, fear takes over, and they cannot learn. Use your imagination and superior brainpower to figure out how to make it less scary for your dog. Think of it as turning down the intensity of the scary object or sound.

c. **My dog won't eat the food.**

First, ask yourself if you are using food that your dog absolutely loves. Just because we think a certain kind of food is delicious doesn't mean your dog does. Test the food when your dog is not stressed and ask yourself if he really loves it. Is it his favorite? Good choices include real chicken, cooked liver, canned tuna, scrambled egg, or cheese. You can even use the canned version of their usual dry dog food. Dogs usually find canned food much more palatable than dry. You might even want to try canned cat food. Make sure your dog is hungry when you begin. You can feed a lighter meal on the days you plan to train. Whatever food you do choose, make sure your dog can tolerate it and that it will not cause stomach upset. Consult your veterinarian if you have any questions about the types of food you can use.

If your dog loves the food you are using but will not eat when you are counterconditioning, another possibility is that you are starting when your dog is already over threshold. When dogs are unable to eat food that they would normally love, they may be feeling too stressed. Try lessening the intensity of the exposure by increasing distance or lowering volume. When your dog is able to eat, you have found the right threshold.

d.  **I don't have an assistant.**

Ask for help. If you have neighbors, relatives, or friends, you can invite them over for a short session, and then reward them with lunch or a cup of coffee with you afterward. Use some positive reinforcement on your helpers. Bake some chocolate chip cookies and reward them! *Good humans!* People are usually happy to help when asked. Thank them profusely each time, making sure you express how integral they are in helping your dog overcome his fears. Another idea is to use a remote reward system like a Treat & Train® Remote Reward Dog Trainer to deliver food to your dog using a remote control. This option is a little more expensive, but it works very well. You would have to adjust what food you use to suit the mechanics of the dispenser as per manufacturer's instructions.

e.  **I can't replicate the sound my dog is afraid of.**

Some sounds like thunder or sirens are difficult to find in real life. The good news is that there are many sounds now available online to download for free. There are sound downloads you can purchase such as the Through A Dog's Ear Canine Noise Phobia™ series. There is also a great app for your phone called Sound Proof Puppy Training© which contains a wide variety of sounds. You can even record your own sounds to use. Make sure you use a high quality speaker so that your sounds are life-like.

f.  **I can't find access to the object my dog is afraid of.**

There are many ways to gain access to what your dog fears. Be resourceful. For example, some dogs are afraid of motorcycles. You can contact your local motorcycle dealer and ask permission to come and observe from a distance with your dog when they are holding a riding class. You can do the same with bicycles and other vehicles. Simply find a nearby dealership or store and ask for permission. Most people are happy to help if they can. If your dog is afraid of other dogs, you can look for a local pet store and work at a distance in the parking lot, watching for dogs that are going into the store. You could find a local dog park and work a block away so that your dog can see the dogs at the park but be at a distance that keeps him under threshold. Use your imagination. There is almost always a way to accomplish your goal.

g. **Consult a professional.**

If you are unsure about how to help your dog or if you are running into any problems, consult a qualified, force-free, positive reinforcement dog behavior professional with experience in behavior modification. Fear is nothing to fool around with. You really want to do this right!

# CHAPTER NINE

# Wylie the Kleptomaniac

## THE TREE FLAGS

Our property was beautiful. It was quiet. It was peaceful. It was forty-seven acres of rolling hills, little streams, and beautiful woods. The trees were plentiful. There were those big red pines, towering over the ground below, casting lots of shade with their enormous branches. White birch, whose bark stood out like painted white stripes, stark delineations among fellow trees. White pine, with their tangle of branches tipped in long, slim evergreen needles. The quaking aspen that the locals call *popple*, whose little round leaves turned a stunning bright yellow against the bluest of autumn skies, shimmering and rustling in the cool breeze. And there were so many more varieties!

What we were missing on our property was oak. The oaks had been harvested for lumber a long time ago, and they were few and far between on our property. That's one tree that I truly love. I remember sitting out under our huge oak tree as a child. It provided the only shade around our house and gave some relief from the summer heat.

No air conditioning meant that the inside of the house was like an oven, so the days were spent outside, only going in to replenish ice cold glasses of Kool-Aid or to get popsicles made of the same stuff. The dogs turned into slow motion creatures, tongues lolling and heads drooping, with little relief from the heat. They flopped down on the grass under that big oak tree to take advantage of some shade.

Back in Highbridge, each fall, the local Department of Natural Resources took orders for a wide variety of tree saplings. They came in bundles of one hundred little trees that were two to three years old for about fifty bucks. There were rules associated with these trees. They had to be planted in Wisconsin — nowhere else — and used only for conservation purposes, and that included growing them for eventual use in forest products, for wildlife habitat, or erosion control. You couldn't use the trees for simple landscaping or for Christmas tree production. We wanted them for wildlife habitat. Tim ordered two bundles of one hundred baby oak trees.

When they arrived the next spring, they didn't look like much, all smashed together, not intimidating at all! We stuck them in a bucket of water, as instructed, and put them in the garage. Our front five or so acres had been stripped of trees at some point and only a bit of new growth had taken root up there. The rest was filled with tall grasses that had to be regularly mowed with the tractor to keep them from taking over and becoming a fall fire hazard. That was the property that abutted the road, so we thought it would be nice to create more cover for us and for the deer and other animals. Great idea!

Tim bought a manual tree planter thing. It's a metal rod, about four feet long, with a handle at the top and an eight-inch metal wedge with a crossbar at the bottom so that you can use your foot to jam the thing into the earth. On a beautiful spring day, we geared up in rubber boots, hats, and gloves, and we set out to plant our two hundred trees with Wylie in tow. Tim had the job of making the hole with the planting tool. I had the job of untangling the seedling and placing it in the hole alongside a little orange marking flag. Without the flags, there was no way to know where the trees were. As soon as the grass grew tall enough to mow, it would totally conceal the trees. We had to be able to clearly see where the trees were so that Tim didn't run over them with the giant mower, so those orange flags were really important.

Wylie's job during all of this was to try to grab the seedlings in her mouth and run around wildly, shaking mud and water from the dangling roots. When she couldn't get a tree out of my bucket, she would run and find a stalky weed, clamp onto it with her jaws, and pull, pull, *pull!* The weed would come loose, giving way to her might, and send her flying backwards. She would tumble and spring up, the huge weed dangling from her mouth, proud as proud could be. Then she would shake, shake, *shake* that thing until she was sure she had killed it. Satisfied, she would drop it and move along to her next victim. Wylie loved this job and being outside with us was her favorite thing to do, so she was in doggie heaven!

I, on the other hand, was not so impressed. I got hot and sweaty (a running theme, apparently) pushing the wheelbarrow through the dense grass and underbrush. It was buggy with flies, and my back started to ache from bending over and placing each of those trees in their holes. After a few hours, I was done. We quit for the day and walked back to the house. From our driveway, we turned and looked to admire our work. There were all the little orange flags, in lovely straight rows, marking our days' effort. Wylie was still romping around the field, weeds flapping up and down from her mouth as she ran. We laughed. How cute our puppy was! I was happy we had a lot of space for her to wreak her havoc. I imagined what she would be like in a more structured environment like a backyard with lovely gardens. Those gardens wouldn't stand a chance!

# Dale M. Ward

Just when I thought our work was exempt, I saw Wylie pluck her first flag. She deftly pulled it out of the ground and stood there, looking at us. "Look, Mama! See what I've got?" That's what her face said to me. Tim and I dropped our stuff and ran towards her — big mistake. She took off running, reveling in this gigantic game of chase. She wasn't that much faster than we were, but she was oh so nimble. She darted and dashed with that flag in her mouth. When she was far enough away, she dropped it. *Oh, good girl!* I thought. Nope. She plucked another one, spat it out. Then another and another and another, all while Tim was running after her, yelling at her to stop.

"No. *No!* Don't do that! Please, *stop it!*" I followed behind, trying to put the flags back by each tree, but it was a losing battle. I couldn't spot them among the long grasses and twigs.

Then, we changed tactics. We stopped trying to chase her. We tried calling her sweetly: "Wylie, come, Wylie. Come over here. Look what I've got!" As I extended a hand, using the *fake-the-treat* tactic. She stopped and started to approach but changed her mind.

"Fine," I said, frustrated, and turned to walk away. I called to Tim, "Let's go back to the house. It's useless now. We can start over tomorrow." As soon as Wylie saw us going home, she dropped everything and ran full speed back to us. She had no interest in the flags, the weeds, or the trees. She only had interest in us. Lesson learned. Don't take your *bandida chiquita* tree-planting with you.

# RAGS, BAGS AND OTHER TREASURES

We spent a lot of time outdoors with Wylie. Having such rich countryside all around us was an incredible privilege. Tim spent a lot of time fixing things. He was a stickler for changing the oil in both of our vehicles, and he spent countless hours taking care of the tractor. He did all of the maintenance on all of our stuff: lawnmower, chainsaw, wood stove, chimney, and anything else that needed work. He spent a lot of time under things. He'd be under the car or the tractor more often than not, or so it seemed. I would either be inside doing whatever, or outside gardening, mowing the lawn or playing with the dog. Wylie was always curious as to what Tim was up to. There was usually something going on when he was working, and usually that meant stuff for her to steal. Her favorites were Tim's leather work gloves, and oily rags and plastic bags filled with oily paper towels. There was something about the paper that she simply adored. She would steal paper at any opportunity, and paper soaked in motor oil? That was the best!

Wylie usually spent her time playing ball with me. She loved that tennis ball more than anything. No food, no other toy, could come close to her obsession with that tennis ball. We bought tennis balls by the dozen! We'd play for a while, then I would make her quit. If left up to her own devices, she would fetch until she dropped of exhaustion. I had to be her monitor and stop the game before she overexerted herself. Most of the time, she was content to sniff around, eat deer and bunny poop, pluck weeds and eat grass while waiting for the next ball throwing session. When Tim was under a vehicle though, she knew fun was right around the corner.

I'm sure that the first time Wylie discovered the treasures Tim produced, it was by accident. She was just interested in why her human was lying on his back, on the ground, outside. When she investigated, to her delight, she found an array of items to play with.

The first time, it was a work glove. She picked one up and trotted off, proud as could be. She didn't run. She didn't know that she wasn't supposed to take that glove. After all, it was just lying there! I saw her grab it, so I walked over to her and took it away. I brought it back to Tim. "Hey, Wylie stole one of your gloves." Nothing. "Maybe you should put them somewhere that she can't reach." I handed it to him. "Okay, thanks," he said. He set the glove back on the ground, exactly where it had been before. "I'll keep an eye out for her" he said. "Okay!" I said, as Wylie and I walked back towards the house.

No sooner had I reached the front door than I heard a voice booming from across the yard. "WYLIE! Get back here!!!" This time, Wylie had snagged a bag full of oily paper towels and had run into the middle of the yard. She dropped the bag and proceeded to stick her head in it, pull out one of the paper towels, and started to eat it. "NO!!! Wylie don't do that! You're going to get sick!" I ran towards her and she darted away, soiled, white paper towel dangling from her mouth like a flag of surrender, except there was no surrender in sight. "Is motor oil poisonous?" I screamed at Tim. "How should I know!" he growled back. "Well, YOUR dog just ate some." (Whenever Wylie did something wrong, she was the other person's dog.) Luckily, she had left the bag with all the other paper towels behind, so I ran over and grabbed it. Ha! At least I won something! I ran after her. She ran away from me, of course, but it seemed like she couldn't eat while she was running. The paper towel was not being consumed. I grabbed her tennis ball and threw it right past her. Wylie dropped the paper towel and gave chase. Another game of fetch won the day.

Wylie's love of paper extended to items inside the house too. We learned that an open bathroom garbage can was a huge mistake. Wylie would come trotting out with used tissues, reams of toilet paper, and anything else she could find. One of the most embarrassing episodes happened when we were visiting my friend Audrey. She had a really nice dog, a German Shorthaired Pointer named Paisley. Wylie and Paisley were good friends. One day, we were chatting in the kitchen when Wylie came strolling through. I look down and I see my dog with a feminine hygiene product in her mouth. I was mortified. I quickly grabbed her, swiped that thing out of her mouth and ran to the bathroom to dispose of said treasure. I apologized profusely for my dog's rude behavior and made sure that all the doors to the bathrooms remained shut for the rest of our visit. From then on, I would make a point of closing all of the bathroom doors in Audrey's house every time we visited!

Wylie loved all paper and would snag magazines, books, even paper off the printer. Life with Wylie meant that we became very good housekeepers. Everything had to be put away so that the little devil dog couldn't get at it. That was a big lesson we had to learn. Sometimes, it's just easier to prevent some disaster from happening rather than to try to train a dog NOT to do something! Just put things away.

## THE SNOWSHOE

Winter came quickly enough, and Wylie was growing into a magnificent, if challenging dog. I loved her beyond words. She frustrated me to no end, but she also made me laugh and made my life so much better. She was almost ten months old at Christmastime and was truly in full adolescent mode. Tim's son, Evan, and our future daughter-in-law, Julie, came to visit for the holidays that year, and Wylie was thrilled to have more humans to play with. I remember that it was brutally cold in late December because we felt so sorry for Julie, who was born and raised in Louisiana. Never having really experienced snow or real cold weather, she had to withstand the kind of cold that took your breath away for her entire visit. The weather was beautiful apart from the cold. The sky was a brilliant, clear azure blue during the day and the sun threw its icy white rays onto the snow, creating a sea of diamonds everywhere you looked. But those sunny rays held little warmth. Our tradition was to take a walk into the woods a few days before Christmas to chop down our Christmas tree and haul it back home. We debated on whether to even do it that year because it was so cold, but Evan and Julie really wanted to have the full experience. We outfitted Julie with proper warm boots, a hat, and mittens. She had a good coat, borrowed from other northern relatives, and some snow pants, so she was ready! Evan was a true northerner even though he had lived in the south for the past several years, so he knew what to expect and was ready for the cold weather.

We all bundled up and went outside, Wylie too. It seemed that nothing was too cold for Wylie. Her black fur absorbed what little heat there was from the sun, and her coat actually felt warm to the touch. We got the axe and the snowshoes out, and Julie's first reaction was to exclaim, "Oh, it's fine, I'll just walk. I don't need to wear snowshoes." Those were the words of someone who had never walked in deep snow! We convinced her to wear them by having her climb up the snowbank and drop down to the other side where the snow lay undisturbed. She sank up to her thighs. Even though we knew what would happen, the look on Julie's sweet face was priceless. She was truly shocked, no doubt about it. Her eyes went wide as she gasped in surprised amazement, and then she started to laugh. We all joined in, having a good laugh at the whole situation: the southern girl, the freezing cold, and the thigh-deep snow. It was a recipe for hilarity. Julie decided that maybe she would try the snowshoes.

We all put on our snowshoes, and away we went. Julie was such a trooper. She is very athletic and hopping around on the snowshoes came easily to her. It was fun to watch her adapt to life in the north. The five of us tromped way back into the woods where the stands of fir trees stood, and we picked out the best one we could find. Now wild balsam fir trees don't look anything like the ones that are tended and manicured and turned into commercial Christmas trees. Wild balsam fir trees look kind of like Charlie Brown Christmas trees. They're skinny, and the branches are sparse, but that also means they're a lot easier to chop down and not too heavy, so dragging our tree all the way back to the house wasn't that hard. We gave Julie the axe, and she chopped down her first Christmas tree.

Meanwhile, Wylie was running around in the snow, jumping over fallen trees, pulling on dead branches, tripping and falling over her own feet, and generally having a blast. The snow was not as deep in the woods because the trees acted as a canopy, keeping some of the snow out. This allowed Wylie to really run! She would tear around us, leaving her tracks everywhere, biting at the snow, eating some of it, and drooling out what she didn't swallow. She was definitely not cold. Everything was fun for Wylie.

The sun was starting to go down in the sky, so we tromped back to the house. We leaned the tree on the side of the house and took off our snowshoes. Traditionally, you stow your snowshoes by shoving them into the snow bank in an X fashion, one just behind the other. It looks cool. I had just gotten some new, expensive ones for both Tim and I as an early Christmas present. They were barely broken in. As we chatted outside, before going in, I noticed a black blotch out of the corner of my eye at the far end of the driveway. I turned to look and there stood Wylie with one of my snowshoes in her mouth. She had a good, solid grip on it. All I could think was "Oh no, those are three-hundred-dollar snowshoes, and she is going to bite right through the straps." I knew she wasn't going to relinquish that snowshoe easily. She wanted to entice us into a game of "chase me, chase me, and catch me if you can!" We were in a standoff, just like the Wild West — a very cold Wild West. With no guns, only snowshoes.

"Oh my gosh," I breathed slowly, "Look what she's got." Tim, Julie, and Evan all turned around and looked at my dog standing there, slowly wagging her tail from side to side, just staring at us.

# Dale M. Ward

"Don't make a move. She'll just run away with it." We all stood there for what seemed like a long time. Wylie was just waiting for us to run so she could make a break for it. I knew she would be off like a shot if we tried to approach her. What to do, what to do? Then, it came to me. A flash of brilliance! "Evan, call her name, really loud, then run away from her, out into the snow. I think she'll chase you."

"*WYLIEEEEE*", Evan's voice boomed like thunder in the cold, crisp air. I could see Wylie's ears perk up, and she stood higher on her toes. Her tail stopped wagging for a second. She paused, intrigued.

"Go now!" I yelled, and Evan took off running. Wylie couldn't resist. She dropped that snowshoe in a New York minute and hightailed it after her favorite boy. I ran over to where she had stood, so proud with her now discarded prize and picked up my snowshoe. No harm done. I turned back to watch Evan and Wylie tumbling around in the snow together, Evan tossing fistfuls of snow at her, Wylie running circles around him. I'm sure that Wylie thought she'd made a good trade. Evan was a much better prize than that silly old snowshoe.

## Wylie the Kleptomaniac

IT'S TRAINING TIME...

# How to Teach Your Puppy to Trade

If you just read the preceding chapter, you may be able to relate to some of those situations. Dogs are very clever, and they learn quickly. If your puppy picks up a random item — a TV remote, for example — your reaction to that behavior will shape how your dog responds. Your reaction, whatever it is, will teach your puppy what to do next. Will your dog learn to run away from you or walk towards you? Will your dog learn to crush or swallow the item, or will your dog drop what is in his mouth when you ask him to? Sometimes, it is difficult for us humans to understand what an enormous impact our own behavior has on the behavior of our dogs.

Before we start, let's look at what can happen if you don't teach your dog how to willingly give up what he has in his mouth.

## Caution

1. Constantly removing items from your dog's mouth can lead to dangerous resource guarding, resulting in a dog that resorts to biting in order to keep the item in question.

2. Forcefully removing items from your dog's mouth can damage your relationship with your dog. Your dog may perceive you as a bully.

3. Children mimic what they see adults do, and so may imitate adults who try to remove objects from dogs against their will. Children could then potentially be at risk of a bite.

4. Not being able to get your dog to give up inappropriate items can be dangerous and lead to major health issues like intestinal obstructions or poisoning.

5. Cornering a dog to remove an item from their mouths can make the dog feel threatened. Further, it will negatively impact your relationship and may even elicit aggression.

## So, let's break it down.

You turn to see your puppy with an expensive pair of headphones hanging out of her mouth. The scene might unfold something like this. Yes, I know this is anthropomorphizing, but I asked my dog if it was okay, and she told me it was fine!

> **DOG:** "Gee, I'm bored, my human is always so busy. Hmmmm, what's this? This is new!" Sniff, sniff. "It smells like my people." Lick. "It tastes like my people. I'll just pick it up to investigate, just for a moment."

> **YOU:** As you are working at the kitchen table, you see your dog, Sadie, across the room with something in her mouth. "Sadieeeeee? What have you got? SADIE! Bad dog!"

**DOG:** "Oh, what? Did I hear my name? What? Did you call me? Are you talking to me? Are you ready to play with me? Yes?"

**YOU:** "Don't you dare eat those headphones!" You jump up and run across the room towards your dog.

**DOG:** "What? Oh, YES! You *are* ready to play! Here comes my human! Yipee! She wants to chase me! It's my favorite game in the world. I'm going to run this way, around the chair, under the table, and into the living room! Go!"

**YOU:** Trying to block her as she runs circles around you, you yell, "Sadie! Get back here! Those things are expensive! *Sadie!*"

**DOG:** Hears "Blah blah blah Sadie blah blah Sadie". Weee! Run, run, run. "Wait, she's not very fast, so I'll slow down a bit and wait for her. She's getting close again!" Zip, zip, zip, run away, and back to the kitchen. Rinse, repeat!

**YOU:** Tired, frustrated, and angry, you give up and stop chasing your dog.

**DOG:** "Oh, is the game over? You're done already? Humans are so boring." She drops the headphones and turns to walk away. Done until next time!

So, ask yourself, in this scenario, "What am I actually teaching my dog to do?" What is your dog learning from you? She picks up a random item. You drop everything and give her your full attention, you say her name, and you physically run after her. Sadie will no doubt look at you, perhaps be a little startled by that immediate and large response from you. But, as you dart towards her, arms outstretched, talking to her in an animated fashion, she will likely run away from you so that you will chase her. From Sadie's point of view, the act of picking up the headphones caused you to engage in play. That's all. Your dog is not being obstinate or naughty. In the future, when Sadie wants to get your attention, she is likely to grab another item with her mouth, knowing that it will likely elicit the same response from you. You have now taught Sadie to grab something, show it to you, and then run away. She now knows you will give her a good chase.

I know that this is absolutely *not* what you intended to teach your dog. You did not intend to teach Sadie to steal valuable items and potentially destroy them so that you could play with her, but dogs really don't care what we intend. They respond to what we do.

So, how does a person get a puppy or even an adult dog to voluntarily drop the item in their mouth? It's very simple. We teach the dog how to trade. Trading is a simple exchange. One exchanges something for something else, and very often that "something else" is some form of currency. In our case, we are going to exchange the stolen item, and our currency is going to be food. Let's go over the rules of the game.

## TRADING RULES AND REGULATIONS
(Simpler than Wall Street)

**Determine what kinds of foods your dog loves most.** Most dogs love meat, so small pieces of leftover steak (no fat) or boneless chicken breast, small pieces of low sodium turkey hot dogs, or some dried liver, even a chunk of cold scrambled egg are all items you could try. Check to see what your dog's reaction is to each of the foods. Does your dog tell you that it's delicious? Do her eyes open wide, is she excited by the smell? Try a variety of foods and rank them from least to most delicious on a scale of one to ten. Save the best foods for difficult trades.

Always check with your veterinarian regarding the suitability of specific foods for your dog. Also, refer to the ASPCA Poison Control for a list of human foods that are toxic to dogs.

**Set up some easy training situations.** Your dog needs to practice trading. Practice a lot, especially at first. Until your dog knows the game and is fluent in how it works, it will not be reliable.

**You must always trade UP.** A dog will not give up what it deems to be a GREAT item, for something as dull as a piece of kibble. (Well, Wylie would because she loved ALL food, no matter what it was, except mushrooms. Mushrooms were valueless.) After all, humans don't make these kinds of bad trades either. Would you trade that twenty-four-karat gold ring for a single Lego block? No. Would you trade that hundred-dollar bill for a ten-dollar bill? No. So why would your dog trade that remote control for a piece of dry kibble? Your dog likely values that remote control because in the past, it meant that you would spend the next fifteen minutes "playing" with her, so yes, that remote is very valuable to her.

**Trading is always optional.** Your dog should have the choice to trade or not. It is up to you, the human with the bigger brain, to select your trade currency with forethought, so that your dog will *want* to trade. "Give up this plastic piece of junk for some chicken? Heck, yes!" That's the reaction from your dog that you are looking for.

**Never lie to your dog.** If you say you're going to trade and your dog drops what they have, you *must* give them the delicious food you promised. Dogs remember. If you don't follow through, your dog will stop trading with you. You will have become an unreliable trading partner. Your dog will not trust you. You'll have to go work on Wall Street with all the other unreliable traders.

## INSTRUCTIONS FOR TRADING WITH YOUR DOG

Here's how you are going to play this game with your dog. Do this right and your dog will LOVE to trade with you, anytime, anywhere.

1. Give your dog a toy that she likes but is not crazy about. When you see that your dog has the toy in her mouth, calmly get up and walk to your refrigerator (or treat pouch) and get a piece of delicious food. That's your currency. Make sure its value is high.

2. Approach your dog. Don't say anything yet. Stand to the side, not directly in front of her. Don't stare at your dog. Don't bend over your dog. Don't corner your dog.

3. Now, say your dog's name and ask the question in a light, happy voice: "Sadie, would you like to trade?" Show your dog the food, then let your dog sniff your *closed* hand with the food in it. Don't let her eat the food from your hand.

4. Toss the piece of food about three feet away from your dog. The idea is that your dog will drop the item and walk over to eat the food. When your dog has walked

away, slowly bend over and pick up the item and hide it behind your back, out of sight. Praise your dog. "Good job Sadie!"

5. In your set-ups, the item will always be a dog toy or object that she is allowed to have. Once you complete the trade, give the item back to your dog. If real life happens and it's something your dog should not have, you keep the item, but give your dog her favorite toy and spend a minute or two playing with her.

Repeat, repeat, repeat. Your dog will come to love trading. You may notice her bringing you things, stolen or not, and dropping them at your feet, hoping for a trade. In this final stage of trading, you don't have to reward every trade. Every once in a while, do reward with a high-value food item. Keep your dog guessing. *"Will I get some yummy food this time?"* Your dog will soon eagerly give up items instead of guarding them, destroying them, or consuming them just based on the chance that tasty food might be forthcoming.

## FAQS

- **Am I not rewarding my dog for taking things?**

  No, you are rewarding your dog for *giving up* the item. This is far, far better than having your dog develop guarding tendencies or destructive habits.

- **What if I don't have any food?**

  While you are teaching your dog to trade, be proactive and have a selection of good currency in your refrigerator or pantry. For example, you can cook a chicken breast ahead of time (I cut the raw chicken up into chunks and microwave it) and then portion it out and freeze it. Then you will always have some valuable currency ready to go. When you are out of the house, bring your treat bag with you so that you are prepared in advance. You can almost always find something in your refrigerator. In an emergency (if the item that your dog has is dangerous, poisonous, etc.) use whatever you have on hand. One small piece of lunchmeat or cheese, or some peanut butter on a spoon, is better than ingesting a battery!

- **What if my dog growls at me?**

Your dog has likely already developed some guarding behavior and that growl is telling you that he feels threatened by what you are doing at that moment. Try moving farther away from your dog, using more than one piece of food, create a "food trail" by throwing several pieces of meat in a row. Start the trail very close to your dog, then throw a piece further, then further, then further, so that your dog has to walk further away from the guarded item. Pick up the item when it's safe to do so and hide it behind your back, out of sight. If you can't safely pick the item up, try going into another room and calling your dog. When your dog comes to you, close the dog in the room while you go remove the guarded item, then go let your dog out. Remove all items that your dog is likely to guard. Call a qualified professional force-free positive reinforcement trainer to help you with your dog's resource guarding. Don't wait. This behavior won't go away by itself.

- **What if it's an emergency and my dog has something potentially toxic?**

Don't panic. Try using more than one piece of food, create a "food trail" by throwing several pieces of meat in a row, very close to your dog, then further, then further, then further, so that your dog has to walk further away from the dangerous item. If your dog will not drop the dangerous item, remove the item from your dog's mouth with your hand, then feed a succession of treats immediately after. This situation should not happen very often. If it does, you haven't practiced enough, and your environmental management may be off. Check that you are keeping dangerous stuff out of your dog's reach. Work on trading more often, with items that are safe, like your dog's own toys. Gradually work up to trading more difficult items such as a shoe or some paper and eventually, something truly important to the dog, a bone or other treasure.

- **Now that I've taught my dog to trade, she is bringing me stuff all the time! What should I do?**

Trade with your dog! It's great practice. You can lower the value of the reward when your dog volunteers to trade. I recommend using a piece of their regular food in these cases. Always remember to add lots and lots of praise too! *Good girl Sadie, good girl!*

# CHAPTER TEN

# Wylie the Nature Freak

The remoteness of our home up north provided an amazing playground for our young sporting dog. Wylie had forty-seven acres of woods, fields, and streams to play in, and she enjoyed every last inch of the property. Most of the time, it was quiet. We had a big wraparound porch that faced a small ravine, and we all loved spending time out there during the day, drinking in the sights and sounds of nature. There was so much wildlife! We had deer, bears, coyotes, rabbits, weasels, porcupines, beavers, squirrels, and skunks. We often came across evidence that the bears had been around, and a few times, we were lucky to see them really close to our house.

One sunny afternoon, the three of us drove up the long driveway, and as we approached the house, we saw a young black bear asleep against the air conditioning unit. We always put a black tarp over the unit for the winter, so at first, we didn't notice him. It was spring, the snow was almost gone, and the little bear looked like he was huddled up against the big black box, perhaps for warmth and comfort. It's hard to know, but maybe his mama had been killed — hit by a car as sometimes happened — and he found himself all alone. As we pulled up, we watched him for a few minutes. He didn't move, so we rolled down the truck window and yelled *HELLOOooOOO!* The bear woke up, seemed a bit disoriented, looked over at us in surprise, and then scampered into the woods.

Another time, we went out to feed the birds and found our feeders pushed over, the metal rods bent, and the feeders lying on the ground completely cracked open. There were several huge pawprints in the mud at the base of the feeders. In early spring, the bears are just waking up from hibernating through the long winter, and they are hungry. There was not much food available yet, of course the berries weren't out this early, and so the birdseed was an easy snack. One summer, we caught sight of a big black bear frolicking in our backyard. We watched stealthily from the deck and suppressed a laugh when we saw the bear lay down, wiggle and roll in the sweet clover. The bear finally noticed us watching its antics and it turned and lumbered away into the woods.

It was such fun to watch them thoroughly enjoying our land, but all these bear sightings caused me to worry about Wylie. I didn't want her to surprise one and end up hurt or killed, so I made her wear a bear bell attached to her collar. That way, the bears would hear her if she was anywhere nearby and they could move away or climb a tree to avoid her. That bell also helped me keep tabs on her when we were out. If I could hear her, I knew she was close by.

The deer were frequently in our yard, both at dawn and dusk. Sometimes, we left dried corn out for them beginning in the fall to help them survive the long, harsh winters. Our abundance of wild apple trees also provided yummy treats for them in the fall and well into the winter months. We had about fifty trees that produced just a ton of small, sour, crunchy apples. We picked and ate a lot, but we didn't come close to picking them all! The deer would eat the apples that fell to the ground or pick the ones they could reach right off the trees. It was entertaining to watch them rear up on their hind legs and balance there for a few seconds while they snagged an apple or two with their teeth.

The deer weren't the only ones to enjoy eating our apples! Wylie absolutely loved them. Whenever we were outside in the fall, she would make a beeline towards the closest tree and gorge herself on the apples that had fallen to the ground. I knew it wasn't good for her to be eating so many apples. At the very least, it would cause digestive upset. At worst, it would poison her. Apple seeds contain cyanide and eating too many is really not a good idea. At first, I tried to manage the situation by gathering up the apples as they fell from the trees closest to the house. That proved to be a completely useless endeavor because I just couldn't keep up with it. In the end, I gave up and let Wylie eat her fill. What else could I do? If I thought she was indulging a bit too long, I would either take her inside, or I would run to another part of the property where there were no apple trees, calling her as I went. She happily followed. In the four years we lived at our house in Wisconsin, Wylie never succumbed to cyanide poisoning, so I guess we did okay! Still, I would have preferred she left the apples to the deer!

All three of us loved to watch the deer out of our windows. It was an almost daily ritual. We knew when to look for them: at dusk, just after sunset. It was important for us to teach Wylie that the deer were nothing to be concerned with and that they were just an ordinary part of her world. It was critical that we teach her not to chase deer. If we didn't, I'm sure she would have gotten lost or hit by a car the first time she gave chase to one. I had no idea how to do this! So, we encouraged Wylie to watch them with us, right from the start, letting her sniff their presence on the air currents so that she would become familiar with their scent. We called them the *Big Dogs*. As a puppy, Wylie was fascinated by them and watched attentively, wide-eyed and nose twitching, as they quietly walked by, nosing the ground, making snuffling sounds and munching on the fresh, green grass that was sprouting up. She quickly learned that when we called out, "Wylie, the Big Dogs are here!" it meant the deer were in our yard and she would run to the window to watch them. I believe that it was this early, benign exposure that allowed Wylie to become so acclimated to them. In all her life, she never once chased or even barked at a deer, even though the opportunity often presented itself. She just accepted their presence as if they simply belonged in her world. I loved that about her.

Once, on a sunny fall afternoon while we were out hiking around our property, Tim and I spotted a young buck about a hundred yards away. We were walking through the field of apple trees. The long grasses were chest high and had turned a golden yellow. Tim kept trails mowed so that they'd be walkable in both summer and winter. The trees were bare of leaves but still full of apples! We could see the deer's head and antlers poking up above the tall grass. As we walked the path with Wylie running ahead, we noticed that the deer was following us. When we stopped and turned to look, he would stop and stand perfectly still, staring at us. We started walking, he started walking. It was kind of spooky. Wylie would run ahead and then back every minute or so to make sure we were still bringing up the rear. That deer got pretty close, only about twenty-five feet away from us at one point. Those eyes! He was beautiful, and I was so thankful that Wylie had no interest in chasing him. When he got a bit too close for comfort, we waved our arms and shouted to scare him off. He turned and ran off into the woods. We knew better than to let a wild deer get too close to us. Deer can be extremely dangerous up close. Their front hooves can easily hurt you if they rear up and knock you over. I was a bit worried that someone had been hand feeding this deer, and that he had lost his fear of humans. If we let him come too close to us and didn't give him food, he could easily have hurt us or Wylie. Deer have been known to head butt, kick, and trample humans — and dogs — if they are fearful or stressed. It was a pretty cool experience though, and Wylie didn't pay any attention to him! She reacted exactly as we hoped and simply ignored the deer. *Good girl, Wylie!*

The local wildlife also included just a plethora of birds! From huge owls that would perch high up in the trees by day and swoop down on their prey at night; to wild turkeys strutting by, unafraid and oblivious to our presence; to sandhill cranes that returned year after year to raise their young. We also saw many bald eagles, both juveniles and adults, soaring overhead, perching in the giant oak trees or diving for fish in the sloughs. From November to April, we would tromp through the snow every morning to fill up our bird feeders with a mixture of seeds and cracked corn, attracting all kinds of birds, from plump little chickadees to graceful grosbeaks. We had a feeder right outside our sunroom window and so we could sit and watch them fly in for a tasty morsel or two.

The squirrels were abundant, too, and they were always trying to get to the birdseed. Sure, they were hungry, too, but they were a bit greedy. We tried to keep them out, but that was an uphill battle; there were so many of them! We mostly had red squirrels — you know, the scraggly rats with quasi fluffy tails. Sometimes, Tim would try to shoot one of the stealthy little thieves, missing more often than not. If he did manage to kill one, he would go out and just toss it onto the snow in the woods, and by morning, some other critter had claimed it for food. Living in the country made me very aware of the circle of life and killing a pesky squirrel didn't bother me if it was going to feed another animal.

One morning, I caught a red squirrel trying its damnedest to reach the feeder outside the kitchen window. He was dangling from a tree branch and then dropped himself right onto its base. Bold. Brazen. Stupid. Tim got the .22, opened the kitchen window, and took aim. You only get one shot at a squirrel because if you miss, that critter is gone! Well, he missed. The squirrel scampered off out of sight. As Tim was leaving for work later that morning, he left the firearm on the table, and told me that I could try to shoot the squirrel if it came back. I know he was thinking that I would never hit it, but he humored me anyway. I had firearms experience from my time working on firearms legislation back in Canada. I used to shoot skeet almost every weekend and had gotten pretty good at it. It was a fun sport. I felt comfortable handling a shotgun. How much different could a little rifle be?

I was getting a refill on my coffee when I spied him. There he was, back in the feeder. He was persistent if nothing else! I slowly and quietly slid the kitchen window open, poked the barrel out the window, shouldered the rifle, aimed, and fired. *Bang!* I gasped. I hit him! I stood there, stunned. I killed a squirrel: a real, living, furry, warm-blooded animal. I felt terrible. I was so sorry! I cried. I promised myself I would never, ever kill another animal again, unless it was in self-defense. I put on my coat and boots and went outside into the cold and snow. I found the little squirrel barely bloody but definitely dead. I was still crying as I picked him up by his tail and tossed him into the woods. I hoped my transgression provided a meal for another animal on a cold winter night. That is my only consolation.

There was always something amazing happening in the nature that surrounded us, and Wylie was exposed to it all. No wonder she could handle just about anything as she grew into adulthood.

# GUNS

Part of living in the north meant hunting. Deer season was a big deal in our area, and most families participated in one form or another. Every fall, the opening of dear season was marked by the sound of early morning gunshots echoing through the still, crisp air. We knew Wylie was going to be exposed to the sound of gunfire whether we wanted her to be or not. We seized the opportunity to introduce Wylie to the sound of gunfire in a controlled way when she was still a puppy so that she would hopefully become accustomed to those sounds. I did not want her to be afraid every time she heard a gunshot. I knew that dogs suffered a lot if they were afraid of random loud noises like gunshots, car backfires, fireworks, and thunder.

We decided to be proactive and try out some "gundog training" to help her cope when hunting season rolled around. Since we lived so remotely, we were able to shoot firearms safely into berms of earth without any problem. Now, let me include a caveat here. What I call "gundog training" and what gundog people call "gundog training" are *not* the same thing. *My* version is just a dog and a gun. All I wanted to do was to make sure Wylie was not frightened by the sharp crack of gunfire. I really didn't know what I was doing, but I decided to put a plan in place. We would start at low volume and far away, gradually increasing the volume by closing the distance. Tim, our gunman, would start with a gun that wasn't too loud, with Wylie and I a good distance away from him. My job was to watch Wylie closely for any signs of stress, feed her some yummy treats, and play ball with her. I would signal Tim with a hand wave to proceed, and he would look back at me between shots. If Wylie reacted in a way that showed she was uncomfortable, I would hold up my fist to signal Tim to stop. Signs of fear, stress, and anxiety in dogs are easy to see if you know what you are looking for. (Refer to the section on Canine Body Language in Chapter 6.)

We chose to start with a .22 caliber pistol. It doesn't have a whole lot of firepower, and so it doesn't make too much of a bang when you pull the trigger. It's still loud, but it's not deafening. Tim set up a station near the ravine in front of the house where he could safely shoot into the wall of dirt. I sat on the ground with Wylie, about fifty yards away, armed with a tennis ball and some treats. Wylie loved her tennis ball, so it was easy to engage her in play. Tim signaled that he was ready. I waved at Tim. He fired a single shot. *Bang!* Wylie dropped the ball and turned to look to see where that big noise came from. As soon as I heard the bang, I started talking to her in a soft, calm voice. "Wylie, what was that big noise? Oh my goodness, what was that?" I offered her a piece of food. She gobbled it up. *Good girl, Wylie, good girl.* We resumed playing as before. I rolled the ball a few feet for her to fetch. She brought it back to me. Wylie acted as if nothing unpleasant had transpired. She seemed to handle the noise without any problem. I waved at Tim. He fired a second shot. Again, Wylie turned towards the sound, and I fed her more food as I babbled on, telling her what a good dog she was. We repeated this a few more times and Wylie stopped paying attention to the loud noise altogether, essentially ignoring it. Instead, she stayed focused on me and her two favorite things: the ball and food!

We took a break. Tim walked over to see how we were doing. He called Wylie, and she ran over, happily wagging her entire body. We tossed the ball around and allowed her some time to relax.

## Wylie the Nature Freak

I was sure that Wylie was ready for a louder gun. We moved up to the .45 caliber pistol. That gun is more than twice as loud as the .22. Again, Tim stationed himself far away from us, and on my signal, he fired. Wylie stopped playing and looked right at me as if to ask if everything was okay. She looked over at Tim and then back at me. I'm sure she was thinking, *Where's my chicken?* I fed her a treat. She ate, she played, she didn't care about the noise. This was going great! We repeated the .45 a few more times and called it a day. We practiced this identical routine several more times over the next few weeks and got the same, unphased reaction from Wylie each time.

I felt that our efforts were successful, but I wondered how this would translate to other loud noises. We hadn't had a thunderstorm yet. They are fairly rare events in northern Wisconsin and usually only occur from June to August. The first time we heard a rumble of thunder, we were all out on the deck. The sky had grown dark, and the air had that sudden, sharp freshness to it. The wind picked up, and the leaves on the trees blew inside out. A storm was coming. We heard the first rumbles from a distance far away. I looked at our dog. She was lying on the deck, chewing on a toy. She didn't react at all. We all went inside, and the rain started to fall in big, fat drops. Soon, it was pounding against the windows. The thunder continued to roll in, getting louder and more intense. Tim and I carried on as if nothing was amiss. I was in the kitchen making dinner, and Tim was sitting on the couch, reading the newspaper. Wylie was on her bed, still chewing on her toys. All of a sudden, there was a thunderous crash. It was loud enough to make *me* jump. I looked over at the dog. She came over, wagging her tail, looking for her treat! She didn't care about the noise, only the food that it predicted. It was looking like our gun training was working!

Another occasion soon arose that would test Wylie's imperviousness to loud sounds. The fourth of July rolled around, and we decided to go see the fireworks from our boat, moored at the Ashland marina on Lake Superior. The fireworks were going to be set off close by, and we would be able to see them directly overhead. It turned out to be a miserable day, cold and drizzly. The fog had rolled in across the lake, and we thought they might cancel the show, but it went ahead anyway. Tim and I were out on the deck of the boat wearing rain gear while Wylie slept inside. The fireworks were barely visible in the dense fog, which just got worse as the night wore on. Each explosion blasted right above the boat. I kept looking in on Wylie to make sure she was okay. She slept through that entire event and I had to actually wake her up to take her home. I guess our *gundog training* was a success after all and, as I'd hoped, expanded to include all of the other loud sounds in Wylie's world.

IT'S TRAINING TIME...

# The Puppy ThunderCookie© Game

## How to Help Prevent Concussive Noise Sensitivity in Puppies

We have all lived with or at least heard of dogs that are afraid of thunder. When a dog is fearful of storms, the effects can be devastating to the dog and owner alike. Dogs are highly sensitive to noises. Their sense of hearing is better than ours.[10] As such, the exposure to loud noises can easily ignite fear in dogs.

In particular, concussive noise — that is, those noises that you can feel in your body as well as hear with your ears — can be especially problematic. Concussive noises include sounds like thunder, fireworks, gunshots, low flying helicopters and jets, heavy construction equipment, etc. There is a big difference between concussive sound and regular sound. In very simple terms, regular sound is heard through air conduction when sound waves that are transmitted through the air are picked

---

[10] *Human hearing: 64 to 23,000 Hz. Canine hearing: 67 to 45,000 Hz. "How Well Do Dogs and Other Animals Hear?", lsu.edu/deafness/HearingRange.html (Louisiana State University).* https://www.lsu.edu/deafness/HearingRange. html *(link verified on 10/13/2021)*

up by the eardrum. Concussive sound has another component; it is heard by way of the eardrum, but it also travels via the bones in the skull. This is called bone conduction. Sound can be transmitted directly through the bones in the skull to the inner ear. Concussive force is most often discussed in reference to combat veterans suffering from hearing loss.[11] However, the extreme sensitivity of our dogs' hearing could make them more prone to "feeling" this type of noise.

So, how can we help *prevent* this potential hypersensitivity from devolving into fear in our dogs?

The younger you can start working with your puppy on concussive noise sensitivity, the better off your dog will be. Using real storms is best, but this is often not practical. If you don't live in an area where storms are frequent, or if you are away from your puppy for long periods of time, just pull up an internet search or download an app for storm sounds and choose one that mimics a real storm as closely as possible. Make sure you use a good speaker so that it sounds realistic. You can use this technique with other concussive sounds, but I will describe steps using thunder since it is by far the most common problem.

## PREPARE FOR TRAINING

1. Set up storm alerts on your phone so that you have some advance warning of the coming storm.

2. Gather some treats for your dog. These treats should be very high-value, whatever your dog loves most (e.g. cooked chicken breast, cooked liver, small bits of cheese). This is not the time to be cheap with treats!

---

[11] *Stanford.edu/otobiomechanics/hearing-through-bone-conduction-pathway.* https://otobiomechanics.sites.stanford.edu/hearing-through-bone-conduction-pathway *(link verified on 10/13/2021)*

Put the treats in a closed container. Keep refrigerated (if necessary) until storm time.

3. Before the storm starts, begin playing with your puppy. You can give your pup something to chew on, or you can play tug or fetch with them inside the house, *not outdoors*.

## THE STORM BEGINS

1. At the sound of the first rumble, say, "Oh, goodie!" Stop playing, and quietly listen to the rumble for a few seconds while maintaining positive, happy eye contact with your puppy. Then say, "ThunderCookies!" in a bright, happy voice (dogs respond much better to this tone of voice) and give a treat. You do not ask for a 'sit' or 'down' or a 'watch me' or any other particular behavior before giving the treat. He gets the treat regardless of what he was doing at the time the rumble occurs.

2. Continue playing with your puppy.

3. As soon as another rumble happens, say, "Oh, goodie!" Listen again with eye contact and say a very happy "ThunderCookies!" Give your puppy a treat or two.

4. Continue this pattern throughout the storm. Play with your dog in between rumbles.

5. If your puppy is frightened, try to reduce the sound as much as possible. Go into an interior room, for example. If your puppy seems totally unfazed by the

noise of the thunder, you can increase the sound by opening a window or the screen door or going out to your enclosed porch (if you have one). If you are using a recording, start with the volume very low, and work your way up. If the dog appears scared at any time, lower the volume. You are raising it too quickly.

6. When the storm is over, say, "All done!" Put the treats away and stop playing with your dog for a little while. This will help her make good associations with the storms. When the storm stops, the play stops, and the treats stop!

Be consistent. Always use the same words. Don't be unfair and not follow through with a treat. Soon, you will see your dog look at you with happy anticipation as soon as she hears the first sound of thunder, hoping that this sound qualifies for the Puppy ThunderCookie Game. Keep playing this game now and then throughout your dog's life to keep her in the storm comfort zone.

These same steps can be applied to any noise, not just concussive noise. However, it has been my experience that if you and your puppy conquer the fear of thunder, fireworks, gunshots, etc., other noises will be well tolerated. If a novel noise startles your dog, simply use your Puppy ThunderCookie Game cue with enthusiasm and follow up with a yummy treat if you can. If you don't have food with you at that moment, play with your dog for a fun few minutes to make a positive association to the new sound. You CAN help your puppy become noise resilient.

# CHAPTER ELEVEN

# Wylie Eats the World

L abrador retrievers love to eat. They are well known for it. If you're not careful, it's very easy to overfeed your Lab, since they always seem hungry. They must have the "hungry" gene or something because they never seem to fill up. That's why there are so many fat Labs. People just assume they are not feeding their dogs enough! Labs are tricksters and will take every opportunity to get an extra bite or two. In fact, scientists now believe that Labrador retrievers may overeat as a result of a genetic flaw, a gene mutation, rather than just because their humans overfeed them[12], so it may not be totally our fault. *Wink, wink.*

When we first brought Wylie home, we fed her the same food that the breeder was feeding the whole litter. It was an okay food, not great quality, but not too bad according to what I had read. Unlike your typical Labrador retriever, Wylie was not a good eater at first. We would put the bowl full of food down for her, and she would pick a few pieces of kibble up and slowly eat them. She never

---

[12] https://thenewdaily.com.au/life/eat-drink/2016/05/08/why-do-labradors-eat-everything/ *(link verified on 10/13/2021)*

finished her meal, sometimes leaving most of it behind. When I took her to the vet for her regular puppy wellness check, the vet told us that she was a bit skinny. I told the vet about her odd eating habits, and he suggested we change her food. Maybe she just didn't like it! Oh, I hadn't thought of that! Just like people, dogs do have food preferences. So, I bought a bag of higher quality food from the vet and went home to try it out.

Lunchtime came, and I mixed the new food in with her old food, about half and half, to try to prevent any digestive issues (if you transition to a new food too quickly, you can cause your dog to get an upset tummy resulting in loose stool, so I didn't want to do that!). I put the bowl down in front of her. Wylie sniffed at it and began to gobble down the food as fast as she could. Wow. It was an amazing difference. Wylie absolutely loved the new food. She was a true Labrador retriever after all! In fact, she loved eating so much that we ended up having to hand feed her! If left to her own devices, she would rapidly gulp up all the food in her bowl, barely chewing it, and then she'd slurp down a bunch of water. About five minutes later, she would throw it all up, leaving a heaping pile of undigested, watery food on the floor.

So, I started to sit on the floor with her and drop a few pieces of food in her bowl while I put my hand in front of her, palm up, like a police officer, and said *Wait* in a long drawl. "Waaaiiit." Wylie couldn't get to the food because my hand blocked her path. I would then immediately remove my hand and say, "Okay!" and encourage her to move towards her bowl. She would quickly gobble up what I had placed in her bowl. I swear that the first few times I did this, she looked at me as if to say, "You've got to be kidding! Are you cheap or what? I'm going to starve!" Wylie quickly got the hang of this new little game. She sat, I put some food in her bowl, she waited, I released her "Okay!", and she ate. Easy.

## Wylie Eats the World

What I didn't realize at the time was just how valuable this exercise was. First, it stopped the rapid ingestion of food and therefore stopped my puppy from vomiting her meal back up. Second, it taught Wylie to be a little more patient and not rush to her bowl. Third, it taught her that a human sitting on the floor with her didn't always mean an opportunity to jump and bite. Fourth, it set Wylie up for learning a really good *stay* later on. We eventually progressed to the point where I would put her bowl down and Wylie would just sit and wait without being asked, and she would stay there until I said "Okay." She got better and better at leaving food alone and, gradually, she was able to apply it to all situations where food was involved. Eventually, we could put food down anywhere, and she wouldn't touch it. We could leave our full dinner plates on the coffee table, at nose level, and Wylie wouldn't even sniff it. She was rock solid on this throughout the rest of her life. For a dog that loved food so much, her mastery of this skill was amazing to me. Regardless of opportunity, she never counter surfed, never tried to snag a snack from an open container, never stole any of our food. *Good girl, Wylie!*

Now, eating stuff that she found outside on the ground was a totally different matter. Wylie was a canine vacuum when she was outdoors. She hoovered up just about anything. It was a challenge to prevent and manage her love of scavenging and foraging. Dogs, in fact, evolved into social scavengers, not domesticated predators, so Wylie's behavior made total sense. Dogs are not hunters, they're opportunistic moochers. That summer, when the dandelions started to appear in all their glory, Wylie noticed them immediately. One lovely, sunny morning, Tim and I were working outside in the yard when I saw her out of the corner of my eye. She walked over to a flower, sniffed it, then plucked just the yellow head, and ate it. She was so cute! I wish I would have been able to capture that moment on video: my four-month-old black puppy, cute as a button, plucking a bright yellow flower, and then *gulp!* It was gone. I knew dandelions were edible, and we didn't use any pesticides, so I wasn't worried about her eating a few. Tim and I spent the rest of the morning doing chores while Wylie amused herself. We all came into the house around noon to get some lunch.

As I prepared our food, Wylie seemed a bit quiet, not her usual rambunctious self. I didn't give it much thought since she had been out with us all morning. I figured that she must be tired. It was such a beautiful day out, not too hot and very sunny, so we decided to eat out on the deck. As we were enjoying our lunch, I noticed Wylie licking the deck boards. Then, she started to lick the screen doors. She was licking anything she could find. Something was wrong.

Tim told me I was crazy. "She's fine! You worry too much!" Famous last words.

Wylie's licking became more frantic. "I'm taking her to the vet, she's obviously not right."

"Whatever, but I think she's fine," Tim said as he looked at me with exasperation.

Just as I got up to go get her, she started to heave. Seeing a puppy try to vomit is disconcerting. Her ribcage contracting and expanding, she was in obvious distress. I was panicking. "Oh my god, what the hell is happening to her?"

Then, all of a sudden, it transpired. A huge heap of dandelion heads erupted from her mouth.

"Holy crap, Wylie! I knew you had eaten a few dandelions, but sheesh! This is ridiculous!"

There must have been about four cups of goopy flowers and leaves, stewing right there in the middle of the deck. As soon as she threw up, vacuum puppy, of course, tried to start eating them again.

"Oh, no you don't!" I exclaimed. I grabbed her and scooped her up into my arms. I looked at Tim and said, "Now, what am I supposed to do for the rest of the summer? Those freakin' dandelions are everywhere!"

Tim shrugged. He was not helpful. He did clean up the mess, though.

On another nice summer Saturday morning, we decided to go out on the boat for the weekend. Lake Superior was calling! As we were getting ready, going in and out of the house with our gear, Wylie was outside as she often was. She was loose, of course. You don't fence in forty-seven acres. Wylie kept checking in with us, per usual, so we naturally didn't think anything was wrong. We were done packing up and so I called my dog. "Wylieeeeee, come Wylie!" She appeared from up the lane in a few seconds, running happily towards me. We were all ready to go.

I had just put Wylie in her crate in the backseat when the heaving began. Nothing makes you move faster than the sound of your dog starting to vomit. I ran around to her side of the truck and flung open the door. Too late. Wylie had thrown up a gargantuan pile of what looked like food waste. There were corn cob chunks, vegetable peelings, slimy greens, and other assorted vegetation. Oh no! Wylie had figured a way to get into the compost pile. Imagine her elation when she discovered a whole stockpile of delicious food, right there in the open, waiting for her! How she managed to get around and over the wire fence, I don't know. Wylie was Wylie, and if there was food involved, she would find a way. I bagged the pile of bile et al. and put it in the trash, changed out her bedding, and off we went for our weekend on the boat. By this time, I was starting to take this kind of thing in stride! Wylie was oblivious, as usual, no worse for wear.

# Dale M. Ward

At Thanksgiving, Wylie ate a sizeable chunk of a whole pumpkin that was *supposed* to be part of my seasonal decorations, not a snack. I was shocked to walk out the door and see the chewed-up pumpkin that she had dragged halfway across the lawn. I don't know why I was shocked. I should have expected it by now! It just never dawned on me that she would even fathom that a large intact, uncarved pumpkin was edible. I mean, how did she even know it was food? Wylie was still enjoying her delicious novelty snack when I found her. "Wylie! What are you doing? Stop!" I said as I ran towards her. Luckily, the pumpkin was too large and too unwieldy to take off with, so she ran away with just her last mouthful.

By our second winter together, Wylie and I had truly formed an amazing friendship. Wylie's puppy antics had calmed down a little, and she was such good company. Tim was away a lot. A *lot*. We had gotten the news that the government project he managed was closing down and that we would be moving to the Norfolk, Virginia area in another year or so. In the meantime, Tim often had to travel back and forth, leaving Wylie and me to fend for ourselves for long stretches of time. It would take almost a whole year before Wylie and I actually joined Tim in Virginia.

Winters in northern Wisconsin are brutal. As a Canadian, born and raised in Ottawa, I thought I was used to the cold. Did you know that Highbridge, Wisconsin, is actually about a hundred miles further north than Ottawa, Ontario? What? How can that be? Canada is north of the United States, isn't it? Well, where I'm from, the geography dips south a little, poking down into New York State. So, yeah, northern Wisconsin winters are hard. More snow. More ice. More cold.

We often got several feet of snow. In some places, the drifts would be chest high. Because Tim was away so often, taking care of our home, including snow removal, was left to me. Thankfully, the town plow came all the way down our seven-hundred-foot lane and around our big circular driveway. That plow left huge piles of snow in front of the Batcave and the house. After a big snowfall, when the plow had finally come (sometimes as late as two days after the storm), I would fire up the tractor and take it out to move the piles of snow out of the way. Then I would shovel the rest of the snow in front of the buildings by hand. I never let Wylie out when I was doing tractor work for fear of running her over. Instead, I left her inside until I was done, and then we would have a game of *Lose the Tennis Ball in the Snow* until we were either pooped out or we had lost all the balls. If the snow was right, sticky enough, I would make snowballs and throw them into the white abyss for Wylie to chase, pounce on, and then ponder their disappearance. It was so much fun!

One bright and frightfully cold morning, I got up and let Wylie out of her crate beside my bed, then rushed out to the front entryway to get dressed and take her outside for her morning constitution. I bundled up while Wylie wove in and out of my legs, excited to go out. I checked the thermometer in the window. Minus forty. Yikes. That's the kind of cold that takes your breath away when you step out into it. I opened the door and Wylie ran ahead to her plowed "spot" beside the big garage to do her business. The sun was glorious, but it did not seem to impart any warmth at all.

I followed behind, walking over to Wylie's spot. When she turned to face me, I almost had a heart attack. Wylie's face was so swollen, she could hardly see. Her eyes were little slits, her ears looked too thick, and her nose was all puffy. Her front legs had lumps all over them too. What the hell? We ran inside, and I called the vet. It was early, around seven, and no one answered their *emergency* number. I tried again. Nope, just a recording. "That's some emergency number!" I said to my sweet, suffering puppy. My heart was breaking for her. "She must be so uncomfortable," I thought to myself.

I knew this was probably some kind of severe allergic reaction, and I knew from personal experience how dangerous this could be. I was afraid Wylie's throat would start to swell and she would ultimately suffocate. I was desperate. I figured I would put Wylie into my 4Runner and drive the thirty minutes into town. By then, the vet should be open, or close to it. Maybe someone would be there early and let us in. I ran back outside. "Come on Wylie, let's go! Fast, fast!" With my swollen Wylie trotting along behind me, I opened the garage door, and boosted my sick dog into the front passenger seat. I wanted her beside me in case something terrible happened. I was trembling. I had an idea that Wylie was allergic to something, but what? I put the key in the ignition and turned it. Nothing. What? My heart pounded. I tried again. And again. Nothing. I couldn't believe it. My truck had *never* not started! Why, oh why, on this day, of all days? I didn't know what to do.

I got Wylie out of the truck and brought her back into the house. It was still really early, but I had to call someone. I hardly knew anyone in the area, but I decided to call someone that I kayaked with in the summer. She and her husband lived about forty minutes from me. I dialed, and the phone rang and rang and rang. I was desperate for help.

She finally answered in an abrupt, ticked-off voice. "Hello."

"Hi, it's Dale and I know it's really early, but it's an emergency, and I really need your help. Tim is away, my dog is really sick, and my car won't start. I need to get her to the vet right away. Can you please, *please* come and help me?"

Surely, she heard the panic and desperation in my voice, but it had no impact. "It's Saturday. John and I sleep in on Saturday. My friends know not to disturb us."

I could hardly process what I was hearing. "What? *Whaaat?* Are you kidding me? Are you saying you won't come? My dog! She's sick!"

"We can't come until ten."

"Fine." I hung up the phone. Wow, some friend. I was so hurt. I was scared. I was crying. I couldn't think of any other options.

Then, it hit me! I'm going to call a tow truck and ask them to take us to the vet! I rifled through the yellow pages and called several companies before I found someone who was listed locally and actually had their truck nearby. A lot of these companies listed Ashland as their physical location, but that wasn't really accurate. They were located a few towns away and their territory *included* our location, but they did not have trucks close by. It would have taken them too long to get here.

I talked to the tow truck man and explained my situation. He said he loved dogs and would leave right away to come and get us. He was only about twenty minutes away. I waited for what seemed like hours when the big white and red truck pulled in. I was so happy to see him! I ran outside with Wylie.

He got out of his truck, took one look at her, and exclaimed, "Oh wow, now I know why you called me!"

His shirt said his name was Brad. He had my truck loaded onto the flatbed in just a few minutes, and he helped Wylie and me up into the cab. Just as we were about to pull out, a car came up the driveway and pulled around the circle behind us. It was the woman who had shirked me earlier.

I rolled down my window and yelled down from the tow truck, "Thanks, but I got it figured out. It was an emergency, and you said you couldn't get here until ten, so I called a tow truck. I was going to call you to tell you not to bother. Thanks anyway!" I guess she must have felt guilty and decided to come out right away. Too bad.

I rolled up my window, Brad stepped on the gas and we took off out of there. Those weren't the words I *wanted* to bellow out to her, but I figured it was enough punishment that they drove out to my place in the freezing cold on a Saturday morning for nothing. Satisfying.

Brad was so nice and incredibly sympathetic. He tried to calm me down and told me he thought Wylie would be fine. I tried to believe him. He called the garage and told them he was bringing in my 4Runner for a new battery and asked if someone could come and get me at the vet when I was done so that I could pick up my truck. They said they'd do better than that; they'd drive it over for me! Thank goodness for the kindness of strangers.

Brad dropped Wylie and I off at the vet and pulled away. By this time, it was a little before nine o'clock, and the vet was pulling in just as we got out. I was so relieved. Wylie and I ran up to his car, and I told him what happened. He hustled us into the lobby and right into an exam room. He gave Wylie a shot of Benadryl® right away, did a quick exam, and pronounced that it had to be some kind of allergic reaction. I was right. But to what? He posited that it might have been some kind of spider bite. Really? It was minus forty outside!

Maybe one was in the house? He couldn't find any evidence of a bite site though and told me that we may never know what caused it. I was to keep Benadryl on hand and give the proper dosage for Wylie's weight if symptoms ever reappeared. I called the mechanic and told him we were done. So was he, and within fifteen minutes, my 4Runner was waiting for me outside, all warmed up and cozy, complete with a brand-new battery. We headed home, me relieved and Wylie zonked out in the back from the Benadryl.

A couple of weeks later, Wylie and I were settling in to watch a movie on a blustery afternoon. I got a fire going, made some popcorn, and snuggled up on the bed with my dog. As we started to watch, I tossed a couple of pieces of popcorn to Wylie as a little treat. She had never had it before but loved it, of course. I had probably given her maybe five popped kernels when I saw something on her front leg. Her fur looked funny in that spot, so I looked closer and ran my hand up and down her leg.

"Hmmmm, what is that?" I asked her.

She looked back at me and her eyes said, "I don't know, but can I have another piece of popcorn, please?"

I felt her leg again. It was a bump. Then, oops, another bump. Then another one. Wylie had hives! She was having another allergic reaction, but this time, I caught it at its onset. It was the popcorn! Wylie was allergic to corn! I ran and got the Benadryl and gave her three capsules, as directed by my vet. Within a few minutes, the bumps had gone down significantly.

"Well, no more popcorn for you, girlie girl!" I always called her girlie girl. I thought that was funny since she was such a bruiser, and not very girlie at all.

She looked back at me. "Popcorn! Please, and thank you!"

"Sorry, Sweet Pea, no more popcorn for you. Ever."

So, if Wylie was allergic to corn, what had caused the severe initial reaction a few weeks earlier? I hadn't fed her any corn that night. Was she allergic to corn *and* to something else? It was a mystery.

A few days later, I was out feeding the birds. I shoved the scoop into my bucket, lifted out a heaping serving, and emptied it into the feeder. The feeder was pretty high and a bit hard to reach. Oops, I accidentally spilled some of it onto the snow below. Wylie made a dash for it. *Ohhh cheezus!* The light bulb went on in my head. Wylie was eating the bird seed from under the bird feeder! The bird seed contained a mix of seeds and stuff, including cracked *corn*. Corn! I quickly shooed her away and scooped up what had fallen to the snowy ground as best I could.

Wylie must have eaten a bunch of cracked corn the evening before I discovered her swollen face. That had to be it. Wylie was allergic to corn: popcorn, cracked corn, deer corn, any corn. From that moment on, Wylie's access to anything with corn in it was strictly outlawed. I made sure that her food and none of her treats contained corn. I switched out the kind of birdseed we fed, choosing one with lots of sunflower, millet, and thistle seeds. No corn!

Once I figured this out, I managed to avoid any exposure to products that would cause an allergic reaction for the rest of Wylie's life. I got her a new identification tag that had the line "Severe Corn Allergy" on it so that if she got lost, no one would accidentally feed her anything that contained corn. I also made sure that her allergy was noted on her new veterinary chart when we moved to Virginia. I still kept the Benadryl handy though, just in case.

IT'S TRAINING TIME...

# Allergic Reactions and Poisoning

Allergic reactions can occur as a result of ingesting or being exposed to a specific substance. The allergen could be from a particular food, something in the environment like grasses or plants, or even an insect bite. Allergies can suddenly appear at any age. Even if your dog was perfectly fine with something in the past, she may develop an allergy to that same substance in the future. Talk to your vet about potential allergic reactions that may appear in your dog. Discuss the appropriate use of Benadryl® to counter a histamine reaction. Make sure you know the proper dosage of Benadryl for your dog's body weight. Keep Benadryl on hand and make sure to replace it when it expires. If you suspect that your dog is having an allergic reaction, take your dog to your vet or the closest emergency veterinary hospital immediately. Allergic reactions can be deadly.

## POISONING

If you suspect that your dog has ingested something dangerous, do not wait, call ASPCA Poison Control at (888) 426-4435 immediately. They are the experts! They will open a case file for you and give you a case number. A small consultation fee will be charged to your credit card. Do not hesitate. Many people think that they will avoid the fee and wait for their vet to treat the dog instead. You should do both! The Poison Control Center will help you immediately and they will help your vet. Your veterinarian will probably be contacting them anyway and passing on the Poison Control Center fee to you, likely with an additional fee to cover the cost of their own staff calling on your behalf. If you call yourself and have the case file number ready to give to your vet, you will be one step ahead in a situation where time may mean life or death for your dog.

The ASPCA even has an app for your phone that contains a plethora of information on potentially poisonous plants, foods, medications and much more. It's free to download. https://www.aspca.org/pet-care/animal-poison-control (phone number and link verified on 10/13/2021)

CHAPTER TWELVE

# Wylie the Thrill Seeker

L ike a lot of other Labrador retrievers, Wylie developed a love of tennis balls very early in her life. I bought them by the dozen. She loved to chase the ball and bring it back for more. "Do it again, do it again, please! Throw the ball! *Weeeee!*" No training required. I introduced the tennis ball when she was a very little puppy. We played in the house then. I'd toss the ball down our long hallway and Wylie would chase after it, her little legs going as fast as they possibly could. She would slide in, like she was stealing second base, grabbing the ball as she skated on by. Then, she would scramble like Fred Flintstone to change direction and run back to me. She loved it. She really was a natural retriever. Her instinct was alive and well from the beginning when we brought her home at eight weeks old. This is where the genetic component of behavior becomes obvious. I didn't have to *teach* Wylie to retrieve, she was bred to do it.

Outside, Wylie would run after the ball, down our long gravel driveway, sometimes going so fast that she would overrun the ball and have to brake hard, snapping backwards to grab it. I enjoyed seeing her enthusiasm and loved to watch her play. Soon, Wylie was asking for more and more ball time. We would go out a couple of times a day, sometimes more often, and have a game of fetch. The sessions were short at first given that she was so young and small. As she grew, so did the length of her play sessions. She was growing like a weed, and she was developing into a very athletic dog. It took longer and longer to wear her out.

By the time she was about nine months old, if we weren't able to give her at least one forty-five minute ball session a day, we just couldn't live with her in the house. She would be restless, get into all kinds of trouble, chew on inappropriate things, and get the "zoomies" where she'd run around at full-speed in circles like a Tasmanian devil. She just wouldn't settle down. Wylie fashioned herself a racetrack: up on the couch, over the end, into the kitchen, around the island, and back into the living room with a good launch up onto the couch again. Repeat. Repeat. Repeat. She spent a lot of time in her crate because I just didn't know what to do with her! My solution was always to take her outside and play ball for forty-five minutes. When we came back inside, she would slurp up a bunch of water and then flop down on the cool floor, absolutely contented and very satisfied with herself.

I tried to take Wylie for a walk every day to help tire her out. One such day, we were wandering along the dirt road on our way back home. Wylie was always much more relaxed on the way home as opposed to on the way out when she was a pulling, choking, hacking freight train. She had her nose to the ground, as usual, checking for anything that she could put into her mouth when in the distance, I saw a big black bear cross the road and run onto our property. I stopped dead in my tracks. I looked down at my dog to gauge her reaction. Wylie hadn't seen it, thank goodness, and kept her interest focused on what was on the ground. A few seconds later, I saw two little bear cubs cross, following their mother. This was not good. *Oh, no! How am I going to get home with this dog?* I had no way of knowing if the bears were right there in the driveway, down by the house, or what! I did not want to risk coming between a mother bear and her cubs, especially with a young, crazy dog! That would have been a very, very bad idea. I was worried about Wylie. Would she smell them? Hear them? Bark at them? I didn't know what to do. I had to get back home somehow. I didn't have a cellphone. It wouldn't have mattered anyway because the only person I could call was Tim, and he was an hour away. He would have just told me to buck up and walk home while I made lots of noise. What to do, what to do?

I paced around for several minutes. Then, miraculously, I heard a car in the distance. At that time of day, it was rare to see a car go by. I could see the dust its tires were kicking up in the distance. I waited until it got closer, then I stood halfway out on the road and started waving my arm while trying my best to hold onto my dog. The car slowed down. Yes! It stopped. It was an old, beat up, light brown sedan with an old, beat up guy in it. He rolled down his window.

"Hi," I said, tentatively.

"Hey", the gruff voice responded, cigarette dangling from his mouth.

"Um, I just saw a big bear and her two cubs cross the road up ahead, and, this is going to sound crazy, but I'm scared to walk home with my dog." I was nervous and trying to evaluate whether or not to ask for a ride.

He just looked at me. "Ah, ya, bears," he said.

I weighed my options: risk walking home and having a bear attack me or my puppy or both of us, or risk getting into a car in the middle of nowhere with a smoky, stinky, middle-aged man I had never met before. I picked door number two.

"Do you think you could give us a ride to my house? I live right up there, see that first mailbox?"

"Ah, sure," he said.

"My dog, too?" I looked into the back seat. It was packed with junk. No room back there for a dog!

"Sure, just get in and put her up in here with you."

"Okay, great, thanks a lot!"

In we got. The front seat sagged so much that I felt like I was sitting on the floor, but beggars can't be choosers. Wylie hopped up onto my lap, I slammed the squeaky door and we were off. We drove about a hundred yards. He pulled into the drive and stopped.

"Oh, um, no. Could you keep going? Our house is way back in there. The bear might be back there." Mental calculation: not smart, now he knows where I live and will see that there is no one home. Ah, the hell with it. He seemed harmless enough.

"Yep, keep going, it's way back." He drove us right to our door. Wylie and I hopped out and thanked him profusely.

"Not a problem." He waved and drove off, never to be seen or heard from again.

I was so relieved. I unlocked the front door; we ran inside and I locked up behind us. I was so happy to be back home! Wylie, of course, was oblivious to it all. This whole adventure changed my mind about taking my dog for a walk. Unless I was with someone, I wouldn't go. I would rather stay closer to home and play fetch with Wylie where we were safer. *Safer-ish.*

I saved walks for when Tim was home on the weekends. The three of us would go for long strolls on our property through the woods, streams, and fields. It was a little corner of paradise, and Wylie definitely loved it. Running and splashing through the shallow little streams was one of her favorite activities. She would find sticks and carry them around, rip up small trees and shake them until they were surely dead, and generally do what dogs do best: have fun.

That first winter, the snow came early. Wylie absolutely loved the cold weather and especially the snow. She had been born in the winter and spent her last two weeks with the breeder outdoors in

April, and spring in northern Wisconsin is mostly still winter. She was a cold weather dog, no doubt about it. It seemed that the colder it got, the happier she was. She could run and run and run and not get hot! That meant she could play longer and longer and longer before running out of steam. Wylie would chase that tennis ball down the driveway and bring it back as quickly as she could, just to do it over again. After a while, she would run back to me, then keep on running past me, right up a snowbank and do a belly flop on top with her entire underside making full contact with the cold snow. She would lay there for a few minutes, panting and resting, then she'd be ready for another bout. I shivered at the thought of that cold snow on her warm belly, but she loved it.

Wylie would stay outside pretty much indefinitely until it reached minus twenty or so. Even then, she wouldn't want to go inside. I knew she had to go in when she would start picking up one foot then hopping onto the other one, back and forth, front and back, like she was walking on something really hot. Then I knew her feet were getting really cold and it was time to hurry inside and warm up. We tried getting boots for her, but she had the bottoms shredded after only two outings. I think they were meant for walking on city sidewalks or something tamer like that. I returned them for a refund and Wylie resorted to going barefoot.

We continued playing fetch but were losing just a ton of tennis balls in the snow, so I shopped around for an alternative that would be easy to locate in our winter wonderland. It had to be something big and durable. I found what we called The Big Orange Ball online and ordered one. From the moment Wylie saw it, she was in excitement overdrive. It was made of really hard, durable plastic, and it was a good weight; not too light, not too heavy. I couldn't wait to see what she did with it in the snow.

I bundled up in boots, coat, hat, and mittens, and out we went. I tossed the ball into the yard, and it skidded across the snowy field with Wylie in hot pursuit. Wylie caught up to it as it was still moving, and she tried to bite it. She couldn't, of course, because it was so big and so hard, so she just propelled it forward. She bit; the ball rolled. She bit again and again and again, and the ball careened across the yard, flying on top of the snow. If Wylie bit slightly off center, the ball would fly erratically to the side. She chased it everywhere, and it seemed that the game always ended the same way; with the ball in the ravine, stuck in a bush, or in a pile of snow. I would trudge down to get it, sometimes thigh deep in snow, and toss it back up, and the game would start all over again. Wylie would have stayed outside and played this game until she dropped, I'm sure. I had to cut her off. I would eventually get cold, and we would go inside. I'd have to put the ball away, out of sight, so that Wylie could concentrate on other things like resting.

One day, we had just come in from a session with The Big Orange Ball, and I was sitting on the couch with Wylie splayed out beside me. I noticed a golf ball sized lump on her front leg, about half way up. It hadn't been there that morning — or, I hadn't noticed anything. It seemed to have materialized out of nowhere. When I touched it, it felt squishy. I immediately called the vet and made an appointment for later that afternoon. We drove into town, and all

I could think of was cancer. It must be an incredibly fast-growing tumor, I thought to myself. Why, oh why did I always assume the worst? Sigh.

The vet examined her, poked and felt the lump, asked a bunch of questions, x-rayed it, and pronounced it a bursa. Wylie had smacked her leg so hard and so often on The Big Orange Ball that it caused a pouch to form and fill with fluid. Oops. No more Big Orange Ball for her! We were instructed to make sure that Wylie didn't smack her leg on anything and to watch it to make sure it went down. In a few days, the bursa was gone, the fluid reabsorbed by her magnificent, morphing self.

I was so sad that I would have to take The Big Orange Ball away from my sweet puppy. It was a source of such sheer joy for her. Of course, she wouldn't really know what happened, only that The Big Orange Ball was missing-in-action. So, we reverted to tennis balls. In the end, she loved them best anyway.

Wylie was growing fast and getting strong. Her endurance was admirable. At least, that's what I thought. I still didn't see the connection between the amount of exercise Wylie wanted and was getting, and her inability to settle down and relax in the house. The two seemed totally unrelated in my mind. After all, a tired dog is a good dog, right? How often have we all heard that? Well, I now know that I was creating a sort of adrenaline junkie. Wylie was getting so many "feel good" hormones from all that exercise that she wanted more and more, and if she didn't get them, she just wasn't happy. So, I indulged her needs and made sure I gave her at least one (but usually two) forty-five-minute sessions of ball play each and every day, rain or shine, cold or blizzard.

That winter, the winter of 2004-2005, temperatures were often in the negative twenties. We got tons of snow. I remember one day in the late afternoon, darkness had just settled in, and Wylie was begging to go outside. I looked out the window. There was a snowstorm brewing out there. I turned on the outside light, and I could see the snow blowing almost sideways against the house. I didn't want to go out, but I loved my dog, so I got out all my snow gear: long underwear, snow pants, fleece sweater, wool socks, down-filled jacket with hood, hat, mittens, scarf, boots. Getting dressed for winter wonderland playtime is no small feat or quick suit-up! All the while, Wylie was bouncing up and down with a tennis ball in her mouth. "Oh boy, oh boy, oh boy, we're goin' out to play, we're goin' out to play!" When I opened the door, the wind blew it out of my mittened hand and smashed it against the doorstop. Wylie bounded out into the snowy darkness without a care in the world. No coat or boots for her! A tennis ball was all she needed.

# How to Teach Your Dog to Settle

I'm sure you've all heard it. *A tired dog is a good dog.* After all, what better way to cope with a growing, energetic, large, playful dog than to wear her out? That way, she will be quieter in the house and simply come inside and sleep when she's played herself out. Mission accomplished: peace and quiet. This sounds like a great idea. What could possibly go wrong?

One of the skills that is often overlooked in more traditional dog training is having your dog settle nicely and quietly on a mat when you ask. Teaching a dog to be calm is not one of the things most of us think of when we think of dog training, but it should be at the top of your priority list! This is how to teach your dog to settle.

## PREPARE FOR TRAINING

### Get a mat.

I prefer a flat mat over a bed. Choose a mat that is big enough for your dog to lie down on. Pick a solid color that is not brown (that's the color of most dog food and we're looking for contrast here). The color should ideally be one that will let your dog easily see a piece of food on the mat. Also, no patterns. A patterned mat will interfere with your dog being able to see food on the mat. You want overt contrast between mat and snack.

## Get the food.

Have approximately fifty *small* pieces of your dog's food in a container. Remember to subtract the amount used from your dog's daily feeding amount.

## Get set up.

Sitting at the kitchen table or on the couch are good options. Place your mat beside you, on the floor, close to your feet. Have your food in a treat pouch or small bowl on the table or on your lap. Take about ten pieces of food and put them in your hand.

## Get started.

1. **Call your dog to the mat.**

   Call your dog over to you as you say, "Daisy, go to your mat." Point to the mat and drop a piece of food on the mat. When your dog walks onto the mat, mark the behavior (Say, "Good!"). Reward by dropping a piece of food on the mat between your dog's front feet. Try not to let the treat bounce or roll off the mat.

2. **Release your dog.**

   Choose a release word. I use "Okay!" but you can also use something like "Free!" or "Release!" Once you choose a release word, stick to it. Call your dog off the mat with your release word. Then encourage your dog to walk off the mat. You may need to walk away to get your dog to move off the mat. That's okay.

**REPEAT** at least ten times.

3. **Have your dog lie down on the mat.**

   Call your dog to her mat. "Daisy, go to your mat." But this time, when your dog arrives, cue your dog to lie down using your hand signal only, no voice cue. As your dog lies down, say, "Settle," in a light, happy voice. Immediately begin feeding your dog, one piece of food after another, in rapid succession, on the mat. Keep your hands fairly close to your dog's face to begin with, to prevent her from getting up to move towards your hand. You must use this rapid rate of reinforcement at the beginning of training this skill. (You will slow down your rate of reinforcement as your dog learns.) After you deliver approximately five pieces of food, stop. Release your dog from the mat using your release word and encourage your dog to get up and walk off of the mat. This constitutes one trial.

   **REPEAT** five trials.

4. **End your session** on a happy note. Ask your dog to do something easy, sit or touch are good options. Reward with a game, whatever your dog loves to do (e.g. tug or ball).

Aim for five trials, three times a day. Do more if you can. Move your mat to different areas of your home so that your dog gets used to settling down on her mat regardless of location.

Remember, as your dog learns, slow down your rate of enforcement!

## Sample Rate Reduction Schedule

One piece of food every second

One piece of food every two seconds

One piece of food every four seconds

One piece of food every seven seconds

One piece of food every ten seconds

One piece of food every fifteen seconds

One piece of food every twenty-five seconds

One piece of food every forty seconds

One piece of food every minute

One piece of food every two minutes

One piece of food every five minutes

One piece of food when you release your dog

**CAUTION:** Do not push your dog past her abilities. If your dog keeps getting up off the mat before you've released her, you are doing too much too fast. Back it up, make it easier for her. If your dog can settle for fifteen seconds but keeps getting up when you try for twenty-five seconds, work at fifteen seconds a bit longer. Then work at eighteen seconds, then twenty, then try twenty-five. You may just be trying to progress in time chunks that are too big for your dog to handle. Build on your dog's successes. It's your job to prevent your dog from failing.

Once trained, you can use this skill in a variety of situations. You can ask your dog to go to her mat when you are cooking in the kitchen, when you are eating dinner with your family, when you want to watch television. Don't abuse this skill though. Your dog is not meant to live on her mat! Remember that she still needs exercise, your attention, and play time!

It's also a skill that is portable! Whether you're at an outdoor patio, at the vet, visiting a friend's home, etc., you can ask your dog to settle on her mat. Just remember that each new situation will be harder for your dog. Adding new distractions means you must reward and reinforce your dog more often and with higher value treats than if you were working on this at home.

# CHAPTER THIRTEEN

# Wylie Makes a Splash

Our home in Highbridge was close to Lake Superior; it was about eighteen miles from our doorstep to the shore. Lake Superior is also known locally as The Big Lake or just The Lake. When someone talked about going to the lake, everyone knew they were referring to Lake Superior, even though there are literally hundreds of lakes sprinkled throughout the northwoods. Now, for those who are unfamiliar with Lake Superior, its name is supremely suitable. It really is superior to all other lakes. It's the largest lake in the world by area. It's like a freshwater sea, and vast! It has big storms, giant waves, and hundreds of recorded shipwrecks. That lake is nothing to fool around with. It deserves respect. It is also very, very cold. Lake Superior is so big that it only completely freezes over once or twice in a century![13] That's saying a lot given that winter is extremely long (November to April) and cold (so much below zero time!).

Ashland, our closest "big town," was located right on the shore of Lake Superior, so we were there quite often. Whenever I took

[13] https://www.nps.gov/apis/faqs.htm *(link verified on 10/13/2021)*

puppy Wylie into town, we tried to make some time to go down to the water. There was a boat landing with a modest stretch of beach and a small adjacent parking lot, so access was easy, and, most of the time, the beach was completely empty.

Although this area had (and still has) incredible potential to be a lovely tourist town with maybe a boardwalk and shops and outdoor restaurants with patios all along the water, it had none of this. Instead, there was a large power plant and an odd mishmash of waterfront businesses: a dentist office, a couple of chain fast food places, an engineering firm, a few gas stations, a pretty stone church, and a few old houses. The church, called Our Lady of the Lake, was one of the most interesting buildings in Ashland. It was constructed in 1888 and, like many buildings in the area, it was built out of brownstone.[14] Pretty. The rest of the waterfront was mostly industrial, except for the marina and a few cheap hotels. The biggest landmark along the waterfront was the power plant[15]; the boat landing and beach were right next to it. This area of the lake was known as The Hot Pond. The water there was warmer than in the rest of the lake due to the discharge of hot water from the power plant. Lake Superior is a frigid lake with average surface water temperatures for July and August barely breaking 60 degrees Fahrenheit (16 degrees Celsius)[16]. The water at The Hot Pond was significantly warmer, and, in the winter, the shore ice would usually be kept at bay. It was a popular fishing spot, and it was a place where Wylie and I could go to play.

---

[14] https://www.wisconsinhistory.org/Records/Property/HI4349 *(link verified on 10/13/2021)*

[15] https://wi.my.xcelenergy.com/s/energy-portfolio/natural-gas *(link verified on 10/13/2021)*

[16] https://coastwatch.glerl.noaa.gov/statistic/gif/avgtemps-s_1992-2017.gif *(link verified on 10/13/2021)*

# Wylie Makes a Splash

(Image Credit: Terry Owen)

It was late spring by the time it was warm enough outside to consider going down to the lake with Wylie. We would take a few tennis balls with us down to the Hot Pond and toss them in the water, one at a time, just a few feet in, and Wylie would run to fetch them. She also loved running after driftwood, pulling whatever she could find up onto the beach. The slope of the sandy bottom is very gradual in that part of the lake and you could walk about 20 yards and still be only up to your knees in water, so it was ideal for a young puppy to get her feet wet, so to speak. Wylie loved splashing around and fetching those sticks and tennis balls. She didn't actually swim at this point in time, she just splashed and ran around. She never cared about the water being cold either. Her thick double coat took care of that for her. This became our routine for the next few months. We would go to the little beach a couple of times a week, usually combined with either doggie daycare or just some socializing around town, to play "run around in the water."

We were lucky enough to have a boat that we could take out on the big lake for day trips or overnighters. The boat was an Osprey Pilothouse, a twenty-six-footer with a spacious outside deck and an enclosed cabin that slept four people, or, in our case, two people and a dog. Wylie always came with us when we went out on the boat. She loved the adventure and was a good little sailor. She was really comfortable in her soft-sided crate, which we bought especially for the boat (the crate wouldn't scratch the fiberglass). We secured it to the deck at the back of the boat when it was nice and warm out and I would sit out there with her, enjoying the sunshine. If the weather was colder, Wylie came inside with us. She loved going down to the marina and easily walked the narrow floating docks. She jumped on board without hesitation.

This part of Lake Superior has some really wonderful boating. The towns along the shoreline are all boat friendly and boast marinas and provisioning options. The prettiest town of all is a little place called Bayfield. Bayfield is small, with a year-round population of a little over five hundred people[17]. It relies heavily on tourism to make ends meet, and the summer population balloons up to about eight thousand people. In the fall, Bayfield is home to Applefest,

---

[17] https://en.wikipedia.org/wiki/Bayfield,_Wisconsin *(link verified on 0/13/2021)*

Wylie Makes a Splash

attracting over *sixty thousand* visitors in the space of three days![18] It's a fun place to be, and to be able to get there by boat and stay at the marina was simply magical.

One weekend in early August, when Evan and Julie were visiting us again, we took a boat trip out to Oak Island, one of twenty-one islands belonging to the Apostle Islands National Lakeshore, a US National Park[19]. Wylie was a little over five months old, and so far, she had only been in water she could walk in. It was a spectacular day, bright and clear, warm and breezy. We sped out from the Ashland Marina and cruised out to Oak Island. We docked the boat, gathered up the dog toys and our stuff, and we were off on an adventure. It was a short trail walk to get to the beach. We were all delighted to find that we were the only ones there!

Wylie immediately ran into the water. She absolutely loved splashing around and running after her ball. This was the first time we had been to this island, and so we were unfamiliar with the bottom terrain at the beach. I tossed the ball into the water, but not too far. Wylie ran in after, snagged it and ran back. *More please and thank you!* This time, Evan picked up the ball and threw it into the lake. He threw it a bit further than we had anticipated. Oops. Wylie ran to fetch it with her usual recklessness, and when she got about ten feet out, all of a sudden, her splashing stopped as she sank beneath the surface. Evidently, there was an abrupt drop on the lake bottom at that spot where a huge, flat rock fell away. Wylie just fell off the edge. For a brief moment, she disappeared, then her head popped up, a look of total surprise on her little face! After all, in her mind, I'm sure she thought that all water was walkable. She had no idea that water could get deep. She managed to keep herself afloat by smashing all four paws up and down in a wild, uncontrolled way.

[18] https://rove.me/to/midwest/bayfield-apple-festival *(link verified on 10/13/2021)*

[19] https://www.nps.gov/apis/faqs.htm *(link verified on 10/13/2021)*

Her front paws came up above the surface of the water and smacked back down at a furious pace. She didn't look like she was swimming; she looked like she was drowning! I was just about to run in after her when she suddenly started to keep her paws just under the surface of the water and started paddling. I can't describe the funny expression she had on her face. I think it said something like, "Ohhh, so *this* is how you do it! Look at *me*, I can *swim!*" From that moment on, Wylie became a total water dog. If there was an opportunity to swim, she took advantage of it. If the swimming also included chasing a tennis ball, she was in doggie heaven. She even learned to jump off the bow of the boat and leap with abandon, a picture of pure joy.

We spent the rest of that summer and the next two boating on Lake Superior almost every weekend. We went to many of the islands including Long Island where the shallow channel water was warmed by the hot sun and where Tim picked up a bad case of poison ivy. On Stockton Island, we anchored offshore to watch the beautiful sunset and spent the whole night getting up every hour to run the motor, cursing the boat batteries that wouldn't hold a charge. We even ventured way out to the farthest island called Devil's Island, where we walked the trail to the lighthouse and got inundated by blackflies that were so thick that they covered all white surfaces of the boat and feasted on us as soon as we poked our noses outside. We boated west to Duluth, Minnesota, getting tossed around by seven-foot seas. I got seasick with a bucket under one arm and Wylie under the other, trying to hold on to my dog to keep her from being slammed against the wall or getting thrown onto the floor while intermittently puking into the bucket. We finally arrived on dry land and met up with Canadian friends the next day to compete in the annual dragon boat races. We boated east to Black River Harbor in Michigan, one of the most remote harbors in the country[20], where we docked, got out of the boat, and tied Wylie to a picnic table while we unpacked our things, only to notice that she had chewed through my brand new, very expensive Teva® sandals in about three seconds flat. I thought I had left them out of her reach. My mistake. We made bonfires, had barbecues, drank wine, swam, and played. It was a wonderful time, made so much better by the presence of my four-legged best friend.

# Boating Safety and First Aid

A large part of summer fun for many lucky people includes spending time on a boat and dogs are often a part of this aspect of summer. There are a few important things to note about boating with your dog.

Most (but not all) dogs are natural swimmers. However, problems occur when they cannot get out of the water. Many drownings happen while the boat is still docked. A dog may fall into the water unnoticed and swim around looking for somewhere to get out, only to exhaust themselves and succumb to drowning. This can be avoided. First, get your dog a life jacket. Pet life jackets are available from a variety of sources and are relatively inexpensive.

They are available in sizes to fit even the smallest dog. *Paws Aboard*™ makes one to fit dogs under six pounds, so there is definitely one out there to fit your tiny dog. Look for a bright color for high visibility, and make sure it has a handle on the top. You can use the handle to lift a small to medium dog out of the water or to guide a larger dog to an area of the boat where they can board.

Once you have life jackets, use them. Life jackets are of no use to you or your pets if they are stowed below.

Also, dogs should be shown how to get out of the water by themselves. There are devices on the market that you can install to help your dog climb into the boat. One such device is called the *Paws Aboard*™ *Doggy Boat Ladder and Ramp*. It is a portable, lightweight ladder that is easy to carry and install. Dogs can learn to use the ladder with some training. Practice, practice, practice, and make it fun! Entice your dog up with a toy or a treat. Be patient. Watch the *Paws Aboard*™ videos for more complete training instructions.

By observing these boating safety guidelines, you and your dog can enjoy a wonderful summer of boating on the water!

## FIRST AID

Okay, so now you and your dog are out on the boat for the weekend or hiking up in the wilderness for the day. What are you going to do, all alone out there, with no veterinarian around, when puppy slices his paw pad open on a piece of glass? Yikes!

Be prepared! Having a pet first aid kit is the first step and knowing what to do with it is the second. Whether you purchase a ready-made kit or make your own, there are some items that you should be sure to include. Ask your veterinarian what you should have in your pet first aid kit or check out the information provided by the American Red Cross.

Your basic kit should include:

- Muzzle — any dog in pain may bite
- Dog nail clippers to trim broken or torn nails
- Styptic powder such as Kwik Stop® to stop nail bleeding

- Non-stick bandages to stop bleeding and keep wounds clean

- Gauze and vet tape for bandaging

- Duct tape for everything!

- **Super** Glue® for closing small cuts

- Hydrogen peroxide to clean wounds and induce vomiting (mark dosage on label ahead of time!)

- Milk of magnesia or activated charcoal to absorb poison (mark dosage on label ahead of time!)

- Antibiotic ointment to prevent infection

- Large syringe (without needle) for administering oral treatments and flushing wounds

- Phone numbers of your veterinarian and emergency contacts

- Means of contacting the Coast Guard or Forest Service

## Common First Aid Treatments

**Cuts:** Clean small, superficial cuts with clean water, and apply antibiotic ointment. See your veterinarian if cuts are not healed within three days.

**Broken or Fractured Toenail:** Apply muzzle. If the loose piece is attached by a strand, trim it away with the clippers. If still well attached, try to superglue it together. It may hold until you can get help. To stop the nail from bleeding, pack it with coagulant (e.g. styptic powder, a bar of soap, flour, cornstarch, or tea leaves from a tea bag will work in a pinch). Hold it there for a minute or two. Seek veterinary care as soon as possible to help avoid complications.

**Lacerations:** Apply muzzle. Deep or long cuts can be cleaned with cool, clean water and a topical antibiotic can be applied before bandaging snuggly. Get to the vet as soon as possible!

**Punctures and Bites:** Apply muzzle. These wounds are deep and may be the tip of the iceberg, so to speak. Flush with clean water and apply topical antibiotic. Watch for swelling or inflammation. Bacteria may become trapped under the skin. See your vet as soon as possible!

**Know your location!** If you call for help, you need to be able to tell someone where you are.

The **American Red Cross** offers online Pet First Aid courses that could prove invaluable if you often find yourself in situations where you and your pet are isolated from help. Take one.

s

## RESOURCES

Paws Aboard Doggy Boat Ladder is available at a variety of locations. Other boat ladder options are also available. http://www.skamper-ramp-store.com/paws-aboard-ladder.html **(link verified on 10/13/2021)**

Outward Hound® life jacket: https://outwardhound.com/dog-gear/life-jackets-and-swimming-supplies-for-dogs.html **(link verified on 10/13/2021)**

Paws Aboard life jackets: https://www.fidopetproducts.com/products/pawsaboard **(link verified on 10/13/2021)**

American Red Cross Pet First Aid Online Classes: https://www.redcross.org/take-a-class/first-aid/cat-dog-first-aid (link verified on 10/13/2021)

American Red Cross Pet First Aid Kit: http://www.redcross.org/images/MEDIA_CustomProductCatalog/m4440087_First_Aid_Kit_for_Pets.pdf (link verified on 10/13/2021)

# CHAPTER FOURTEEN

# Wylie Walks her Human

Wylie was a challenging dog, as you have probably already surmised. I was a regular person who had very little knowledge on how to train a dog. A lot of what I knew was based on what I learned when I trained Roxy all those years ago. It was outdated to say the least!

The hardest things for me to live with were Wylie's jumping up on people, especially me (she was big and overly enthusiastic) and her incessant pulling while attached to a leash (she was big and overly enthusiastic). We had found the head halter in class, thanks to our wonderful trainer, and it worked pretty well most of the time. Wylie didn't like it. She fought wearing it. Every time I put it on her, she would paw at it, dive to the ground and rub her face in the dirt or grass for a minute or two, then give up in sad resignation. I felt bad. She would still pull on the leash when she wore it, but much less. The loop on her nose would tighten as she pulled, and it tugged her nose to one side. She eventually wore a grove in her nose where the strap was. It must have been very uncomfortable. It didn't feel good to me either! That head halter worked because it was aversive. I was passively punishing my dog for pulling, and I didn't like it. Also, it did nothing to teach Wylie how to walk nicely on leash without it. I figured that if I wanted Wylie to show any semblance of calm, she would have to wear it forever. I was not happy with that idea, and neither was my dog.

Whenever we went for a walk on the road or in town, I would use the head halter. However, when we decided to walk our property, which was often, Wylie was off leash. She loved running through the woods, splashing in the creek, and loping through the fields. She was pretty good at coming when called, even though she rarely came close enough for us to catch her when she returned to us. We didn't really need to; she would always follow us, even if it was from a bit of a distance. Looking back, I think that all of this freedom may have contributed to my difficulty in teaching Wylie to walk calmly on a loose leash. After all, if I were Wylie, I would rather be out running around freely too!

When Wylie was about seven months old, Evan and Julie came back from Louisiana for another short visit. Tim and I wanted to show them some of the natural beauty our area had to offer. We lived right beside the Chequamegon National Forest[21] (pronounced

[21] *https://dnr.wi.gov/topic/parks/name/copperfalls/ (Link verified on 10/13/2021)*

shə-WAH-mə-gan, not the way I pronounced it for the first six months I lived there, i.e. check-wa-mee-gone) and very close to Copper Falls State Park and the Great Divide, a geological line that basically splits northern Wisconsin. North of The Divide, rivers flow to Lake Superior. These waterways are full of rapids and waterfalls, making river travel almost impossible. South of The Divide, calmer rivers run south to the Mississippi River. We picked a hike to Morgan Falls and St. Peter's Dome along The Divide. Tim and I had hiked it once before, and the views at the top were simply spectacular.

On a sunny Saturday morning, I packed a picnic lunch, and we all piled into our respective vehicles and drove to the trailhead. Dogs were allowed on the trails but had to be leashed. I liked that idea because it meant that we weren't likely to encounter loose dogs. I thought it would be nice to let Wylie have a bit of freedom though, so along with her head halter and short, six-foot leash, I brought her long, twenty-six-foot retractable leash. My plan was to use the head halter and short leash until we got to the rough part of the trail, then I would switch to the retractable leash attached to her regular flat collar.

I was excited about the hike. This trail is absolutely beautiful. The walk to Morgan Falls is easy and fairly flat. It's a wide gravel path so Wylie was on her head halter as we walked along, passing a few other hikers along the way. It's not far — about half a mile and then you come upon the seventy-foot-high Morgan Falls. Beautiful. Everything was going well. We then headed for the trail to St Peter's Dome.[22] Unlike the Morgan Falls trail, this one was pretty rugged with some steep climbs and exposed rock. You really have to watch where you're stepping and, in some spots, the trail is only a few feet wide.

---

[22] https://www.nrs.fs.fed.us/rna/wi/chequamegon/st-peters-dome/ *(Link verified on 10/13/2021)*

I switched Wylie from her head halter to her flat collar and retractable leash. We started off in single file along the trail. Wylie went first, of course. No one would have been fast enough to be ahead of her! I followed Wylie, holding the big handle of the retractable leash. Tim followed, then Julie, and Evan was bringing up the rear. I was in charge of managing the dog. I could tell Wylie was excited to be semi-free, less restrained. She ran ahead, darting left and right, into the woods, around the trees, getting tangled in the bushes. I was left following behind, locking that stupid retractable leash device, trying to untangle her.

"Wylie! *Wylie!* Wait! Just a minute — wait — let me just get this... *Wait!* Damn it! Just wait!" I was hot, sweaty (a common theme by now), and getting more and more frustrated by the minute. I put her back on her regular leash and put the retractable one in Tim's backpack. If Wylie was going to be such an idiot, she wasn't going to be an idiot on a retractable leash! This just wasn't working.

We climbed a bit further, but all I was doing was yanking on the leash, trying desperately to get Wylie to walk with me on the trail. No way. Wylie was *not* cooperating. There was no way I was going to make it. I was so self-conscious. *Stupid dog,* I thought. *You ruin everything!*

I stopped. Wylie came to my side, looked up at me with those beautiful amber eyes, tongue lolling to one side, thoroughly pleased with herself and obviously having a grand old time, oblivious to my plight. I, on the other hand, looked down at her with resentment, frustration, and anger. I didn't say anything to her.

I spun around and barked at Tim.

"This isn't going to work. Give me the keys."

"Why, where are you going?"

"Home."

"What? Why?"

# Wylie Walks her Human

"Why? Why do you think? I can't get this stupid dog to walk with me! You guys go on and enjoy the view. I've seen it before anyway. Have a picnic at the top. Have fun. I'm going home with this goddamned dog."

I took the keys from Tim and turned back, dragging the dog with me. I could hear them all talking as I left. When I turned back to look, the three of them had started up the trail again. *Goodie for you*, I thought to myself.

By the time I got to the truck, I was crying my eyes out. I couldn't do anything with this stupid dog! No hike for me, no picnic, no gorgeous view of the Chequamegon Bay and Lake Superior, no nothing! I boosted Wylie into the cab of the truck and climbed in after her. I sat there. I looked at her and was so mad! She stared at me, panting from her joyous effort. She licked my face. She was so happy. I looked at her and felt an enormous rush of love come over me, mixed with undeniable frustration. I started to laugh. She was ridiculous! I was ridiculous! I turned the key in the ignition, blasted the air conditioning, revved the engine, and we drove home. I loved this stupid dog way more than one silly hike. I guess I would have to do a bit more work before we attempted to do that again!

When the trio got home several hours later, they found me and Wylie snoozing on the couch. Wylie jumped up and greeted them all in her wildly enthusiastic manner (a little jumping was involved) with much tail wagging. Evan and Julie absolutely loved the hike and the view, and all three were happy they kept going and made it to the top. We all had a good laugh at Wylie's antics and her less than stellar hiking abilities. I felt a little sorry for myself, but in the end, I was just happy to be with my dog.

That same summer, Tim and I took several excursions on our boat to the Apostle Islands. Our area of Lake Superior really is a boater's paradise. On another bright, beautiful, sunny summer day, we left our home base at the Ashland Marina and headed out to sea (in our case, lake, but that doesn't sound as good). We were headed to Oak Island again. We loved it there and were eager to go back. After about an hour of carefree boating, we approached the Oak Island dock. Wylie was in her soft-sided crate as she always was when we docked. Tim smoothly guided us in, and I jumped out and tied up. Perfect landing. The day was spectacular, so we decided to go for a walk on the Loop Trail before lunch.

I got Wylie out of her crate and Tim got our backpack, locked the boat, and we all started up the trail. Wylie was on her retractable leash and was doing well! She would run ahead a little bit and back to me every so often to check in before running ahead again. She was really enjoying her freedom. We had gone a little more than halfway around the Loop when Wylie ran back towards me again. But instead of stopping in front of me as she had been doing, she kept running past me to see Tim. Rather than turn and walk back to me, she decided to go behind Tim and then around to his other side. She then got the urge to run full speed straight ahead. Picture this: the line on the retractable leash went from the handle in my hand, back behind Tim, around both of his legs, then back up to me and then fifteen feet ahead to where Wylie abruptly stopped as she ran out of rope.

I heard Tim yell, "Jesus Christ!" I turned to look and saw him tangled in the line. I dropped the retractable leash and it clattered against the rocks, rushing towards Tim, smashing its way behind his feet, and chased Wylie up the trail. Wylie took off running.

"Wylie! Come back here! *Wylie!*"

I was so happy to see her stop, turn, and run back to me, dragging the plastic leash handle behind her, *clackity clack clack clack*. She sat in front of me, looking all innocent. *Phew,* I thought as I picked up the leash, *crisis averted.*

In my mind, I assumed Tim was okay, just angry that Wylie had done yet another silly thing. He showed me the back of his leg.

It looked like the cord had given him a bit of a burn when it pulled tight against his calf. "No big deal," I said and continued along the trail. "You'll be fine." I was trying to minimize the disaster that my dog had caused.

I knew that it was a dangerous thing for Wylie to have done, but I tried to shrug it off. There was nothing I could do about it now! Tim's a tough guy, but he continued to curse at us and then basically stopped talking to me. He was mad! When we finished our little hike and were walking on the dock, back to the boat, Tim was walking ahead of us so that he could unlock the boat cabin. I finally saw the seriousness of his injury. That retractable leash had burned a slice into the back of his right calf that looked to be about a half-an-inch deep.

"Look at your leg!" I exclaimed.

Tim looked at me as though I was crazy. "I know! Tell me about it!"

I felt so bad. "I'm sorry! I'm so sorry." I felt like it was totally my fault, first because it was my dog and second because I made light of it.

Tim forgave me, and he forgave Wylie. That injury took a long, long time to heal, and he still has that scar today. It's a souvenir from Wylie that he will always wear, like a tattoo, except incised against his will. Ouch.

Wylie's leash escapades were frequent during the first few years of her life with us. Loose leash walking was the skill that I had the most trouble teaching her. It looks so easy, but I know that it's not. She got the hang of it eventually, but I was a terrible teacher. If only I had known then what I know now! Isn't that what we all say?

# How to Teach Your Dog to Stop Pulling While on Leash

Why does my dog keep pulling me? This is the question I hear over and over from people who are trying their best to walk their dogs on a regular basis. Short of giving up, they suffer the embarrassment, danger, and sometimes pain of walking a dog who pulls like a freight train. Before I became a dog trainer, this was the one skill that Wylie and I could not master. Even after learning loose leash walking techniques in a basic obedience class, many people (including me) still struggle with this often-frustrating ability.

(blank/by Shutterstock.com)

Leash pulling is one of the most exasperating and common problems faced by dog owners. This is especially problematic for people who have big dogs because it involves not only the safety of the dog, but also that of the person walking the dog. Big dogs can easily overpower their owners and drag them into the street, perhaps even into oncoming traffic. That's why the pet industry has exploded in its design and marketing of quick fix solutions to this pervasive problem. The invention of cruel devices like prong collars have found a niche in today's dog world because owners who have "tried everything" essentially give up and are willing to inflict pain on the dogs they profess to love to get them to stop. This leash pulling problem occurs with small dogs too and with much the same frequency, but owners will often overlook it because a small dog's pulling doesn't pose any real hazard other than being annoying. Either way, pulling while on leash is an almost universal problem we have with our dogs. Let's look at leash pulling more closely.

Always remember that it takes two to tango, as they say. A leash is pulled taut between two ends: one attached to the dog and one attached to the human. If either the dog or the human stops pulling, the resistance goes away. Most of the time when dogs pull the leash tight, they are either trying to get to something or away from something faster than we want. When humans pull the leash tight, we want dogs to pay attention to us or leave something they are interested in to come with us. Either way, we pull or the dog pulls and the result is a tight leash.

In all instances, the dog is resisting our request to either slow down or to come with us. This struggle has been referred to as "resistance to coercion."[23] In all of these cases, the human is trying to *coerce* the dog into doing something he does not

[23] *Eileen and Dogs: "Opposition Reflex: What Is It Really?" Resistance to coercion,* https://eileenanddogs.com/2016/04/16/opposition-reflex/ *(link verified on 10/13/2021)*

want to do. The secret (okay, it's not really a secret) is to get the dog to *want* to walk with us at our pace. Giving the dog choice — letting him *choose* to come with us — will always win the day! When a dog chooses to comply, coercion goes out the window.

Incidentally, you may have heard of the term *opposition reflex*. This 'reflex' is sometimes cited as the reason that dogs pull on leash. The *opposition reflex* posits that dogs have a natural resistance to pressure and if pulled in one direction, they will automatically pull in the other direction. Just to let you know, there is no science behind this idea, but it has made its way into dog training via urban myth and sticky theory[24]. It has no bearing on our discussion or on leash training in general. If you hear someone use it as an excuse for pulling, know that the person is likely just repeating something that they heard from someone else who didn't know that it wasn't a proven concept.

It's always a good idea to put everything in your favor before you start trying to teach your dog how to walk politely on a leash, so let's look at some important factors.

## KEYS TO SUCCESS

1.  **Identify the right problem and teach your dog to be patient in other situations.**

    Some leash pulling problems have nothing to do with loose leash walking. Instead, they are rooted in other issues and situations. For example, I once had a client who brought her two young Labrador retrievers to doggie daycare several times a week. When they

---

[24] Made to Stick *by C&D Heath, Random House, 2007.*

arrived, the dogs were frantic to get inside, their arousal levels sky high. As soon as she opened the back hatch of her car, the dogs came crashing out, dragging her to the front door. This became dangerous because the dogs could have easily overpowered her and caused her to fall or the dogs could have gotten loose and run out into traffic. The problem in this case was not walking to the door; it was the crashing out of the car. Teaching the dogs to wait before being asked to exit the vehicle helped calm them to the point where walking them inside was less of a problem. So, it's important to separate out the skills your dog needs in order to perform the behaviors you are looking for. Teaching calm in a variety of situations will help your dog.

## 2. Switch to a harness

Switching to a proper fitting two-point attach harness, like the Balance Harness® by Blue-9, the Freedom No-Pull Harness, the PerfectFit Harness, or the Ruffwear Front Range® Harness (these are four harnesses that I like, but there are many others on the market[25]) will actually decrease pulling and give you more control even without changing anything else. Clipping your leash to the front attach point will help you a lot. It sounds counter intuitive, but it's true.

---

[25] *For a review of dog harnesses, please refer to The Whole Dog Journal article entitled "The Best Harnesses of 2018", first published in the April 2017 issue, updated 07/19/2018. This review is published annually so check for new reviews.* https://www.whole-dog-journal.com/issues/20_4/features/Best-Dog-Harnesses-2017_21622-1.html *(link verified on 10/13/2021)*

### 3. Exercise your dog *before* going on a walk

Trying to teach your young, exuberant dog to walk politely on leash when he has not been adequately exercised is, in itself, an exercise in futility. Dogs have so much pent up energy that if they are not exercised, they simply cannot focus, cannot walk slowly, and cannot listen to you. A good romp in the back yard or a game of fetch will expend some of that energy, making it easier for your dog to focus and understand what you want him to do. Don't go overboard. You know your dog best and know how much exercise keeps them happy, but five or ten minutes of running and playing should be enough. If you don't have access to a fenced yard, you can expend some of that energy indoors by engaging your dog in some scent games. Using their nose is enjoyable for dogs, and their amazing olfactory system burns a lot of energy. Be creative and spend a bit of time doing what your dog loves.

I don't really consider leash walking as exercise for most young, healthy dogs. Humans walk incredibly slowly from a dog's perspective. Dogs must think we dawdle and are pretty boring, mostly walking in a straight line, not stopping to smell the roses. However, walking is good for your dog and adds to their overall sense of wellbeing. Going on regular walks with your dog can increase their social skills, provide necessary mental stimulation, and is a wonderful time for them to explore the world while bonding with their humans. But exercise your dog first, before you walk.

## 4. Your walks are training sessions

Remember, your dog is learning from you all the time. When your dog is first learning to walk nicely on a leash, you should consider all walks to be training sessions. All training sessions, whether practicing the basics like sit and down or learning loose-leash walking, should be short and fun. There is absolutely no point in trying to take your unskilled dog for a three-mile walk. You will just get frustrated, the dog will get frustrated, and you will be tempted to give up. Go slowly and be patient. If you feel the need to go on a long walk, go without your dog until he has learned this skill and is ready to go with you.

## 5. Learn the right technique

You'll definitely need some help to master this skill. Here are some tips, including one method of teaching your dog to walk nicely with you while on leash.

- *Find a good class.* Take a basic obedience class in your area that includes walking on leash. You can never get too much good coaching.

- *Make sure the trainer uses positive reinforcement.* The trainer should use positive reinforcement techniques to teach your dog and should not advocate the use of choke collars (sometimes referred to as training collars), prong/pinch collars, or shock collars (sometimes referred to as e-collars or electronic training collars). There is absolutely no need for these types of devices.

- *Wear a treat pouch.* Get one that will allow you easy access to the treats. Magnet or hinge closures work best. Don't get one with a drawstring because it makes it harder to reach into the pouch to get the treats.

- *Select high-value treats.* You will be using a lot of them, so make sure they are healthy and tiny (pea-sized or smaller).

- *Pick a Side.* Choose which side you would like your dog to walk on: your left or your right. I prefer the left for a couple of reasons. If you are going to participate in competitions with your dog, your dog must usually walk on your left. Also, if you are walking on a street with no sidewalks, you walk facing oncoming traffic. If your dog is on your left, he will be walking on the shoulder instead of being on the road, close to traffic.

- *Reduce distractions and think small.* Start in your house when no one else is around. Call your dog to you as you walk away from him and reward him when he comes to your left side. Take one step forward, and your dog should follow. Say *Good* and reward. If your dog doesn't follow, encourage him to do so by calling his name and patting your left leg. Repeat, repeat, repeat. Add a step: take two steps, *Good,* and reward. Repeat several times. Then, move to three steps, then four, then ten. You get the idea. Now, put his harness on, snap the leash to the front clip, say *Good,* and feed your dog a treat at your left side by your knee. Take one step forward and reward, then two steps and reward, the same as you did without the leash. Repeat. Aim for short sessions, less than five minutes at a time, several times a day. When your dog is happily trotting by your left side in the house, it's time to take it outside.

- *Move outside and define your zone.* Start in your driveway or right in front of your home. Pace out an area of about ten steps that you will be walking back and forth with your dog. This is your starting zone. You are taking the skill your dog has learned inside to a whole new level. There are a *ton* of distractions outside, so expect that your dog will be excited.

- *Begin again.* Stand at the top of your driveway with your dog on leash and don't move. Let your dog smell and see what's going on. If your dog pulls, wait for the leash to slacken then say *Good* and reward. Wait for some calm. Reward. With your dog at your side, start at the beginning again. Take one step, *Good*, and reward. Also reward every single time your dog makes eye contact with you. Repeat until you can add a step, then two, etc. Stay within your ten step zone until your dog is happily trotting along beside you.

- *Expand your zone.* Add a few more steps beyond your initial zone, either down the driveway or in front of your house. Then, turn and go back. Remember to reward eye contact. Your dog is paying attention to you! Reward that! Add more and more steps until you are actually walking a whole block. Your job then becomes adding more steps between rewards until you are rewarding only occasionally, for eye contact, or when there are added distractions.

- *Don't expect too much.* Your dog will not learn this in one session or even ten sessions! Learning how to walk nicely on a leash may take weeks, depending on your dog. Many short teaching sessions are better than one long session. Dogs learn faster in short spurts.

- *The world is your oyster.* Walk wherever you want. Have fun. Sometimes, let the dog choose the route. When you get to a junction, ask your dog which way he wants to go, right or left. He'll show you with his nose! Then go! Remember to add some breaks along the way so that your dog can sniff and do dog things. Enjoy!

Sometimes, a basic obedience class just doesn't cut it and more intensive training is called for. If you are having trouble, seek out the help of a qualified force-free trainer and take one or two private lessons. By concentrating on a single skill, both you and your dog should be able to learn faster, practice those learned skills with guided feedback, and succeed through positive reinforcement of desired behaviors.

Remember, dogs learn faster and better if they are given a choice. The idea of letting your dog decide whether or not to relax the leash may seem novel to many dog owners, but it is essential if your dog is going to learn to voluntarily walk nicely with you while on a leash.

# CHAPTER FIFTEEN

# Wylie Lives a Wonderful Life

Before we knew it, Wylie's puppy months were over, and she was a young adult dog. By the time she was three, she was starting to become a more manageable, livable, biddable dog. Don't get me wrong; she still had her moments, but I continued to work hard at her regular training on a daily basis. We ran through all that she knew — sit, stand, down, stay, come, leave it, take it, fetch — almost every day. Wylie loved to work.

One day, Tim came home and announced that the Department of the Navy was closing down the project he was responsible for. His job was being cut and the whole project, two huge locations in two states, was being terminated. They would need him to stay to close everything down over the next two years (a very long and complicated process), but we were going to have to decide what we wanted to do. Tim could either quit and find some other job, and we could stay in Highbridge, or we could move, and he could take a job in Norfolk, Virginia. There was a lot to consider. If he quit, that would mean losing healthcare and a great retirement plan. It would mean finding another job in a place where jobs were really hard to come by. I put my foot down when he came home one day suggesting that he could be a long-haul truck driver. I did not get married to have a husband who was never home! If we moved, that would mean selling our brand new house and uprooting ourselves to move to a place neither of us had any desire to live in. Tim was almost fifty and would only have to work a few more years to be eligible for retirement, so it seemed foolish to throw that all away. He already had something like twenty-five years invested. I thought it might be fun to get back to a more urban environment. As much as I loved our home in the wilds of the northwoods, sometimes I missed Ottawa. In the end, we decided to move.

Over the next two years, Tim did a lot of traveling back and forth to Virginia and to Michigan, where the second site was located. Wylie and I were often on our own during that time. I don't know what I would have done without her, isolated in the middle of the woods like that. I never felt alone when I was with Wylie. She was my constant companion. It took a long time to sell our house given the depressed market coupled with the depressed area. Tim eventually had to start work in Norfolk without it being sold. He rented a crappy little apartment in Virginia Beach only a few miles from his new office, and that became his home for about eight months. I stayed behind and tried to sell the house. Wylie and I weathered an entire northern Wisconsin winter by ourselves. *Big deal*, you might be thinking. It was hard. We had a ton of snow that winter. I remember lots and lots of shoveling, running the tractor and plowing snow, dealing with heating problems and frozen pipes, stress upon stress upon stress. Wylie was oblivious, of course, but her enthusiasm for everything was infectious, and she made everything better.

Over the months apart, Tim made several trips home, and I went to visit my new home state. I flew once or twice, leaving Wylie in the capable hands of her daycare/boarding friends, and I drove out a couple of times with Wylie as my sidekick. It's a long drive from northern Wisconsin to southeastern Virginia! It took us three days. Since I didn't have a real job, I could take as long as I wanted. All that car training I did with Wylie in those early months of her life really paid off. I never had any issues at all with her riding in the car. She happily hopped up into her soft-sided crate in the back of my 4Runner, her nose at my elbow, and we drove endlessly. She snoozed while I sang my favorite tunes. She was the only one who ever liked — or at least tolerated — my singing. We stayed in Tim's crappy little apartment and went house hunting almost every day. Prices were sky high, and we were getting disheartened thinking that we would never find anything even remotely as nice as what we had in Highbridge.

It was a real marathon, but after almost a year, we finally sold the house. We had split the property, carving off ten acres that we sold with the house, keeping the other thirty-seven acres just in case we got homesick and wanted to move back at some point in the future. Soon, the moving company was packing everything up and we were having a giant garage sale. We sold leftover lumber, spare windows and doors, household equipment, Tim's motorcycle, the tractor, and bunches of other stuff. I had already made the big purge when I moved from Ottawa a few years earlier, but this was hard on Tim. He had a lifetime of treasures that had to be parsed and sold. Soon, the big moving van was parked at the top of our driveway. A company representative had paid us a visit a few days earlier to check out the turning radius that our driveway allowed, and he assured us that the rig would be able to make the turn. Tim doubted it. When the big truck arrived, sure enough, the driver was unable to make the turn. That turned out to be the first hurdle we encountered that day. The moving company had to arrange for a smaller truck to drive over from Duluth, Minnesota to ferry our stuff out to the big truck, one load at a time. That meant loading and unloading and loading it all again. Thank goodness we had a moving company to do most of the work! It took them two days to finish.

At the end of the first day, Tim asked me where his laptop was. I didn't know. We frantically searched everywhere for it. We hoped that one of the packers had accidentally packed it into a box or placed it somewhere out of the way. Tim had had it that afternoon, showing some photos to the truck driver. That was the last time we saw it.

That computer had all of our photos of Wylie on it. This was back when you had to take photos with an actual camera and download them to your computer with a hard connection. There were no smartphones back then, so no handy dandy cameras at your fingertips. We had downloaded most of the photos from the camera to Tim's computer. I had hardly any of the photos of Wylie on mine. We confronted the driver the next day, but he denied having seen it after our little photo show. He asked everyone else, and they all denied taking it, too. Of course. We reported it to the moving company, but there was nothing they could do since it wasn't part of the tagged inventory. That computer was useless to the thief because of encrypted security technology but losing all those photographs of Wylie really broke my heart. It pains me to this day that all of the photographs of Wylie's early years are gone, likely in a landfill somewhere.

We finished loading the last few boxes and saw the big rig roll away, taking our belongings to be held in storage until we found a house to live in in Virginia. We were sad. We didn't want to go.

House hunting was proving to be impossible. It was the height of the housing bubble in 2006, and all we could afford seemed to be shacks on postage stamp sized lots. It was so depressing. We looked and looked and wore out our poor real estate agent. She tried hard, but there was nothing within our budget. I'm sure she thought we were being totally unrealistic, and I suppose we were, but we wanted a clean, sound house with a decent backyard for Wylie. The adjustment was going to be hard enough on her going from forty-seven acres of pristine wilderness to a different kind of wilderness, one made of concrete, asphalt, strip malls, and noise.

## Wylie Lives a Wonderful Life

Ah, but the ocean! We were close to the ocean! Wylie loved swimming and would happily spend most of her time in and around the water if she could. The first time we brought her to the ocean, we took her to the beach at Fort Story in Virginia Beach. This beach is on a military base, so there were no crowds. It was a nice introduction to waves. Wylie had never seen ocean waves or tasted salty water before and didn't quite know what to make of the whole thing. We threw her tennis ball in the water and she sprinted after it, running until her feet didn't touch bottom anymore, swimming out to fetch it. She met her first wave as it crashed over her head. She popped up and kept swimming like nothing had happened. I should have known. Wylie didn't care! It was water, and so it was good! I'm sure it was no different to her than when she leapt off the deck of the boat and crashed into the lake. It was the same sensation of water smashing her in the face.

# Dale M. Ward

We ended up renting a house for a year, which turned into three, to let the housing market calm down. We moved to the city of Chesapeake, adjacent to Norfolk and Virginia Beach. They're really all just one big blob of city, divided only by some imaginary lines. They all look pretty much the same. Chesapeake seemed a bit newer, a little further from the ocean, and quieter, less touristy. Tim found a nice neighborhood called Stone Gate, where the homes and yards were well tended, the lots a little bigger than the norm, and it seemed pretty quiet. The house was nice, if cookie-cutter in style. There was a man-made pond right behind the house and huge power lines running between us and the houses beyond the pond. When we were looking at the property, we walked to the back of the yard to check things out. I was wearing sandals and could feel little electric shocks, like sharp scratching, tingling all along the edges of my feet where my skin touched the grass. I asked the landlord about it.

"So, what about the electric current I feel in the grass?"

He looked at me like I was crazy.

"What do you mean? We've never felt anything. You must be overly sensitive or something. No, there's no problem with the power lines."

"Okay then. It must just be me."

Later that summer, when I was taking the metal tomato cages down in the garden at the back of the yard, I lifted one off the tomato plant and swung it up over my head to clear the plant. As it rose up, I felt an incredibly painful shock run right through my hand and down my arm. I screamed and threw the metal cage across the yard. No problem, sure thing! I just nearly got electrocuted by a tomato cage while gardening in the backyard, for goodness sake! Who would ever want to actually *live* here? I pondered that question many, many times over the next three years. The answer was always the same: not me.

Wylie's first impression of the house was fun to watch. She ran around and sniffed her little nose off. Another Lab had lived there before her, and Wylie was thrilled. She seemed to like the yard, running and fetching and plopping down in the heat. She didn't seem to notice the shocking grass. Oh, yes, did I mention the *heat*?

So, here I was again in another new place. I had lived my entire life in one place until I met Tim. Forty years in Ottawa. I was slowly coming to the conclusion that I didn't know how to adjust to new surroundings. I had no coping skills. Tim went to work every day, and guess what I did? Yep, nothing. Me and Wylie. Doing nothing. Again.

One day while I was sitting outside drinking coffee and throwing the ball for Wylie, I got the brainy idea to look into dog training. I loved training Wylie and I did a really good job, or at least I thought so! I saw what the trainer in Wisconsin taught us, and I thought I could do that. It was Wylie that was the impetus for my career change. I figured if I could train a dog as bad as Wylie, I could train any of them! How hard could it possibly be?

I searched around online and stumbled across the program at Animal Behavior College. It wasn't too expensive, and it included hands-on mentor training. I had no idea what to look for in a dog training school, but it looked good to me. I broached the subject with Tim one evening over dinner.

"So, I think I know what I want to do."

"What now?"

"Well, I thought I could become a dog trainer."

"How do you do that?"

"You go to school, like anything else!"

"How much?"

"Only two thousand dollars or so."

"Okay, go for it."

I signed up the next day. I plowed through the online portion of the course. I took the exam and passed with flying colors. Easy so far! *Good girl, Dale!*

The school gave me the name of my mentor trainer. She was a dog trainer at a big, new dog training and boarding facility in Virginia Beach. I went to our first meeting and there were three students already there, all having completed the online portion of the course. I thought to myself, *You've got to be kidding. Four of us in this small geographical area? All at once? This is going to be really competitive. I'll never get any clients!*

The mentorship was divided into three parts: audit an eight-week class, attend an eight-week class with a dog (Wylie would be my student dog), and then co-teach an eight-week class. It seemed to be a thorough apprenticeship. Every Wednesday evening, I would make the drive to Virginia Beach to attend class. After each class, when all the people and their dogs had left, the five of us would sit in a circle, and our mentor would critique us, quiz us, and teach us. She was (and still is) a fabulous trainer of both people and dogs. I was beginning to realize that dog training was more people training than dog training. Training the dogs was easy compared to training their owners! Maybe all those years working in the corporate world would come in handy after all!

In the meantime, I went in search of employment. I found a dog grooming place and applied since I had *so* much experience *(not!)*. I got hired on the spot for minimum wage. I worked there for a few months. I didn't like the way they handled the dogs. They were too rough, so I quit. Before I left, I asked some of my coworkers for a recommendation for a veterinarian for Wylie. They told me to go to Centerville Animal Hospital, so I did. Our first appointment happened to be with the vet who owned the practice. Wylie got her exam, and I chatted about dogs. A couple of days later, boom, I was interviewing for a position at the hospital. I was hired and ended up working there in various capacities for the next three years. I learned so much during my time there. The experience was invaluable. It helped me deal with Wylie's many ailments and served me well in my dog training career.

Upon completion of my ABC mentorship, I applied for a business license with the City of Chesapeake and set up shop. I had a little office in my house and concentrated on building up a client base through my work at the vet. I started teaching basic obedience classes in my backyard. Wylie became my *demo dog* for every class I ever taught. At the first class, when there were no dogs, only humans, I would bring her out near the end to greet everyone and then I would show the class how to teach some basics to work on that week with their own dogs. Wylie absolutely *loved* her role as doggie ambassador.

I continued my studies through conferences and seminars, other courses, competing, and expanded my dog training repertoire over the years. I learned AKC Rally® with Wylie as my sidekick. We competed at American Kennel Club® (AKC) competitions and she earned her AKC Rally Novice title. We were getting ready to compete at the Intermediate level when I noticed that Wylie wasn't enjoying her training as much as she used to. I think her hips were bothering her and all that sit/stand/down stuff was hard on her. If Wylie wasn't enjoying it anymore, neither was I. We quit. I did teach AKC Rally classes myself for several years after that and Wylie continued to demonstrate her amazing skills. That's all I asked of her, no more competitions, and she was happy to deliver. We shelved the more intense training required for competition. I am thankful and proud that Wylie helped hundreds and hundreds of dogs in her lifetime, showing them the ropes, so to speak. I absolutely loved working with her. We were a great team. *Go Team Wylie.*

# Dale M. Ward

Wylie's three loves were water, tennis balls, and fetching. If you combined all three, she was in doggie heaven. I saw a poster for an event coming to our area called DockDogs®. I had never heard of it before, but it looked like Wylie's kind of fun. It involved sit, stay, run, jump, swim, fetch, swim. Not too hard. I signed her up. Wylie had jumped off plenty of docks in her time in Wisconsin, and she jumped off the boat like a champ. I knew she would be good at this DockDogs thing!

Wylie and I went to our first competition in a neighboring city called Suffolk. We got there well before our appointed time. I'm always early, no matter where I go, but when I'm nervous, I over-compensate. We had lots of time and watched a bunch of people go before us just to get an idea of what was going to happen. Some dogs ran and jumped. Some ran and stopped right at the edge of the dock, refusing to jump. Some ran fast, and others strolled along. Some wouldn't stay at the far end of the dock and followed their human to the pool. Some dogs chased tennis balls, like Wylie, but others ran for rubber chickens, frisbees, bumpers, and other assorted floating toys. And the dogs! There were a lot of Labrador retrievers, as one would expect, but there were also Chesapeake Bay retrievers, doodles, spaniels, and mutts. Most were big dogs, but there were some little ones, too. It was such a mix! If you ever get the chance to go watch a DockDogs competition, go! You won't be disappointed. It's fun and extremely entertaining. There's even an announcer, booming the names of the dogs and handlers over the airwaves, providing background information and live commentary on each of the jumps.

Soon, it was our turn. The announcer's voice bellowed from the loudspeakers. "And up next, it's *Wylie One of Highbriiiiidge!*" He continued to read some of her bio as Wylie and I climbed up the stairs. I led her to the far end of the forty-foot long dock covered in artificial turf. It was so long that it looked like a runway. I was armed with Wylie's tennis ball, and she was amped up! She had been watching all the other dogs jump, chase toys, and swim, so she was chomping at the bit to get into that water. Wow, she was loving this!

At the other end of the dock, there was a massive blue pool of the same length but set two feet lower than the dock. It looked a bit intimidating; I must admit. Wylie was walking beside me, sort of, spinning and jumping at her ball. We got to the back of the dock, and I had Wylie sit. I gave her the hand signal and asked her to stay. Her stay was rock solid, so I was confident she would get this part of the game.

I got half way down the runway, and I heard the announcer. "Oh, no, there she goes!"

I turned to see Wylie following me very slowly, creeping along, looking something like, *Um, I'm coming with you. You're not leaving me down here, right? All the fun is up there!* Gulp! Maybe we wouldn't be able to do this at all! I felt my face flush red. I did not want to fail — not in front of all these people.

I walked Wylie back to the starting position. I asked for a sit/stay, again. This time, I kept my eye on her and kept my hand signal visible, palm out, like a police officer. *Stay*. I got to the end. Phew!

Then, I released the beast. *"OKAAAYYYY!"*

As she started running, I threw her tennis ball into the pool. Wylie increased her speed when she saw the ball and jumped. *Splash!* It was like she had been a DockDog all her life. The crowd burst into applause! Wylie's head barely went under water as she swam to her ball and snagged it. But instead of coming back to me, she kept swimming, right to the end of the pool where the people were standing and cheering. There was a ramp that the dogs are supposed to swim over to, to get out of the pool. I was standing on the ramp, trying to get my dog's attention.

"Wylie! This way! Come! Wylieeeeee! Wylie, this way!"

It was hard to make myself heard over all the noise. All Wylie wanted to do was swim back and forth along the edge, saying hi to all the people. The spectators finally caught on to what was happening and helped guide Wylie over to the ramp and up she came, ball in her mouth, proud and happy as could be. *Good girl, Wylie!* Shake, shake, shake, she soaked me! We had completed our first jump! We jumped in one more wave (that's what heats are called in the sport of DockDogs) that afternoon and then we went home. We decided, Wylie and I, that we had found a great sport that we could do together. We both loved it.

The next time we competed was a few months later. We packed up everything for a day at DockDogs: a picnic lunch, chairs, cooler, and dog supplies. Wylie was registered in two waves. This time, when we got up on the platform, we knew what we were doing. There were a lot more people in attendance and a lot more dogs competing. This event was way bigger than the first one. Well, we would give it our best, right Wylie? Wylie was her same excited self, maybe even a bit more so because she knew what was coming. We set ourselves up at the end of the platform. Wylie stayed and I walked to the edge of the pool. I released her and threw the ball. Wylie was off like a rocket and launched herself through the air. *Splash!* Big applause!

Then, I heard the announcer say, "And that was Wylie One of Highbridge. A fantastic jump at eighteen feet."

*What? Eighteen feet?* Wow, that was amazing. I was so proud of my dog!

We had a break before we jumped again, and Wylie had another great jump. I can't remember the exact length, but it was another good one. A bit later, Tim and I were sitting around, watching the other dogs, thinking we were done for the day when I heard Wylie's name over the loudspeaker. I didn't catch what he said, so I went over to the trailer that seemed to be the hub of administrative activity. I asked about Wylie.

"Oh, you didn't pick up your medals," she said.

*Wait, what medals?*

She handed me two medals on colorful ribbons, one blue and one red for first and second place. I was shocked. Wylie had come first and second in her National Big Air Waves. Then the woman told me that we had qualified for the Big Air Pro Finals. Wow. We were jumping again with all the Big Dogs, the real jumpers, in the PRO finals! So, we jumped again and came in eleventh. Not too shabby for a novice. We got another medal, big and shiny, on a red, white and blue ribbon. Three medals in one day, and this was only her second competition. *My dog is amazing*, I thought to myself. *Good girl, Wylie!*

The next day, Wylie seemed fine, if a bit tired. That was to be expected after her big day of competition. That afternoon, I went into the bedroom to relax on our bed and read. Of course, I invited Wylie up too. Wylie jumped up and let out a high-pitched yelp in mid-jump. She cowered on the bed, ears flattened against her head.

"Wylie, what happened? Are you okay?" I scrambled close to her and put my head near her ear. I whispered to her. "You okay, Sweet Pea? I'm here. You're okay."

Wylie whimpered. She was obviously in pain. When she jumped, she must have pulled something, or at least that's what I thought. Overexertion from yesterday was my best guess. I kept her quiet for the rest of the day and made an appointment to see the vet the next day. That was our first appointment with Dr. Betty Riedel. She was the other vet at the animal hospital, and I liked her immediately. She was kind, compassionate, knowledgeable, and she connected with Wylie right away. Wylie loved her at first sight. After an examination, Dr. Riedel suggested that we do some x-rays. That's when we discovered that my wonderful Wylie had the first signs of hip dysplasia. There was some malformation in the hip joint. My heart sank. No more jumping for Wylie. No more DockDogs.

Wylie made a quick recovery after a few days of rest. She got back to her regular activities as if nothing had happened. I was disappointed that Wylie's competition days were cut short, but I kept telling myself that Wylie didn't know that! She was oblivious. Life in its entirety was fun in her eyes, so if she never jumped off a dock again, she didn't care. After all, there was still going on walks, playing fetch, swimming, chewing things, swimming, doing stuff for food rewards... and more swimming. Guess which one was her favorite? Gosh, how she loved the water!

## Wylie Lives a Wonderful Life

One of our other favorite activities was to take long walks along the Great Dismal Swamp Canal Trail. The "trail" is really the old two-lane highway (since replaced by a new four-lane one that runs parallel) that stretches out of Chesapeake south towards the North Carolina border. This nine-mile-long stretch of trail (paved road) is bordered by the Canal on one side and some swampy jungle on the other. We affectionately called it "The Swamp." It's quite picturesque and is fairly well sheltered by the tall trees, perfect for walking, running, or biking. No motorized vehicles are allowed on the trail, so it's nice and quiet. In the cooler months, from October through March, it's practically deserted. It's much more crowded in the summer, which I do not understand since summer around here is hot. *Too* hot. The locals like the heat. Not me, and not Wylie. Winter, on the other hand, is lovely. Temperatures ranging from the low sixties to around freezing are normal all winter long. It rarely gets cold enough to snow. For northerners like Tim, Wylie, and me, it was perfect.

Most weekends, the three of us would go for a long swamp walk. Tim would run, and Wylie and I would walk. I always brought a tennis ball and her slip leash with me. All dogs were supposed to be leashed while on the trail. I always followed the rules *when* I thought they were necessary. I used a slip leash for a quick on/off. I never walked Wylie on a slip leash! A slip leash is the same as a choke collar, a definite *no-no* in my opinion. But it served me well in this situation and I kept one handy in case of emergency.

In the winter, when not a soul could be seen for miles down the trail, I let Wylie off leash. *Shhh!* Don't tell anyone. Wylie had an excellent recall and loved to run after that darned tennis ball, so I just had to let her go. If the coast was clear, I set her free and threw the ball, and she gave chase. The ball bounced really far on the smooth pavement, and Wylie tried to catch it on the first bounce. She always brought it back to me, always wanting one more toss. Much of the time, when I thought she had run enough, I let her trot ahead of me, carrying her ball in her mouth. Wylie never strayed from the paved road and shoulder into the woods or the swamp. She'd get maybe two hundred feet ahead and turn to see if I was coming. This gave me a great opportunity to practice her recall many times during each walk. When she was far enough away, I would call to her. *Wylieeee!* She would stop and turn. Always. *Come!* And she would run back and sit in front of me. I slipped the leash over her head each time. *Good girl, Wylie!* Then, I slipped the leash off, back over her head and released her. *Okay! Go play!* And off she would run. We must have done this thousands of times over the years. If ever I saw someone coming, or saw a bear in the distance, or the Trail Police in their white trucks, I needed her to come to me quickly and reliably. I would have to leash her up fast for her own safety and so that I wouldn't get fined by the park people. That's why the slip lead was so efficient. It was a quick on and off. By leashing and unleashing her so many times, Wylie never developed the fear that coming to me would mean that her freedom was over. She always happily let me slip that leash over her head with no issues.

We tried to pick days when we knew the temperatures were going to stay low. After all, Wylie was a snow dog, born and raised in a cold climate. She thrived in freezing temperatures, and so did I. We both hated the heat. Sometimes though, especially in the spring, we would start out when it was cool, but as so often happens in southeast Virginia, it was pretty warm by the time we finished our walk. I always had fresh water in the truck and Wylie loved to have a good slurp when we were done.

On one particularly warm day, we were getting close to the end of our walk and the fresh, cool water at the truck. Wylie was panting from running around so much. I knew she was warm and thirsty. She was walking ahead of me with her tennis ball, as usual. All of a sudden, she stopped and turned to look at me, dropped her ball, and headed for the swamp. *Splash!* I was frantic.

"Wylie, no! Wylie, come. Get back here!" My recall wasn't working! It just couldn't trump her thirst. Biology before trained behaviors!

Wylie had never run off the trail before. We'd been there so many times, I thought I could trust her! I had some ideas about what could possibly be in that swamp. We were in Virginia now, not Wisconsin. There are deadly things here, like snakes. Water moccasins got their name because they live in the *water*!

"Get out of there! Wylie!" I guess my panic was evident because Wylie ran back onto the trail, but not until she had gulped down a bunch of swamp water. Oh, great. This whole thing was totally my fault. I should have brought a bottle of water with me so that I could have given her some on the walk. If I had, I know she wouldn't have run into the swamp to quench her thirst. *Bad girl, Dale!*

The next day, Wylie started throwing up. She was lethargic and wouldn't eat. I was worried about her and knew she had ingested that slimy swamp water the day before. Then, the diarrhea started. Something was definitely wrong with my dog. I took her to see Dr.

Riedel. Wylie had likely picked up some bacteria or parasites from drinking swamp water. I felt so bad. It was totally my fault! We put Wylie on a protocol for a bland diet, withholding food and water for a few hours, then eased her back on a diet of chicken and rice. Wylie started to feel better the next day and was back to her old self in no time at all. From that day forward, I made sure to bring bottled water with me on every walk. I didn't want a repeat performance of that scene happening any time soon! Lesson learned.

Wylie's love of chasing tennis balls posed other problems at The Swamp. I would throw the ball ahead of her. *Bounce, bounce, bounce, roll.* She would take off like a bat outta hell, giving chase and skidding to a stop as she flung her body sideways to pick up the ball that she ran past, going too fast to stop.

One day, when we got home, I noticed some blood on the floor. *Oh, oh, what the heck was that from?* I called Wylie and checked her over. I picked up her feet looking for maybe a thorn or something. Oh no, Wylie had worn off the pads of her feet. They were raw. Her enthusiasm for tennis ball chasing was causing injury. It must have been painful, but she didn't seem to care. *No more chasing tennis balls at the swamp for you!* I thought to myself.

Wylie healed well in a few days, and we were able to go back to the swamp the next weekend, *sans* tennis ball. Oh, my goodness, Wylie was totally confused! No tennis ball? *Come on, Mom, this is ridiculous!* She was lost. She would walk ahead of me for a bit, then come back looking for the throw. No throw. I'd show her my empty hands, *all gone!* I would continue walking, getting ahead of her this time which rarely happened. I'd turn around to find her just standing there, looking sad and forlorn. She didn't understand why she couldn't play, and I couldn't tell her why. Sigh. We didn't walk very far that day, and when we got home, I took Wylie out in the backyard to throw the tennis ball for her. She could run in the grass with no problem.

I hated to see my dog so sad, so I came up with the brainy idea to get Wylie some boots to wear at the swamp to protect her feet. Wylie had worn boots once before when she was a puppy. I remembered that those booties didn't last long before the bottoms were shredded. Cheap boots, I guess. I went searching for better ones on the internet. I read reviews and chose the best ones I could find. They were supposed to be much more durable. I ordered them in red. When they arrived a week later, I took them out of the box and examined them. The foot part was molded rubbery stuff, good for gripping, I thought. The upper part was made of red neoprene, comfy. The boots came up higher on her legs and were fastened with velcro straps. They looked great. *This would do the job*, I thought. *Wylie would be able to get back to her swamp running!* I called Wylie over and put them on her feet. That was more difficult than anticipated, not because Wylie didn't want to put them on, but because she wouldn't hold her legs stiffly. Instead, she lay on her side and she let me take each floppy foot and try to stuff it into the boot. It was really hard to get them on straight! I managed to get three on, two on the front and one on the back, before Wylie decided that was quite enough.

She got up and stood stock still. She wasn't moving. I grabbed some treats and called her to me. She started to *walk* over. What ensued was one of the funniest moments of my entire life. I have literally never laughed so damned hard. Poor Wylie. Being the food-driven dog that she was, she tried to walk over to me. It was like her feet didn't work anymore and each one was on a separate switch or something. She would pick one front foot up really high, move it forward in a jerky sort of way, and place it on the floor with a *thunk*, then pick up a back foot and hold it high in the air for a moment. She'd move it forward, *thunk*, then the other front foot, and so on.

She made it over to me and ate her treat. I was in hysterics. I walked a few steps away and encouraged her to come to me. She got a little faster, but with that same awkward high step. Every few steps, she would donkey kick. I was howling with laughter, doubled over, tears streaming down my cheeks. I got my phone out and took some video, memorializing the moment forever. She was so funny.

A big part of me felt sorry for her. She was obviously uncomfortable, but I thought she would get used to wearing the boots. A little discomfort for the pleasure of chasing tennis balls. I weighed those two choices in my head and was sure that if I could ask her, Wylie would choose to soldier on, so we did. I kept that first session short, feeding Wylie yummy treats the whole time, then took off her boots after just a few minutes. I repeated this several times. She did get a little better, but not much. *Idea!* Maybe if I took her outside, in the back yard and played fetch with her, she would acclimate faster! After all, she loved her tennis ball more than anything else in the whole wide world, even more than food. And that's saying something! Excellent. I put her boots on and out we went.

I threw the ball, and Wylie gave chase. She wasn't as fast as when she was barefoot, but she chased. She got to the ball, picked it up, turned around and looked at me, then lay down in the grass on the spot. I called her. Nothing.

"Wylie, come! Wylie!" She stared at me with the ball in her mouth. She slowly got to her feet and clumsily trotted back. She dropped the ball at my feet.

"Are you ready? Fetch!" I threw the ball. Wylie looked excited for a moment, started to run, and then slowed to a walk. She got to the ball and flopped down into the grass without even bothering to pick it up. I called her again. Nope. This time, she was not coming back. She just lay there. I walked over to her and looked down at my sad, sad dog.

"I'm sorry Sweet Pea, I was just trying to help." I took the boots off. We were done. No more torturing my dog. What was the point if I was robbing Wylie of her joy? When the last boot came off, Wylie jumped up and pranced around like a puppy. She wanted to play! We had a lovely game of fetch before going inside. I took the boots over to the closet and put them on the shelf where they stayed until I donated them to a search and rescue organization several years later. Those boots are in Italy now, keeping a dog safe from injury.

I have so many more memories of my dog that I can't possibly pack them all into a single chapter. Instead, I would like to share some Wylie snippets with you. These are highlights that stand out in my mind as memories that live warm and whole in my heart. Oh Wylie, you were such a good girl!

## WYLIE WAS SMART

She learned the names of thirty toys over her lifetime and could bring each one back to you from the pile in her toy basket if you asked her. Thirty. That's a lot. I'm sure she could easily have learned more, but Tim thought we had enough toys in the house and we were running out of creative names to call them. Tim couldn't remember the names of all of them! Wylie could. She could also play basketball. *Get the ball!* I tossed it. Bounce, bounce, bounce. Wylie ran after it and picked it up. *Dunk it!* Wylie ran to the red bucket and dropped the ball in. Then she'd run to me for a treat. *Good Girl, Wylie!*

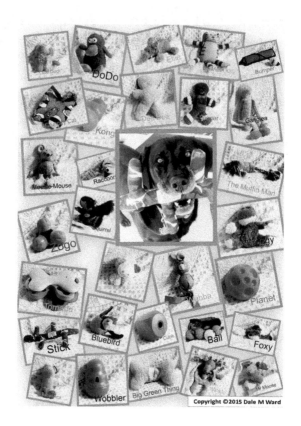

## WYLIE WAS KIND

One morning, we were out in the yard when Wylie started to follow a scent in the grass that ended in the flower garden adjacent to the house. She seemed overly interested in what she found, so I walked over to investigate. There, in the shade of the crepe myrtle tree, under the broad leaves of the hosta, was a nest filled with smooth white eggs. Each one was big enough to fill the palm of my hand. They were duck eggs! *Oh no*, I thought. *How am I ever going to keep Wylie away from them*! How stupid was a duck that would come up into a yard where a dog clearly lived and lay eggs? Any other dog would have eaten the eggs. *Stupid duck.*

I remembered something I had taught her a long time ago. Maybe it would work, but I had my doubts. I said my cue. "Wylie, not for you!" My sweet Wylie moved away. She allowed that duck to lay her eggs in the backyard garden, never touching the eggs or bothering the pair when they were in the nest. I had taught her that cue years earlier. It meant *leave whatever that is alone please*, and it applied to whatever I wanted her to ignore. We had started with rabbits that would cross our path when we were out on walks. Wylie would perk up when she saw one, ready to chase. *Not for you*, I'd tell her, and I would walk her away from the bunny. It was hard at first, but Wylie eventually got the hang of it. I only had to ask her to leave the eggs and ducks alone a few times, and she never bothered them again. Sometime later, I looked out the window, and there was the adult pair of ducks, walking in the middle of the yard towards the pond, with their brood of little ducklings following them all in a row. They were finally leaving the nest. *Good girl, Wylie!*

# WYLIE WAS OBSERVANT

Early one morning, Wylie and I went downstairs to start the day. I let Wylie out right away so she could do her business, as usual. She was always quick and ran right back in for her breakfast. This particular morning, I let her out, and a few seconds later I heard frantic barking. Wylie never barked, so I immediately knew something was wrong. Was there someone in the back yard? Was Wylie being threatened? I dropped everything and ran outside in my pajamas to find Wylie standing a few yards from the solid fence that separated us from our neighbor, barking at what seemed like nothing. She would bark, back up, bark as she moved forward a little, then she backed up again, repeating this pattern. That was definitely fear. I walked up to her and called her name as I went so as not to scare her any further.

"Wylie, what's wrong, what is it?" She ran over to me for a moment then turned and went right back to barking at the fence.

I looked and looked before spotting a tiny orange flower about the size of my little finger that was poking its head over the six-foot fence, swaying in the breeze. The neighbor had planted a flower garden on the other side of the fence, and for the first time, one of their flowers grew tall enough to reveal itself at the top of the fence. Now, that was pretty easy for me to puzzle out. I recognized it as a flower and I knew flowers could grow tall, and I knew that there was a garden on the other side of the fence. Easy.

Now, think of it from Wylie's perspective. She'd been in her yard daily for several years by this time. Nothing had ever poked over the fence before. It hadn't been there yesterday or the day before or ever! It was orange, which looks like a dull gold color to a dog, and it was moving back and forth. Wylie had no concept of a garden on the other side. So, what was it? In her mind, it might have been the tip of a big orange monster, ready to jump over the fence and eat her! She had no way of knowing what it was and couldn't make sense of it. Sometimes, people are quick to dismiss their dog's barking and fear as *nothing*. Dogs don't normally bark at *nothing*. Once I figured out what was causing the fearful barking, I was able to calm Wylie by touching the flower and calling her over.

"See, Sweet Pea? It's just a flower. It's nothing. All good!"

Wylie approached, stretched her neck up to sniff and checked it out, then turned away and went back to her normal, easy-going self. And that was the end of that.


## WYLIE WAS FRIENDLY

One afternoon, Tim and I were getting ready to go somewhere. I don't even remember where now, but that's not important. I let Wylie out to pee before we left. Usually, I would turn and see her waiting at the door to be let back in but not that day. I thought she was just out there enjoying the sunshine. We continued our preparation, and about fifteen minutes later when we were ready to go, I opened the door and called Wylie. Nothing.

"*Wylieee!*" I ran outside but didn't see her. I hurried to the side of the house, and as I turned the corner, I saw our gate swinging wide open, and Wylie was nowhere in sight. Now, everyone who has ever lost a dog knows what I was feeling: PANIC.

I dashed back inside and yelled, "Tim! Tim! Wylie's gone! The gate is open, and Wylie is gone!"

"What? What do you mean she's gone?"

"The gate is open. She's gone. Wylie's *GONE*! Oh my God, oh my God, *oh my God*!"

I rushed to get my jacket and keys, grabbed a leash and some treats and screamed at Tim.

"Let's go for @#$% sake, she's gone, and she was out there alone for over *fifteen* minutes! She could be anywhere by now!"

Tim grabbed his coat and shoes as I was already in my 4Runner, and he flung himself into the passenger seat. I stepped on the gas and took off.

"Slow down!"

"No."

"Slow down!"

"*No!*"

"You're going to kill somebody!"

"I don't care. Roll down your window and yell her name!"

We both did. "*Wylieee!*"

I was driving around our suburban streets like a maniac. Tim kept yelling at me to slow down.

"Yell for the dog, not at me!"

I was only going about fifty. Sheesh. The speed limit was twenty-five. There were parked cars, kids, bikes. It was suburbia. I kept driving too fast and yelling for Wylie. I'd slow down when I saw someone and ask if they had seen a black Lab. Nope. No one had seen her. Tim was getting madder and madder.

"Stop acting like a maniac. Slow. Down."

"Fine."

I turned back towards home and pulled up in front of our house.

"Get out and take your own truck then!" and I pulled away, leaving Tim standing there looking a bit dumbfounded. I didn't care. Where was my dog? I was so worried that she'd get hit by a car. She never did learn what traffic was all about. Her country roots hadn't imparted that skill. I drove and drove and drove calling her name.

# Wylie Lives a Wonderful Life

After about forty-five minutes of searching, I decided to take a swing back to the house to see if Tim was there. As I drove down my street, I could see something in the middle of my front yard. As I approached, I saw that it was Tim sitting in a lawn chair holding a beer in one hand and a leash in the other hand, a big smile on his face. A black head popped up. There was Wylie, lying in the grass, enjoying the sunshine! She was home!

"Oh my God, oh my God, *oh my God!*" I screamed as I pulled into the driveway. I jumped out and ran across the lawn. Wylie jumped up and pulled towards me, straining against her collar. I dropped to my knees in front of her and kissed her sweet face.

"Oh Wylie, where were you? Where did you go? I'm so glad you're home."

Wylie wiggled and wagged and licked. Oh, how I loved that dog!

"So, what happened? Did you find her? Where did she come from?" I was full of questions.

Tim then told me the story of getting dumped off by his wife (sorry honey, not sorry) and deciding to walk the neighborhood. He had gone inside to get a leash, filled a plastic bag with some of her dog food and set off on foot. He had walked for about ten or fifteen minutes, calling her name, when a black SUV with dark, tinted windows pulled up and a man rolled down the window.

"Hey, you wouldn't happen to have lost a dog, now would you?"

"Yes! How did you know?"

"Umm, the leash and the bag of food kind of gave it away."

"Oh. Yes, a black Lab. Have you seen her?"

"Yep, she's in the back."

Tim recounted the man's tale. His wife and daughter had been out for a walk when all of a sudden, this black Lab came running up to them out of nowhere. They petted her but then told her to go home.

They turned to walk away but the dog just followed them, wagging, seemingly very happy to be going for a walk with them. They shooed her away several times, but the friendly dog just wouldn't go. So, they let her walk home with them. They walked in their front door and Wylie went right in with them. They all agreed that she was lovely, but that she must belong to someone in the neighborhood, so the man decided to put her in his SUV and drive around. That's when he found Tim.

I have no idea why Wylie wasn't wearing her collar and identification tags that fateful day. She always wore them, especially since her tag listed a warning about her corn allergy. Well, I guess she didn't *always* wear her collar, obviously. This episode serves as a good reminder to make sure your dog is wearing identification.

After I got over my elation at finding her, I only half-jokingly told Wylie I was mad at her and that she could go live with her new family. That became a running joke for the rest of her days. I would often say to her, "Why don't you just go live with your new family? You liked them better anyway."

## WYLIE WAS WISE

After three years of living in rental suburban hell, we finally bought a house in the country. We moved to North Carolina, just south of the Virginia border. We had a nice house and eight acres of land. Yes, we were back in rural America! Our new property was nothing like our Wisconsin piece of heaven. This house was built on farmers' fields. There was not a single tree on our property, save the little newly planted few. The corn grew higher than those tiny trees. It was pretty empty and very flat.

# Wylie Lives a Wonderful Life

The first thing we did when we moved was to get a company to come out and fence in a big backyard for Wylie. It was nice to be back in the quiet countryside. Oh wait, *bark bark bark*, incessant barking from behind the neighbor's fence. If we were out and their dogs were out, it was non-stop barking. Wylie never barked back. She didn't care if they barked. Those invisible dogs were of no concern to her. On the other side of our yard was a field that we rented to a local farmer who grew soybeans on it. We would get paid a percentage of the harvest in exchange for use of our land.

On a lazy, late afternoon, Wylie and I were relaxing out in the backyard. Wylie was lying down in the grass beside my chair snoozing in the open air. She was facing the soybean field, I was facing the opposite way, watching Tim wash his truck in the driveway. Suddenly, Wylie woke up and slowly raised her head and elongated her neck. Her nose started to twitch, air scenting, picking up a trace of something. She lowered her head and stared hard. Then she stood up, very slowly and very deliberately. She was unnervingly still. I had an eerie feeling creep up the back of my neck. *What is it Wylie?* I turned around in my chair and what I saw made my heart skip a beat.

Out of the tall, green soybeans came a big cat. Wylie must have smelled it on the air currents. When I say big, I mean big. It was bigger than Wylie. Way bigger. At first, I thought it was a bobcat, but it seemed to be too big. It took one, then two stealthy strides. I knew the cat was coming for Wylie. I stood up. The cat stopped. Wylie stood stock still, not moving a muscle, burning a stare right into that cat. She instinctively knew we could be in big trouble. I don't know where I summoned the courage, but I started waving my arms in the air and shouting.

"Hey, get out of here, go away!" The cat paused, assessing the situation. I knew it could easily jump the six-foot chain link fence. We all stood stock still, staring at each other. Then, the cat slowly turned around, showing its long tail as it disappeared back into the soybeans. That was no bobcat. That was a mountain lion!

As soon as it was gone, I let out a huge sigh of relief. Wylie ran across the yard, over to that side of the fence to get a better sniff. I walked over too, talking loudly to make sure it was really gone, not just lurking, waiting for another opportunity. Wylie and I ran back and told Tim the amazing story. He thought it must have been a bobcat, but the tail! Bobcats don't have tails. I called my dog and we went inside. That was enough outdoor excitement for the day. Wow, I was so impressed with my dog. *Good Girl, Wylie!*

## WYLIE WAS SENSITIVE

Wylie enjoyed the big yard and the sunny deck and screen porch a lot. We were able to put in a vegetable garden because she was beyond her youthful need to dig everything up and eat it. That was for puppies! Wylie didn't bother with any of that stuff anymore. She still loved chasing her tennis ball and sunbathing. That was about it. Oh, and swimming!

I was feeling a little sorry for her one day and so I brought her home a fresh beef marrowbone from the grocery store. It seemed like everyone I knew, all the professional trainers, were giving their dogs raw bones. I felt bad that I was denying Wylie this great pleasure. I gave her the bone outside to chew on. She absolutely loved it, and in true Wylie fashion, she managed to eat all of the marrow out in about twenty minutes. I could hardly believe it. That was a lot of marrow! I didn't think much of it until the next day. She was so sick! She vomited so many times and got terrible diarrhea. I took her to the vet. It was pancreatitis, the first of several bouts. It turned out that Wylie had a very sensitive tummy. Who knew! From that point onward, we battled with her delicate gut.

I cooked for Wylie for about a year. I prepared mountains of sweet potatoes, chicken breasts, and eggs. For a long time, that's all she could tolerate. Anything else caused her issues to return. She went to see a specialist who performed an endoscopy and did some other tests. Results were inconclusive, but it looked like Wylie had delayed emptying of her stomach. She was put on medication, lots of it, but it didn't seem to help. Every once in a while, Wylie would have what I called an *episode*. They usually happened at night. She wouldn't be able to settle, panting and pacing, sometimes going out in the yard to walk in circles for what seemed like hours. I would go with her, walking and talking beside her, trying to reassure and calm her. When the episode was over, she would go back to her usual self. I thought she was having stomach pain.

Wylie was losing weight. I couldn't feed her enough low-fat foods to keep the weight on her. The specialist put her on a prescription diet, and I credit that move with giving us an extra year with her. It was hard to believe that our iron-stomach puppy had turned into such a food sensitive dog.

# Dale M. Ward

Wylie's *in-between* years, those from puppyhood to senior dog, were filled with joy, happiness, and great doggie adventures. She lived life to the fullest each and every day, even if that meant snoozing on the couch all day. She loved everything in her world. That should be a lesson to us all: no matter what you're stuck in, look for the light. It's there somewhere.

# The Premack Principle: Using What Your Dog Wants to Get What You Want

When I was training Wylie's recall and leash up, this is what I did.

I tossed the tennis ball.

Wylie ran after it and picked it up.

I called her back to me: *Wylie, come!*

Wylie came to me.

I slipped the leash over her head and immediately took if off. *Good girl!*

I tossed the ball again and encouraged her to run after it.

She brought the ball back.

I slipped the leash on and off again.

I tossed the ball...

I repeated this over and over.

I rewarded Wylie for coming back to me and letting me put the leash on by sending her away to chase the ball and play another round of fetch.

I was using the *Premack Principle*, also known as the *relativity theory of reinforcement*. This principle states that more probable behaviors will reinforce less probable behaviors. Simple.

You've probably been aware of this principle for most of your life. Have you ever heard a parent say, "You have to eat all your vegetables before you can eat any dessert"? This is the Premack Principle at work. The second behavior is a high frequency behavior (eating dessert); the first behavior is a low frequency behavior (eating vegetables). The idea is that eating dessert acts as a reinforcer for eating vegetables.

In Wylie's case, she had to let me put the leash over her head (low frequency behavior) in order to play fetch (high frequency behavior). I gave her a head start with one initial toss so that she understood that we were playing her favorite game. Playing fetch became a reinforcer for coming back to me and letting me leash her up. The likelihood that Wylie would return to me and let me leash her increased because it was being reinforced by her favorite game.

You can use the Premack Principle in a whole host of situations with your dog. Here are some examples.

| Low Frequency Behavior | | High Frequency Behavior |
|---|---|---|
| Loose leash walking | REINFORCED BY | Letting dog sniff the grass |
| Sitting calmly at the door | REINFORCED BY | Opening the door to go play in the yard |
| Sitting and waiting when the front door is opened | REINFORCED BY | Allowing dog to go greet the person |

| Low Frequency Behavior | | High Frequency Behavior |
|---|---|---|
| Coming when called | REINFORCED BY | Sending dog to chase the ball |
| Dropping the toy | REINFORCED BY | Game of tug |

As you can see, the Premack Principle is useful because it's win/win. You get what you want, and your dog gets what he wants! This type of reinforcer is also sometimes called using *life rewards*.

A word of caution: sometimes a high frequency behavior can be so over-arousing for a dog that he can't think clearly. A good example of this is chasing squirrels. With certain dogs, trying to get the dog to sit before being let outside to chase squirrels will be nearly impossible. They are simply too distracted by the squirrels. It would be much easier to teach a calm sit first using food reinforcers. Increase distractions gradually until the dog is able to sit inside by the door with a squirrel in the yard. Then, transition to the Premack Principle. In fact, most behaviors should be trained using food as a primary reinforcer first, and then you can transition to using the Premack Principle if you so choose.

# Recall Training
# aka Coming When Called

One of the most important cues you can teach your dog is to reliably return to you when you call him. Recall is the "life saver" cue, the one that you absolutely need in case your dog gets loose and is in danger. It's also a cue that helps minimize the frustration of having a dog that just won't come back to you.

So, tell me, why don't dogs come when called? Is it because...

They're stubborn?

Defiant?

Dominant?

Unintelligent?

Afraid of being punished?

They never listen?

They don't want to?

That last one is probably the closest to the actual reason. Dogs don't come when called because it almost always means the end of fun. Simple. When do we normally call a dog to come inside? When we are about to put him in his crate, or we ask him to leave whatever he's doing — sniffing moles, chasing squirrels, nosing a toad, playing with the kids or another dog, chewing on a stick — and when he finally does come to us, we either leash him up, put him in the car, or put him in the house and ignore him or leave altogether. What fun is that? Remember, when you call your dog back to you, you are competing with so many things in the environment that are far more interesting than boring old *you*! You have to figure out a way to make yourself more interesting than all that other stuff.

## Set Yourself Up for Success!

First and foremost, you must establish and nurture a good relationship with your dog. This is at the heart of all good training and is especially important if you want your dog to come to you when you call him. If you don't have a good, solid relationship based on trust, you can't expect your dog to want to work with you. Assuming you have this bond securely in place or are in the process of establishing it with your new puppy, how do you teach your dog to come when you call him? Let's break it down.

1. **Select a treat** that you will use as a reward for coming to you when called. Your recall treat should be plentiful and amazing! Meat is usually a good choice. Real cooked chicken breast, low-fat low-sodium turkey hotdogs, and string cheese are some good choices. Whatever you choose, your dog must love it. This special treat should only be used for recall training. Cut the treats up into tiny pieces no bigger than the size of a pea (if you have a small dog, make them even smaller), and keep them in a container in the refrigerator. Freeze some if you prepare more than needed for a two or three day period.

2.  **Choose a cue** and hand signal. Your verbal cue should be short and clear. I like punchy words that start with a hard sound. You must not use this word for anything other than recall training. Most people automatically think they have to use the word *come*. Not so. If you think you are going to use the word *come* in other situations, like asking your dog to pay attention to you, or to get your dog to walk closer to you when on a leash, or to just move, then pick another word for your recall cue. Start with your dog's name, and then add your cue. *Sam, COME,* or *BAM, POST,* or *PRESTO* are some other options. I try to choose a big hand signal, mine is a fist straight up in the air, so that in an emergency, my dog can see my signal from a distance, if need be.

3.  **Start inside** your house in a quiet location where there are no other distractions. For example, don't start training if your kids are in the next room having some loud fun because it will be too hard for your dog to pay attention to you. Begin with your dog in front of you. Take a piece of food in your hand, bring it to your dog's nose, and let him smell the food (don't let him eat it), and immediately say your cue — *Sam, come!* — and take one step backwards as you move your hand from your dog's nose to your knee. When your dog follows, use your verbal marker — *Good!* — and give him the food from your hand while still holding it close to your knee. Repeat, taking another step backwards. Do this several times. Your dog should be eagerly following you around the room at this point.

4. **Add a collar grab**. Repeat as above but when your dog comes to you and is eating the food out of your hand, use your other hand to hold onto his collar. Just slip your fingers under his collar and lightly hold. Don't pull or push, just hold. Many dogs don't like being held by the collar and reaching to grab their collar is often avoided by moving back and away from you. If you have to recall your dog in an emergency situation, you will need to hold onto them until you can get them leashed or to safety. By including a collar grab every time you practice recall, it will create muscle memory for you so that you remember to do this while you are in a panicked state, and it will make your dog expect to have his collar held, and so he will not try to avoid it.

5. **Add a few steps**. Now repeat this same exercise but take two steps backwards instead of just one. Repeat a few times. Then add three steps backwards, and five steps, and keep increasing until your dog is enthusiastically following you around the room when your use your recall word. Don't forget your collar grab each time. Repeat this exercise three or four times a day in short sessions under five minutes for several days.

6. **Add extra rewards**. We know dogs love food, but they also love to play, especially when it involves you! After each round of recall training, add in a few minutes of your puppy's favorite game. It could be tossing the ball across the room a few times or a short game of tug — whatever your dog loves. Your dog now associates his recall cue with fabulous food *and* a game with his favorite human. Who wouldn't want to come when called if *this* is the result?

7. **Test Comprehension**. Warm up by doing a couple of repetitions of step one. Now let your dog wander off to the other side of the room or you can move away from your dog. Ignore your dog for a few moments until he has lost interest in you. Now say your cue. *Sam, come!* Your dog should stop what he's doing and run to you. When he is in front of you, close to your knee, feed him a piece of recall food. If your dog hesitates, encourage him to come to you by clapping your hands, patting your legs, crouching down, saying *good boy, good boy,* but don't repeat your cue. If your dog is slow to respond like this, go back to the previous step, and spend more time on it.

8. **Make it better**. Now that Sam likes playing recall, you're going to make him love it. You are going to reduce the frequency with which you play the game. Yes, *reduce*. This is also when I add my hand signal (punch straight up into the air). I use my hand signal at the same time as I say my cue. Sam is still going to play this game a few times a day, but only one repetition at a time. For the next two weeks, use your recall cue two or three times a day, varying the time of day you choose. You are *not* going to do multiple repetitions. For example, recall your dog once before work, at noon, and then after dinner. On another day, you might skip before work and add another one at the end of the day. Just vary it so that your dog doesn't anticipate what's coming. Make sure you have your recall treats ready in advance. Instead of only giving your dog one piece of food when he successfully runs to you, you are going to

give him five pieces in rapid succession, one at a time. Then you are going to say something like, *Okay Sam, let's play*, and then play with him for a few minutes.

9. **Move it outside**. Put your dog on a long line (fifteen to twenty feet) and take him into the backyard. If you don't have a backyard, you can do this in a quiet field or park. Just make sure you always hold the end of the long line for safety. To start, make it easy. Move a few feet away from your dog and call your dog with your cue. Make it harder by adding distance. Drop the long line and stand on the end. This will make it seem more like your dog is not attached since the line will be lying on the ground rather than in your hand. Repeat. When your dog is coming reliably and if it is safe to do so, let him move further away from you while dragging the long line, then recall your dog. Reward.

10. **Proof it**. Now it's time to take this show on the road. Proofing your training means to practice and make sure your dog is successful in a variety of situations and locations. You might add some distractions to your yard, like having the kids out there playing. You might add a chew toy or bone. You can change locations to a friend's fenced yard or a fenced empty field. Remember, when you make it more difficult, always have your dog trail that long line at first so that it will be easier to catch him if you've made it too difficult too quickly. If this happens, reassess, and think of ways to make it easier for your dog. Then, gradually build up to the more difficult situations.

# SOME RULES

- Always be prepared for recall training with some amazingly delicious food treats.

- Don't repeat your cue. Say it once (unless your dog truly was not able to hear you). Repeating it will lessen its potency.

- If you use your recall cue, always follow it with a food treat or a game your dog loves to play — or both.

- If your dog has done something amazing like stopped chasing a squirrel when he heard your recall cue, give him a jackpot of treats: four or five pieces delivered one right after the other. I want your dog to know how amazing he is! He deserves a big *thank you* for coming!

- Never use your recall cue to call your dog for something the dog considers unpleasant, if at all possible. That includes the end of a play session, going into his crate, being left alone for the day, etc. In these instances, simply go get your dog.

- If you know you are leaving at a certain time, 8 am for example, call your dog in at 7:30, and play with him for a few minutes. Then, continue getting ready to leave. When it's time to leave, your dog won't associate his recall with your leaving. Instead, he will associate it with the game of tug you had.

- Reward your dog with praise whenever he comes to you whether you called him or not.

- You can use food, play, and petting/praise in combination to reward your dog if he really likes those kinds of rewards.

- Practice your recall. Don't let it slide. You need to keep it fresh in case you need it in an emergency. If you don't practice, like any skill, it will fade.

- Have fun!

# CHAPTER SIXTEEN

# The End

The end came unexpectedly for the Wylie One of Highbridge. I had always thought that it would be her gut that failed her, that she wouldn't be able to eat anymore. She had had so much trouble in the past two years. That's not what happened.

The first seizure happened on a Sunday night at around eleven. Wylie was lying at the foot of the bed sleeping when I heard a weird noise. I looked down and saw that she was awake. Her jaw was chattering, and she was salivating. I thought she was going to vomit, so I helped her off the bed and half carried her to the laundry room where the floor was tile. She collapsed onto her side and started to seize. Tim was in the kitchen.

"Tim, come quick. It's Wylie, she's having a seizure!"

Tim came running in. "What's wrong? What's happening?"

"She's seizing. Come help me, quick! Grab some towels. Move her head away from the wall. Don't let her hit anything." I put a towel between her head and the wall, to protect her.

Wylie's body was stiff and shaking, and her eyes were vacant. The seizure lasted about thirty seconds, and then she was still. She was breathing. In a few minutes, she had regained control of her limbs and was able to stand up. She was a bit disoriented but seemed okay. I was so thankful at that moment for my experience working at the veterinary hospital. I knew what a seizure looked like, and I mostly knew what to expect. I knew that sometimes dogs had one seizure and never had another. I also knew that some dogs had repeated seizures and had to be on medication for the long term. I wasn't sure which it was going to be with my Wylie. Wylie slept with us on the bed. It was a peaceful night.

Her second seizure happened on Monday morning at 9:50 am. I had called the vet first thing and reported the previous night's events. I had an appointment at 10. Tim had gone to work since Wylie seemed to be okay. Wylie and I were almost at the hospital when it began. We were stopped at a red light one block away. Wylie was in the back of my car, where she always rode. She had been snoozing quietly and then sat up abruptly. I watched her in my rear-view mirror and saw the jaw chatter start again. *No, no, NO!* I was almost there! I got on my phone and called the vet to tell them Wylie was seizing again and to meet us in the parking lot. I pulled in in under three minutes. By that time, the seizure had stopped. There was silence in the car. I jumped out and opened the back hatch, fearing the worst. Wylie was lying on her side. She was completely still but breathing. Two young women came rushing out but didn't know what to do when they saw my unresponsive dog. One went in to get the stretcher. Just as we were delicately trying to put Wylie on the stretcher, Karen, Wylie's favorite Vet Tech came running out to the car. She slid her arms under my dog and scooped her sixty-five-pound body up as if she were a bag of feathers and walked inside.

Dr. Riedel came into the room immediately and started her exam. By that time, Wylie was coming around again. It took longer for her to recover this time but recover she did. A battery of tests was ordered, a catheter was inserted into her front leg, and blood was drawn. The catheter stayed, just in case. She was put on medication.

Dr Riedel asked to keep her for observation for the afternoon. She told me to go eat something, so I went and got some lunch.

The third seizure happened at the vet that afternoon while I was out, and again, Wylie recovered. When I returned at around 3:00, I was taken back into the main treatment area. Wylie was sleeping in a crate. I sat on the floor beside her. She sensed my presence and roused a little.

Dr. Riedel said I could take her out for a while, so I got her collar and leash and brought her out. She was happy to see everyone. She wagged her tail and greeted all her friends in her usual happy way, but she just wasn't herself. She paced a lot, continuously walking in circles around the large room with me following behind, holding her leash. The only way to get her to stop circling was to put her back in a crate. Dr. Riedel wanted her to rest. Wylie went into the crate willingly, as always. I sat beside her and talked to her. I sang to her. I told her everything was going to be okay.

We stayed at the vet until closing at 8:00. They sent us home with instructions on how to give Wylie an anti-seizure medication. If she had another seizure, we were supposed to administer it if it went on beyond two minutes. I had Dr. Riedel's phone number in case I needed her.

The fourth seizure occurred at around nine on Monday night. It was short. The fifth and last seizure was at three in the morning. Nothing prepared me for this. *Nothing.* Wylie started to seize. She was sitting up and thrashing. Tim held her, and I started timing. Thirty seconds. One minute. Two minutes.

I told Tim to hold her tight. I administered the medication rectally as instructed. Nothing changed. Wylie started screaming. Over and over and over. Her scream was like nothing I had ever heard before. It was a deep, wild scream, expressing pain, fear, and agony beyond comprehension.

# The End

I called Dr. Riedel to see if there was something else — anything else — I should be doing to make it stop. She said that there was nothing that could be done but to try to keep Wylie from hurting herself. The seizure had to run its course. I was crying, screaming into the phone.

"It's not stopping! It's not stopping! There has to be something I can do!"

There was nothing to be done but wait. On and on the screaming and thrashing went. It was deafening. Tim sat cross-legged on the floor with Wylie on his lap. I went and got his hearing protection and slipped them on his ears so that he would not be deafened by her screams. He was holding her in a giant bear hug, his hands trying to hold her head still. He was sweating from the effort. I was stunned by the violence of it.

It lasted for forty minutes.

Then it stopped. Silence. Wylie collapsed into Tim's arms from sheer exhaustion. She was still breathing. We quickly grabbed blankets, pillows, bottles of water, and the emergency bag I had packed for Wylie earlier, and Tim carried her out to the car. He sat in the back with her in case she had another seizure. There was no way I would be physically able to hold on to her if that happened again. I drove us to emergency vet, about an hour and a half away.

Wylie was out cold, sleeping deeply. Finally, she whimpered a little as her head rested on Tim's lap. She was still with us! We arrived at the emergency vet and decided to let Wylie sleep since she was stable. We sat in the parking lot, Tim in the back seat with her, stroking her softly down her side. If Wylie showed any signs of distress, we could bring her in to see the emergency vet in less than a minute. After a couple of hours, Wylie roused, stood up, and looked around. We helped her out to let her pee if she needed to. She had trouble standing and walking, but she peed. We lifted her back into the car and covered her with blankets. We waited in the dark and watched the sun come up for the last time with our sweet dog.

We drove to her regular vet and were waiting in their parking lot when they opened at 8 am. Dr. Riedel wasn't working until noon, so we saw the other vet. Wylie was able to walk but circled and panted a lot. Her pupils were dilated, big and blank. We kept her at the vet for assessment that day to see if she would come back to us. There was nothing more for Tim to do, so he went home to grab a shower and went to work. I was going to stay with Wylie and keep him posted.

Wylie barely recognized me. The pacing was exhausting her. In the crate, she would eventually lie down and rest. Out of the crate, she would pant and pace, walking in circles, always in the same direction. Clockwise. And those big black eyes! She would turn and look at me if I called her name a few times, but there were no tail wags. She was voracious and wanted to eat, eat, *eat* everything in sight. She spotted my ring and came over and tried to bite it. She eyed the container of cotton balls on the counter as if it might be food. I fed her, and she gobbled it all up, looking for more. It was like she had returned to a more primal version of herself.

Then, more panting and circling. I spent hours with her in the exam room. I took a couple of videos. I talked to her. I told her stories. She paced. She hunted around for food. She would not lie on her blanket. She would not touch her toys. She paced. She panted.

I don't think she heard much of what I was saying, or she didn't process it until I gave her some familiar cues. *Wylie! Sit! Wylie, touch.* It was like those words sliced through the thick fog that clouded her brain, and finally, she understood. She could hear and process those few words. Wylie, sit, touch. Those three words she recognized. Wylie walked over to me and sat. I gave her food. *Touch.* She touched my outstretched hand. I gave her food. I like to think that *mama* made it through the fog too, but I'm not sure. *Come see mama!* I said. She stared at me with a blank look in her eyes.

# The End

I left her with the vet for an hour to go get a coffee. I sat in Starbucks staring at a piece of paper in front of me. It was the decision tree from *Merle's Door*. I had given that decision tree to so many people in the past, hoping it would help them make this most difficult decision. I knew Wylie could not live like this. Her brain was fried. She peed on the floor. She would *never* do that. She would have been so embarrassed. I couldn't let her go through another seizure like that last one. It seemed so painful and frightening for her.

I will *never* forget that night.

I went to the grocery store and bought some chicken and roast beef for my sweet Wylie. I wanted to give her some tasty last treats. I stood there crying as the deli lady handed me my packages.

That last seizure took a big piece of Wylie away. Tim and I made the decision that it was time to let what was left of Wylie go.

After the clinic closed at 8:00 pm on Tuesday, September 30, 2014, we put her blanket on the floor. I sat down on it and held Wylie close to me, talking softly, whispering her name, and telling her how much I loved her, how she was the best dog ever. The absolute best. Tim sat on the bench talking to her, stroking her head, kissing her sweet face.

We finally said to Dr. Riedel, "Okay." She injected the drugs into Wylie's catheter. Wylie quieted, her panting stopped, and she slipped peacefully away in my arms.

She was so still, so soft, and shortly became cool to my touch. I was surprised at how fast her body cooled. I lay her down across my lap and stroked her silky coat for the last time. They came in and clipped a little of her fur for me to keep and made a clay imprint of her right front paw for me. They had called the crematorium for pick up that same night, so that Wylie would not have to be put in the freezer. They came and wrapped her in a clean sheet, put her on a stretcher, and took her body away. I walked with her as far as I could go.

Tim and I thanked everyone, and we walked out of the hospital for the last time. Tim carried Wylie's blanket and toys; I held an empty collar and a leash. The tags jingled. We drove home in stunned silence.

When we came into the house, it really hit me. Everywhere I looked, all I could see was Wylie. Her toys, her beds, her crate, her water bowl, her medicine, her house! I looked at Tim.

"What are we supposed to do now?" I started to cry. I held up the empty collar and sobbed. Tim wrapped his arms around me and squeezed. I hugged him back. He was crying too.

"I don't know," he said, "I don't know." I wept all night.

By morning, I was exhausted. Tim got up and made coffee. We sat in bed drinking it, missing our sweet dog. I confessed that when Wylie was deep into that horrific seizure, I actually considered getting the gun and shooting her to stop her suffering. Tim admitted that as he held her head up with his hands, trying to keep her safe, protecting her, he considered the same thing. It was unbearable.

We got up and dressed. Tim looked at me and grabbed Wylie's long line off the counter, the one we used to walk her up the long driveway to get the newspaper every morning. "Let's take her with us", he said. Tim coiled the long line, making loop after loop, placing each coiled length across the palm of his hand, just like he had done hundreds of times before. I held Tim's hand and together we held onto Wylie's line and walked out the door.

We walked in silence, deep in our own thoughts and memories, the pain raw, sitting right on the surface. We got to the end of the driveway and Tim handed me Wylie's line while he crossed the road to get the newspaper. I can't describe the feeling of holding that rope with no dog on the end of it. It was weightless. And it was so, so heavy.

## The End

The next day, Tim went to work, and I was alone. Really alone. No Wylie. Ever again. I saw the long line on the counter where we had left it the day before. Without thinking, I grabbed it and bolted to the car. I drove to Coquina Beach on the Outer Banks. Wylie's beach. She loved that beach. It was a warm sunny day with a nice breeze coming off the water. I walked.

I walked where we had walked together so many times, both of us happy and Wylie so full of life. I watched the birds. I sat in the sand and watched the waves roll in, one after another, after another. I could see her in my mind's eye, running far down the beach, right at the shoreline, water splashing up in her wake. I broke down in tears, crying for my dog.

When I had nothing left, I dragged myself to the car and drove home. When I approached our driveway, I just kept going. I blew right past it and drove to The Swamp. I walked our walk, still holding that empty long line. I sang Wylie our silly song, the one I sang to her on every single walk, a huge knot in my throat, choking on the words.

You are my sunshine, my Wylie sunshine,

You make me happy, when skies are gray,

You'll never know Wylie, how much I love you,

Please don't take my Wylie One away.

As I walked, I looked up through the branches of the giant pine trees at the clear blue sky. It was a beautiful day. Wylie would have loved it.

# Epilogue

For months, I grieved. I barely functioned and was really lost. Wylie had been my whole world. Those first weeks are still a bit of a blur. I just couldn't believe Wylie was gone. Tim wrote the most touching eulogy for her and posted it on his Facebook page.

> *Wylie One of Highbridge*
>
> *21 February 2004 to 30 September 2014*
>
> *It is with deep sadness and a sense of loss that we provide news about our close friend, companion, and family member Wylie. Dale and I spent many hours with her on Tuesday and made the difficult decision at the end of the day to let her continue on her journey ahead of us. Thankfully, we were able to take some time to hold her in our arms, tell her how much we loved her, and give her gentle hugs, pets, and kisses before she had to leave us. We were there at her side for as far as we could travel with her and then we had to say good-bye as she crossed over the bridge and entered lush green fields of clover filled with eternal sunshine, gentle breezes, cool water, bunnies, and happy times.*

*Wylie, you were truly a "one-in-a-million" personality who was loved not only by your Mama Dale and Papa Tim, but also by all those who got a chance to meet you during your incredible life. You taught us so much about what it means to have a big heart and how to share it with others without any thought for your own well-being, as you knew we would always be there to take care of you. You gave us all you had to give throughout your wonderful life. You were the best doggone doggie ever and we will miss you so much.*

*We look forward to seeing you again when it is our time to cross over the bridge and we can join you for more long walks along the water and through the woods. Until then, watch over us and be at peace our Little Booboo Bear Wylie.*

I wrote one too.

*Wylie One of Highbridge*

*February 21, 2004 to September 30, 2014*

*Tonight, I am so sad, so lonely, so terribly lost. I am missing my wonderful, sweet dog Wylie. Tim and I walked with her, as far as we could go, then, in my loving arms, as I hugged and kissed her goodbye, we helped her slip peacefully away. Many of you knew Wylie, others only knew her through me. She was a soul so very sweet, eyes the color of burnt sugar, soft velvet ears and a shiny, silky coat. She was so smart. She loved people above all else. She brought so much happiness to our lives, from her sheer joy of fetching tennis balls, to her love of the water, when the two were combined it was Wylie's idea of heaven. Today, I went for our walk along the trail with her leash in my hand. I went to the ocean and watched the waves crashing on the shore where she loved to play. I know she is at peace now, running free, chasing bunnies, rolling in the sweet, cool grass. We will see you on the other side my Sweet Pea. I love you more than I can express in words. Dear friends, Wylie and I thank you all for your kind words and prayers. I miss her so very, very, much.*

My vet clinic posted this one on their Facebook page a few days later.

*There are beautiful dogs...smart dogs...loving dogs...special dogs. And there was Wylie Ward, who embodied all of these qualities. Wylie was our salon spokesmodel and a part of our Centerville family. Along with her mom, Dale, she was an active participant in helping owners and dogs build stronger, happier, life-long relationships. Wylie crossed the Rainbow Bridge on Tuesday. In honor of Wylie, we ask that you spend a little extra time with your beloved dog or cat, doing whatever he or she likes best. And if you can, comment about it so that the Wards can see how Wylie's legacy of love and companionship continues.*

Friends sent cards and flowers. I loved that.

I picked up Wylie's ashes and brought them home a week later. Tim and I made the trek to Coquina Beach and scattered some of her where she loved to run and play. It wasn't fun this time. We scattered more ashes at The Swamp where we all walked together so many times.

I spent hours looking for the right container to keep the rest of her ashes in. I sent some ashes away and got them swirled into a hand-blown glass ball that I could hold in the palm of my hand.

If it hadn't been for Tim, I'm not sure what would have happened to me.

I have always been prone to depression. Losing Wylie made me lose myself. I plummeted into a big black hole head first. I hid from everyone. Tim's solid, reliable presence gave me some structure to follow. He got up every morning and made coffee. He brought me my coffee in bed (he's been doing that every morning since we got married — every, single, morning for sixteen years. I'm very lucky.) We drank our coffee. We'd get up and get dressed, take Wylie's long line and walk to get the newspaper together. We did this every morning for months. We just couldn't stand the idea of stopping. I made dinner every night. Went to bed, and I silently cried myself to sleep every night.

I didn't take any clients for weeks. I had a conference scheduled in the middle of October. I was going to cancel and see if I could get my money back, but friends changed my mind. I went. I drove all the way to Hartford, Connecticut, ten long hours. I don't remember the drive, only a lot of time to think about Wylie. I cried a lot at that conference. People who didn't know me must have thought I was crazy. My friends hugged me tight. I was glad to be with them.

I don't remember much about those first months, other than I felt very lonely, sad, and empty. I couldn't imagine how I was going to face year after year like that. It was overwhelming.

Tim said, "You should get another dog."

*No.* I wasn't ready.

I skipped Christmas that first year. I didn't put up any decorations. No tree, nothing. I did no holiday cooking. My friend Nancy invited us to visit her in Quebec for Christmas, knowing how painful it was going to be for me to spend the holidays without Wylie. *Great idea*, I thought, and gladly accepted. Tim and I drove for two days, our first trip without a dog in many years. It was hard. I cried a lot. Nancy and her family were wonderful to us and helped make getting through the holidays so much better.

On the way home, Tim said, "You should get another dog."

"No. I'm not ready. I don't know if I'll ever be ready, so *no*."

I didn't want another dog. It was just too hard to lose them.

I dipped my toe back into the dog ownership world by fostering for Lab Rescue. I thought that would be easier. It was fine, and I was glad to help some dogs on their way to finding permanent homes. One dog, her name was Belle — we called her Belle-Belle because

Tim said she was a ding-a-ling — stayed with us for months. I know Lab Rescue thought we would keep her. *No.* I wasn't ready for another dog. We finally found a home for Belle after her long stay with us. I cried when the interim foster came to pick her up. See? I get too attached.

Tim said, "You should get another dog."

*No.*

Months went by. It felt like years. No dog. I went to a conference in the summer where there were puppies. They were mostly Golden retrievers, but there were some others. There were black Lab puppies. I held one. I cried.

My friends told me I should get another dog.

*No. I'm not ready.*

One day, on a whim, I started to look at puppies online. They were so cute. Then, I started to look at breeders. Slowly, I eased into it. I found a breeder I liked that wasn't too far away.

Tim said, "You should get another dog."

"Okay."

"What? Really? That's great! You need another dog!"

We went to visit the breeder and met the parents: both beautiful, lovely dogs. Both had impeccable health test results and friendly, outgoing temperaments. We saw the incredible setup the breeder had and were very happy with what we observed. I filled out a really long questionnaire, was accepted, and put down a deposit. The puppies were to be born in early September 2015, a year after Wylie's death. That year without her felt so incredibly long and lonely. Did I really want to go through this again? As the days passed, I started to get cold feet. Did I really want a puppy? I was scared of getting too attached. I knew I could never love another dog like I loved Wylie. She had only been gone for a year, although it felt more like five years. I didn't want a new dog to take Wylie's place.

## Epilogue

The puppies were born on September 3, 2015. Ours was ready to come home at the end of October, but we didn't pick her up until November 3rd. I was in no rush. She was nine weeks old when we brought her home. We struggled with a name but somehow came up with Rhubarb. Her full registered name is Summerwood Sweet Carolina Rhubarb Pie.

I know it's all supposed to be a bed of roses when you get a new puppy, but this wasn't the case for me. For the first three months, I resented her. Every time I looked at her, all I could see was Wylie. It was too soon. I wouldn't let her share Wylie's toys. I bought her new ones instead. I didn't like her. Having Rhubarb around made me miss Wylie even more. It brought the grief up to the surface again and I found myself crying a lot when I was supposed to be happy. I didn't want her. I changed my mind. She made me angry and sad and confused. Then, she would have a cute moment or do something amazing, and I started to fall for her.

Brat. She was making me do it.

# Dale M. Ward

Slowly, I gave her one or two of Wylie's toys, those that were Wylie's least favorite. Then, maybe a few more. She already had Wylie's crates and beds, so what the heck. Pretty soon, that little puppy had wriggled her way into my heart and took her place right beside her big sister. Wylie and Rhubarb live there now, side by side. And I love them both equally, to the moon and back.

As I write this, Rhubarb is stretched out sleeping on the couch beside me. She is now three years old. I can hardly believe how quickly time has gone by. She is my Service Dog and helps me get through my life every single day. I don't know what I would do without her. She is very different from Wylie. Of course, I am a professional dog trainer with over a decade of experience now, so I guess it *should* be easier. And my Wylie was a good teacher. She taught me so much about dog training. *Good Girl, Wylie!* I didn't make the same mistakes this time with Rhubarb, a soft dog and easy puppy.

Especially compared to the Wylie One of Highbridge, the absolute BEST worst dog ever.

# Resources for You

*The American Veterinary Society of Animal Behaviorists (AVSAB)* is an organization for the veterinary community that focuses on animal behavior. This group issues position statements which they publish on the AVSAB website for use by veterinarians, trainers, breeders and the public. Go to https://avsab.org/resources/position-statements/

*The National Canine Research Council-Research Library* houses, in one searchable database, descriptions of canine studies from peer-reviewed literature. This resource is free, and you can browse or search by Author, Content Type, or Topic. Go to http://www.nationalcanineresearchcouncil.com/

*ASPCA Animal Poison Control Center* phone number is (888) 426-4435, their website is https://www.aspca.org/pet-care/animal-poison-control

Join the *Pet Professional Guild (PPG)* Canine Division as a Pet Owner Member free of charge. Use the trainer-search function to locate a professional member near you. Go to https://www.petprofessionalguild.com/Find-a-Member/

Join the *Fear Free* movement to help make your dog's veterinary visits less stressful. Go to https://fearfreehappyhomes.com/

Browse the *Victoria Stilwell Positively* website for information on a whole host of dog related topics. There are excellent articles, videos and much more on this site. Use the trainer-search function to locate a certified and licensed VSPDT professional near you. Go to https://positively.com/dog-training/find-a-trainer/find-a-vspdt-trainer/

Check out *Family Paws Parent Education (FPPE)* for information on dogs and babies/toddlers/young children. Use the trainer-search function to locate a licensed FPPE professional near you. Go to https://www.familypaws.com/find-a-fppe-educator/#!directo

Subscribe to *The Whole Dog Journal.* It is relatively inexpensive and provides you with so much wonderful information. Your subscription includes (as of the date of publication of this book) a printed monthly magazine, but what I find most valuable is the online access to all past articles in its archives. You can find just about anything on dogs in that archive. Some of my favorites are the annual dog food review and the dog gear reviews. Go to https://www.whole-dog-journal.com/

(All links verified on 10/13/2021)

## Trainers and channels to watch on YouTube

- Nando Brown and Jo-rosie Haffenden — School of Canine Science
- Emily Larlham — Dogmantics and Kikopup
- Chirag Patel — Domesticated Manners
- Claire Staines — Lothlorien DS
- Victoria Stilwell — Positively

## Some of my favorite authors

- Linda P. Case
- Jean Donaldson
- Patricia McConnell
- Karen Pryor
- Ken Ramirez
- Kathy Sdao
- Victoria Stilwell

## Some of my favorite blogs and websites

- The Science Dog by Linda P. Case
- Eileen and Dogs by Eileen Anderson
- Victoria Stilwell Positively
- Dognition
- Dog Star Daily
- Bright Spot Dog Training
- The Labrador Site
- Say Yes Dog Training

# ON DEATH AND BEREAVMENT

The Cummings School of Veterinary Medicine at Tufts University staffs a grief support line and also provides links to several internet support groups. You can find more information here http://vet.tufts.edu/petloss/pet-loss-support-hotline-support-group-link/ (link verified on 10/13/2021)

## The Decision Tree

Bernard S. Hershhorn DVM, author of the book *Active Years for Your Aging Dog*, created the decision tree I used in assessing Wylie's quality of life. The decision tree is also reproduced in a book called *Merle's Door* by Ted Kerasote, who added three questions. The decision we must make regarding end of life is so immense and so personal, unique to our own set of circumstances. For me, this decision tree helped give me an objective measure against which I could weigh each aspect of Wylie's life. Here it is.

1. Is the condition prolonged, recurring, or getting worse?

2. Is the condition no longer responding to therapy?

3. Is your dog in pain or otherwise physically suffering?

4. Is it no longer possible to alleviate that pain or suffering?

5. If your dog should recover, is s/he likely to be chronically ill, an invalid, or unable to care for him/herself as a healthy dog?

6. If your dog recovers, is s/he likely to no longer be able to enjoy life, or will s/he have severe personality changes?

If one's answers to all six questions are yes, the dog should be euthanized. If the answers to questions 3 and 4 are no, then perhaps the dog should be allowed to die naturally.

And in his book *Merle's Door*, Ted Kerasote added these three questions.

1. Can you provide the necessary care?

2. Will such care so interfere with your own life as to create serious problems with you or your family?

3. Will the cost involved become unbearably expensive?

Hershhorn, Bernard S. DVM. Active Years for Your Aging Dog, Dutton Adult, First Edition 1978.

Kerasote, Ted. Merle's Door: Lessons from a Freethinking Dog. Houghton Mifflin Harcourt, 2007.

There are no right or wrong answers here. Be open and honest with your veterinarian. Discuss it with your family and close friends. Listen to what your mind, your heart and your instinct are telling you. Remember, it's far better to be one week too early than one day too late.

I believe that a peaceful passing is the most difficult thing you will ever have to do for your dog. But it is also one of the most precious gifts you will ever give them. Be there for them.

## Grief Comes in Waves

I had lost a lot of people by this time in my life; my family, many good friends, other animals, but nothing came close to the piercing grief I felt when I lost Wylie. I didn't think I would survive. This advice, written by a self-described old man on Redditt, is what helped me most during that very dark period.

"As for grief, you'll find it comes in waves. When the ship is first wrecked, you're drowning, with wreckage all around you. Everything floating around you reminds you of the beauty and the magnificence of the ship that was and is no more. And all you can do is float. You find some piece of the wreckage and you hang on for a while. Maybe it's some physical thing. Maybe it's a happy memory or a photograph. Maybe it's a person who is also floating. For a while, all you can do is float. Stay alive.

In the beginning, the waves are 100 feet tall and crash over you without mercy. They come 10 seconds apart and don't even give you time to catch your breath. All you can do is hang on and float. After a while, maybe weeks, maybe months, you'll find the waves are still 100 feet tall, but they come further apart. When they come, they still crash all over you and wipe you out. But in between, you can breathe, you can function. You never know what's going to trigger the grief. It might be a song, a picture, a street intersection, the smell of a cup of coffee. It can be just about anything...and the wave comes crashing. But in between waves, there is life.

Somewhere down the line, and it's different for everybody, you find that the waves are only 80 feet tall. Or 50 feet tall. And while they still come, they come further apart. You can see them coming. An anniversary, a birthday, or Christmas, or landing at O'Hare. You can see it coming, for the most part, and prepare yourself. And when it washes over you, you know that somehow you will, again, come out the other side. Soaking wet, sputtering, still hanging on to some tiny piece of the wreckage, but you'll come out.

The waves never stop coming, and somehow you don't really want them to. But you learn that you'll survive them. And other waves will come. And you'll survive them too. If you're lucky, you'll have lots of scars from lots of loves. And lots of shipwrecks."

From a Redditt post, dated c.2012 by GSnow https://www.reddit.com/r/Assistance/comments/hax0t/myfriendjustdied idontknowwhattodo/c1u0rx2/ (link verified on 10/13/2021)

# ACKNOWLEDGMENTS

First and foremost, my love and gratitude go to my husband Tim, for sticking by me for the past seventeen years and trusting me with this story. Tim, you have shored me up more times than you will ever know. To my friend and colleague, Abigail Witthauer, I truly appreciate your knowledge, advice, generosity, and most of all, your friendship. To Nancy Tucker, my Canadian cohort, colleague and friend, you are always there when I need advice, guidance, and counsel. Thank you, dear friend. I also want to acknowledge and thank the tremendous pool of talent and kindness that lives within the Victoria Stilwell Positively Dog Training (VSPDT) community. My fellow VSPDT trainers are simply amazing people; incredibly knowledgeable, generous and kind. And to Victoria herself, who brought the VSPDTs together in the first place, and who has done so much to further the cause of using kind methods with our dogs, my gratitude is yours.

My heartfelt appreciation goes to Wylie's veterinary team at Centerville Animal Hospital, for their dedication, care, and support throughout the years. Your commitment to your profession is admirable. To Dr. Betty Riedel, thank you for taking such good care of us, and for helping Wylie find her way to the other side.

I'd also like to thank the many dog training and behavior professionals who have inspired me, taught me, and helped me over the years: Dr. Jenny Beard, Nando Brown, Linda P. Case, Dr. Susan Friedman, Jo-Rosie Haffenden, Dr. Lynn Honeckman, Dr. Patricia B. McConnell, Chirag Patel, Ken Ramirez, Kathy Sdao, Grisha Stewart, and others too numerous to mention individually.

# Dale M. Ward

Last but not least, I am grateful for all my clients. Each one of you has taught me something more about dogs and the canine-human bond. You have been some of the best teachers of all. I am so very happy that many of you actually had the chance to meet Wylie. Thanks for sharing your dogs with me over the years!

# ABOUT THE AUTHOR

Dale M. Ward is the 2020 winner of the Dog Writers Association of America's prestigious Maxwell Award for best book in the category of Human/Animal Bond. She is the owner of Dale's Dog Training Academy LLC, located in South Mills, North Carolina. She works mainly in the southeast Virginia, northeast North Carolina geographical area, but also consults online, with clients from Alaska to the UK, to Beijing. She is a well-known dog trainer and behavior consultant who has been working with dogs and their humans for nearly 15 years. Before becoming a dog trainer, Dale was a senior Business Analyst in the Information Technology field. She worked for the National Archives of Canada before venturing out on her own, starting a small IT company in Ottawa, Ontario. Dale closed up shop in Ottawa in 2002 when she moved to northern Wisconsin.

Dale is proud to be a licensed and certified Victoria Stilwell Positively Dog Trainer (VSPDT), a Fear Free Certified Professional (FFCP Trainer & Veterinary), and a former Family Paws Parent Educator (FPPE). She holds two university degrees and is always augmenting her knowledge and skills through continued study. Dale has helped thousands of dogs and their owners overcome obstacles to live their lives together in harmony. She currently lives in South Mills, North Carolina with her husband Tim and their black Labrador retriever named Rhubarb.

# Dale M. Ward

## Contact Information

Dale M. Ward, BAHon, MA, VSPDT, FFCP (Trainer & Veterinary)

Email:      ddta.dogs@gmail.com

Website:    https://worstdogever.com/

                 https://daleward.positively.com/

Facebook:  https://www.facebook.com/TheWorstDogEver

                 https://www.facebook.com/DaleTrainsDogs/

Instagram: https://www.instagram.com/the_worst_dog_ever

                 https://www.instagram.com/daletrainsdogs_/

# Index

Printed in the USA
CPSIA information can be obtained
at www.ICGtesting.com
LVHW021104031023
759761LV00074B/1563